"Not only has Lee Wedlake been there years, but he was exceptionally attentive and took copious notes. Without doubt, Lee Wedlake's *The Kenpo Karate Compendium* will be one of the most significant and beneficial resources available to Kenpoists worldwide."

—Rich Hale, Senior Professor and President, Ohana Kenpo Karate Association

"Lee Wedlake has been in service to the Kenpo community for years with his written material. This book will be a go-to reference for students and teachers in the years to come."

—Bob White, 9th degree black belt, Kenpo Karate

"Professor Lee Wedlake is the consummate martial artist and teacher. I highly endorse his work."

—Dr. Ron Chapél

"Mr. Wedlake conveys his martial authority in amusing and practical ways. This volume deserves consideration and will rivet your attention."

—Tom Baeli, T'ai Chi Instructor.

"I am constantly amazed at how Lee Wedlake puts together a body of work that not only educates, but provides the logic of the art of Kenpo. This book will inspire to succeed!"

—Stephen LaBounty, 9th degree black belt

"This book is an invaluable aid to understanding the forms and sets of American Kenpo, written by someone who truly understands the structure and nature of the subject matter contained within. If you are a serious student of Kenpo then this book is a must for your Kenpo library."

—Gary Ellis, 8th Degree Black Belt, Associate Master of the Art of Kenpo Karate

THE KENPO KARATE COMPENDIUM

THE KENPO KARATE COMPENDIUM

The Forms and Sets of American Kenpo

LEE WEDLAKE

BLUE SNAKE BOOKS
BERKELEY, CALIFORNIA

Published by Blue Snake Books,
an imprint of North Atlantic Books
P.O. Box 12327
Berkeley, California 94712

Cover art public domain
Cover and book design by Brad Greene
Printed in the United States of America

The Kenpo Karate Compendium: The Forms and Sets of American Kenpo is sponsored and published by the Society for the Study of Native Arts and Sciences (dba North Atlantic Books), an educational nonprofit based in Berkeley, California, that collaborates with partners to develop cross-cultural perspectives, nurture holistic views of art, science, the humanities, and healing, and seed personal and global transformation by publishing work on the relationship of body, spirit, and nature.

North Atlantic Books' publications are available through most bookstores. For further information, call 800-733-3000 or visit our websites at www.northatlanticbooks.com and www.bluesnakebooks.com.

PLEASE NOTE: The creators and publishers of this book disclaim any liabilities for loss in connection with following any of the practices, exercises, and advice contained herein. To reduce the chance of injury or any other harm, the reader should consult a professional before undertaking this or any other martial arts, movement, meditative arts, health, or exercise program. The instructions and advice printed in this book are not in any way intended as a substitute for medical, mental, or emotional counseling with a licensed physician or healthcare provider.

Library of Congress Cataloging-in-Publication Data

Wedlake, Lee.
  The Kenpo Karate compendium : the forms and sets of American Kenpo / Lee Wedlake.
      pages cm
  ISBN 978-1-58394-851-4 (trade paperback : alk. paper)
  ISBN 978-1-58394-852-1 (ebook)
  1. Karate—United States. I. Title.
  GV1114.3.W4334 2015
  796.815'309—dc23

                                                              2014034692

1 2 3 4 5 6 7 8 9 UNITED 18 17 16 15 14

Printed on recycled paper

Table of Contents

To all those who have pursued the arts, endured its trials,
and who hold and pass on the knowledge.

Acknowledgments

Thanks to my colleague Mr. John Sepulveda of Boise, Idaho, for writing the new foreword and for being a sounding board. For the photos: Steve and Ross White and Jim Peacock of New Hampshire, Gary Ellis and Mark Richards of Plymouth, England, and German kenpoists Marc Sigle, Nadja Wolz, Lennart Steinke, Thomas Kozitzky, and Claudia Neumann. Also Ed Cabrera of Tampa, Florida; Jack Nilon in Sydney, Australia; Graham Lelliott and Pete Valdez in Fresno, California; and Daniel Delenela of Round Rock, Texas. Hibben knife photo by Mike Carter, courtesy Linda Hibben. Footwork notation graphics by Don McCullough. The medical and legal sections were written by Marc Rowe, MD, and Frank Triolo, Esq., respectively, both from Florida. Thanks also to my editors Erin Wiegand, Kathy Glass, and Louis Swaim at Blue Snake Books for their efforts.

And to my first Kenpo instructor, because you can learn what not to do from the bad ones.

"Death is no more than a rebirth into another sphere. In this sphere, resurrection will allow us to exist in various degrees of glory."

—ED PARKER, *ZEN OF KENPO*

Edmund Kealoha Parker, Sr.,
March 19, 1931–December 15, 1990
Photo by Brad Crooks, from the author's collection.

Foreword by John Sepulveda

I was at Mr. Parker's West Los Angeles school in the late 1980s when I met Lee Wedlake for the first time. I remember Mr. Parker mentioning him many times in the years prior, always saying how knowledgeable Lee was and that he had a unique ability to communicate the art on any level. Lee and I shared many of our thoughts and ideas that first day. I found Lee to be unassuming, very knowledgeable, and very willing to share that knowledge. The key was, you only had to ask. I learned many new things in our conversation, as I still do to this day. I felt from that initial meeting that we were going to become friends on and off the mat, and twenty-five years later, we are.

Lee and I have taught at several events together, from coast to coast as well as in several countries in Europe. We have shared and compared our ideas and consulted each other. True to form, Lee has always been open-minded and willing to share his thoughts and ideas. When I first learned of his idea to write a series of books on the forms (*Kenpo Karate 101–601*), I thought it was brilliant. To consolidate the whole series of books into this one volume is genius. As Lee has previously stated, it is "notes for the new student and the seasoned instructor."

Lee's understanding of the forms is obvious. He shares his insights of not only "how" but "why." He gives many answers while also guiding or leading you to many other answers, trying to get you to think. As Mr. Parker often said, "When all else fails, you have to think." This book will definitely be a great reference tool that we will all benefit from.

To quote Mr. Parker, "Lee has become an authority and celebrity in today's Martial Arts world" (Preface, *Kenpo Karate 101*). I absolutely agree and often refer my students to Lee's books on the forms as well as encourage them to attend his seminars.

Although Mr. Parker encouraged all of us to evolve, we must retain the integrity of our art as he intended it. This book has accomplished that. Thank you, sir, for sharing your knowledge, and for all your time and effort in preserving Mr. Parker's art. This book will definitely be in my library.

—John Sepulveda
Ninth-Degree Black Belt, Student of Kenpo
Founder/President, American Kenpo Training System
September 2013

Not often will you find a Black Belt from an offshoot Kenpo school who is willing to discard or sacrifice his previous status and rank in order to gain knowledge that he firmly believes will lead him to higher levels in Kenpo. Lee Wedlake is just such a person. He was willing to digress in order to progress—a quality not shared by others who are so often thwarted by ego. It is because of Lee's willingness to keep an open mind in pursuing higher levels of Kenpo that he has become an authority as well as a celebrity in today's Martial Arts world.

The content of this book personifies my teachings. It voices the principles, concepts, and theories that I firmly believe to be true. To be sure of my beliefs, Lee has made every effort to authenticate his writings by conferring with me personally and by phone. We have spent hours discussing the logical approach to the study of Kenpo and the merits derived therefrom.

It has always been my policy to allow my students freedom to expand and expound not only on the principles they have been taught, but those thoroughly learned and understood. A thorough understanding of principles is the key that allows one freedom to become self-correcting within the bounds of logic. If an understanding of principles is lacking, freedom can be detrimental and, therefore, lead to distressing detours.

I am proud to say that Lee Wedlake is a rare student who has studied with me diligently and has been able to meet obstacles and roadblocks with renewed vigor. He not only enthusiastically welcomes challenges, he pursues them with logic, assured that his efforts will lead to avenues of progress and overwhelming satisfaction. I am proud of Lee as well as other students exemplifying the same qualities under my tutelage. They are more than a tribute to me.

I highly recommend this book and feel that it should be added to your library of Martial Arts literature. It highlights methods of pursuing knowledge from a logical viewpoint. Such thinking inevitably leads to practical methods of application that are functional in our present environment.

—Ed Parker, 1987

Years ago, it was said that Ed Parker had seven protégés (some say up to eleven) with different specialties, and I was asked what mine was. I had to think, because I did not consider myself a specialist, just more of an all-around practitioner. I realized that my specialty is teaching. I am very good at synthesizing information into an understandable presentation. Through my magazine articles, seminars, classes, and now this book, I hope to expand the horizons of those working in and being touched by our system.

The Kenpo Karate Compendium was originally written as a series of much shorter books in which I tried to capture the essential concepts of the Parker system. Each one focused on a different segment of the Kenpo karate system. I wrote that series with two types of people in mind: new students and seasoned instructors. I am happy that my work has been helpful to so many practitioners of the system around the world. Many have told me they wished they had this information when they were coming up through the ranks and thanked me for my writing. There was very little written about the Parker forms prior to my efforts. The present book compiles and expands that work; and for the first time it is being made available to a much wider audience.

Please bear in mind that I wrote this as a reference, not as The Way. To those in related or offshoot systems: while the forms are done differently by different people, and there are always arguments about their aspects, my intent is to make this information available to anyone from any lineage interested in expanding their knowledge, regardless of who their teacher was. In my years of traveling and teaching I have found that many of the points I make here were not known by many practitioners I met. My intent is to present the information as I understand it. If this book helps you make more sense of the forms then I have done my job.

This compilation is not complete and was never intended to be. It may be instructional, informational, or corrective and is intended to act as a key, a supplement to help you make sense of the big picture of Kenpo that the forms represent aspects of. I can't (won't) give you "the secrets" in a book or video. It is your time and your physical and mental effort that result in knowledge and proficiency. Along with a qualified instructor, this book will help guide you to the many discoveries that lie within the system. There is a wealth of information about logical motion in the forms. I have not disclosed much of the hidden movement and application in the Parker forms. To do so would be a violation of trust and a break with Ed Parker's "pull teeth" precept of teaching. He said if you "pulled teeth" (meaning worked hard) to get the information instead of it being handed to you, it meant more to you. He was right. This book is the result of a whole lot of thinking based on what I was taught in more than forty years in the arts: both right, wrong, or gleaned from another system. In the process of writing this book I sent drafts to some of the more senior Kenpo people I know for their comments. The most common reply I received was that it is written in such a way as to make people look for their own answers, beyond the fact that it has a lot of information in it. That, I believe, is a part of the legacy Ed Parker left us.

Since a form is motion, the best way to learn it is to see it and do it—better yet, to teach it. A video would or should be the medium of choice for presentation of this information. Yet the written reference always seems to have a place and fills a void. The martial arts are intangible and a book makes them tangible. When I do my forms I am living the history of the art, since they were passed to me by some of the foremost practitioners of this art variously called Kenpo Karate, American Kenpo, Chinese Kenpo, and Parker Kenpo. Yet there is something rather comforting to being able to have in my hand the written works of SGM Parker (that's Senior Grand Master), or the notes I wrote during my lessons with him. It is my hope this book works like that for you.

As I wrote in the foreword to *Kenpo Karate 301*, I was fortunate to encounter people who could point me in the direction I needed to go. Through a series of events in my life I was able to train with some of the world's best martial artists, never thinking, as a kid from Chicago's south side, that I would be traveling the world teaching an art taught to me by Ed Parker, one of the world's most influential karate men. That I would meet people around the world wanting my perspective on the art never crossed my mind. My attitude and ability have been so shaped by these people and events, including the death of two of my teachers, that I truly feel fortunate and blessed for all I've experienced. These teachers were the late Michael John Sanders, Frank Trejo, Richard "Huk" Planas, and Ed Parker (who passed away in 1990). Mike was the first real Kenpo man I met; he was fast, accurate, and powerful. Trejo could do everything well—forms, fighting, and self-defense. Huk Planas taught me a tremendous amount on technicalities. Then there was Mr. Parker, who taught me and so many others, and brought us all together. So many others, really, that he could not teach us all and he wanted and needed some of us to help him do the job in the years before his passing. They all allowed me to pass this information to you.

Mr. Parker told a story about "Sam," the gardener to a wealthy man. When the man bought something for his children and tried for hours to assemble it but failed, he called Sam. Within a fraction of the time he had spent, Sam had it built. The employer asked him how he did it. Sam's reply was, "Boss, I can't read. So when you can't read, you've gotta think." Many of us who took Mr. Parker's classes and seminars remember him telling that story. It served to drive home his point—think about what you are doing. Pay attention to your teachers, attend seminars with the traveling professors, and ask questions! The rest is up to the next generation of instructors who never met the man but carry his legacy in their hearts. I believe this book will help preserve, perpetuate, enhance, and evolve the system, *our* system, as he liked to say. I keep an "attitude of gratitude" toward Ed Parker, my other teachers, my students, and readers and trust this is a suitable contribution back to them and the system that gave me so much. I have learned a lot and have quite a bit more to learn.

—Lee Wedlake
Round Rock, Texas, 2013

I created this to help visualize directions without the confusion of laying out the entire form. That's something you should do. As I developed it I realized that it looks something like the "Aresti System," a standardized notation used by aerobatic pilots for airshow and competition routines. Having been an aerobatic pilot, I'd have to say I was probably subconsciously influenced. You won't be upside-down at 150 mph when you use this book, but I think the notations will help.

Laying out the form means you actually draw out the patterns—on the floor with chalk or on paper to see the directions. This is a task a student should take on to get a good idea of what the foot patterns are and how they overlay as one progresses.

A line represents a point of origin or a base line (not an attention stance), or a direction on the clock. That base line may be crossed or reversed at times.

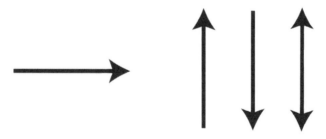

indicates direction of travel, both lateral and longitudinal, forward and reverse

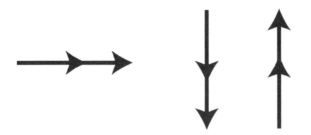

indicates direction of travel for two steps in the same direction, often from the last step of the previous technique

indicates two "sides" of a technique and the directions executed; includes "non-sided," ambidextrous attacks (e.g., a full nelson)

indicates a type of switch

indicates a step up to a horse stance

indicates a step back to a horse

"7" or "reverse 7," depending on which way the arrows point

indicates a 360° direction change

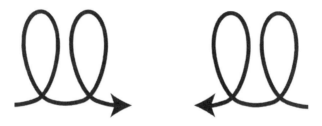

spin (arrow indicates direction of)

cheat (arrow indicates direction)

indicates moving forward and back on the same line

1.

What Is This Stuff?

Kenpo means "law of the fist;" karate means "empty hand." Thus Kenpo Karate is "The Law of the Fist and Empty Hand." Kenpo Karate, for us, is the Ed Parker system. Mr. Parker learned Kenpo in Hawaii as a teenager, where it was taught as a combination of hard and soft[1] systems of self-defense. With that in mind it is not too hard to envision him creating his innovative system—an American system based on a Hawaiian version of a combination of arts. While Kenpo is similar to karate and kung-fu, it is also very different. The name "Kenpo Karate" was used in Hawaii to attract servicemen to training who did not know what Kenpo was. The name stuck. There are also Japanese and Okinawan systems of Kempo, spelled with an "m," that look similar to hard-style karate. (Kenpo normally refers to the Chinese versions.) The methods of motion are different from system to system.[2]

In the U.S. today there exist many versions of Kenpo. Even the Parker system goes by different names—if you learned the system in the early years (the 1950s and '60s), it was Kenpo Karate (according to Steve

---

1 "Hard" and "soft" refer to methods of executing the art. A hard style is external, using muscular power. A soft style is internal, being more fluid. Both use the concept of centering, bringing energy from the *hara,* the body's energy center just below the navel. Hard uses more tension than soft. The difference is like being hit with a two-by-four versus a whip. They are different and they both hurt. Hard and soft also refer to natural weapons and their execution. A punch is a hard weapon; a finger whip, soft. It also refers to attitude and posture, which are related. Hard and soft may be combined in systems like Kenpo. Your response to an attack can be hard, soft, or medium as well.

2 You can read the definitive Kenpo history in Parker's *Infinite Insights into Kenpo,* Volumes 1 and 2.

LaBounty, one of the most senior students in Kenpo).[3] In the '70s it was called Chinese Kenpo. By the time I started training with Ed Parker in the late '70s, it was being called American Kenpo. In about 1980 or so, it had taken on Mr. Parker's name, becoming "Ed Parker's Kenpo Karate." After 2000, the system became popularly known by an acronym, EPAK: Ed Parker's American Kenpo.

The Parker techniques exist in offshoot systems—in whole, part, or a variation—and they bear different names. Some instructors call their system Ed Parker's Kenpo Karate but qualify it by saying that what they teach is the way it was done back in another period; they are teaching Parker material, but what he was doing in the '50s or '60s rather than in his later years. It is true that what he taught varied through the years since he was innovating with what he had learned. Therefore what a student learned from Parker in the '50s was different from what Parker taught in the '60s, which was different from the '70s, and so on. The system was first standardized in 1970. There were some changes after that, but the system known as Ed Parker's Kenpo Karate was essentially formulated then. There are schools using Parker material with totally different names for the techniques, forms, and the system, which makes classification even more confusing.

When the system is changed by others intentionally or mistakenly, the products are called "offshoots." When an instructor intentionally adds or deletes information or changes sequences of movement, he (or she) essentially changes the system. When they do this because they misunderstood or forgot parts of what they learned, it has the same effect. There are even systems that are offshoots of the offshoots—they are just a different type of Kenpo. An example is "New England Kenpo," a brand developed and taught in New England and unique to the area. It is tough to sort out for the beginner. Referring to the Family Tree mentioned in the next sections helps you find out if you are in a Parker school.

---

3 When the Tracy brothers left Ed Parker, the system was called Kenpo Karate in their schools, then Tracy's Karate and Chinese Kenpo in some of its (Tracy's) variations. In 1972 when I learned Kenpo in a school that was a break-away, also known as an offshoot school, it was even called Kenpo Kung-Fu. This was probably an attempt to cash in on the kung-fu craze of the time. LaBounty was the third black belt the Tracys promoted.

Who Was Ed Parker?

In 1999 *Black Belt* magazine listed Ed Parker as one of the top ten influential masters of the century. Information about him is easy to find: Read the biographies in his books. Check the Internet. Read back issues of almost any karate magazine back to 1963, when martial art magazines were starting to be published. You will find references to Parker everywhere and enough articles on him and the technicalities of his system to keep you reading for some time.

Ed Parker told me that he never claimed to be the first to open a karate school in the United States. He did claim to be the first to open a *commercial* karate school here. "If you wanted to be technical," he said, "the coolies who built the railroads in the 1800s were the first practitioners of the Oriental martial arts here." Robert Trias, the founder of the United States Karate Association (USKA), claimed to have started the first dojo here. Trias, Parker, and Jhoon Rhee were to share the limelight as the biggest names in pioneering American martial arts in the twentieth century. Magazines fanned the flames of the "feud" between Parker and Trias about who was the real father of American karate. In the end, Ed Parker simply said he was labeled by the magazines. He had enough firsts on his list: Recapping his list from the back cover of *Infinite Insights into Kenpo, Volume 1,* Ed Parker was the first to teach a university karate class and be a faculty member, the first to be an authentic karate technical advisor for TV and movies in the U.S., and the first to publish a rule booklet for freestyle tournament competition. He was also the first in the U.S. to publish a series of books on Kenpo Karate, starting with *Kenpo Karate, Law of the Fist and Empty Hand* in 1960 and ending with his definitive series *Infinite Insights into Kenpo* and the *Encyclopedia of Kenpo.*

In my humble opinion, Ed Parker was a genius as well as a physical powerhouse. He was six feet tall, about 200 pounds of muscle in his prime. Even when I met him, in his late forties, he was as fast as lightning and hit twice as hard. He was aggressive and loved physical contact, but these qualities alone do not make someone a world-renowned martial art master. Parker could analyze in minute detail how things work. Joe Palanzo told me a story about how an alarm clock in Ed Parker's room did not work. After taking it apart, Parker figured out the workings and fixed it. He was not a watchmaker, but he understood the concepts of motion and was able to apply that skill to solve a problem. Once he understood how things worked, he related that to other things. That was his categorical mind at work.

Parker learned the original Kenpo forms from Professor William Kwai Sun Chow, and he must have seen how they categorized movement in an embryonic way. As the years went by, Parker created expanded versions of these original forms, those being Form One and Form Two, to preserve more of the categories of motion. More of his advanced ideas were placed in the higher forms, preserved for those who persevered in the system. Parker also created a sophisticated system of self-defense techniques that laid out concepts and principles in a progressive manner (in parallel). For example, he spoke about his "Web of Knowledge"—a breakdown of his system into groupings such as holds, punches, kicks, and so forth. He spoke of dead, semi-live, and live attacks. He discussed these in more detail in what he called the "categorical breakdown." He wanted the information taught in a particular order: first, grab defense (dead), then push (semi-live), then punch or kick (live). When you look at the forms, you see that the self-defense forms starting with Short Three use the same pattern. Short Three is used for grabs (dead attacks); Long Three for grabs and pushes (semi-live); and Four is utilized against live attacks. Combination attacks and weapons are also live.

When someone takes that long and puts that much thought into something to get the message across, and it works, that is genius.

As a family man Ed Parker exemplified the concept of yin and yang: the same hands that could (and did) put you where he wanted you held his grandson Blake with tender, loving care. Ed Parker traveled, wrote, taught, organized, planned, choreographed, visualized, and managed to support his extensive family. He looked after his wife

Leilani, five children, their spouses, and the grandchildren. Many of them worked directly for him at the house, running the International Kenpo Karate Association (IKKA). He was under pressure but he made things happen.

Ed Parker had an extensive network of friends, and he influenced the careers of many martial artists. As promoter of the famous International Karate Championships (IKC), which he held in Long Beach, California, each August, he set the scene to expose the public to some now-famous practitioners for the first time. It was the film he shot at the 1963 IKC of Bruce Lee's demonstration that opened the doors for the world's first Chinese-American international film star. Later in that same venue Chuck Norris became a world champion. In fact, many people who competed at the IKC wound up in the movies, as did others associated with Ed Parker in some manner. It was Ed Parker who introduced Dan Inosanto to Bruce Lee; Dan later taught Jeff Imada, the "balisong man," who has been in many movies spinning a butterfly knife. Douglas Wong was at the tournament almost every year I was, and his students Albert Leong and Jimmy Lew were bad guys in such movies as *Big Trouble in Little China* and *Lethal Weapon 4,* among others. Former IKC champs (the late) Joe Lewis and Chuck Norris made movies, as did Mike Stone. Even a Parker student and my friend Frank Trejo were captured on film. Many other IKC competitors have had parts in television shows and movies achieved through their martial arts, although none are as well known as Lee and Norris were when the genre started.

It was the 1991 film *The Perfect Weapon* with Jeff Speakman that put Kenpo on the map. With Parker's help choreographing, Jeff's first movie showcased our system—and it was a hit. (Sadly, Ed Parker died about one month before the movie was released.) Parker was himself in several movies including two of Peter Sellers's Pink Panther movies, playing Mr. Chong from Hong Kong. He also starred in a picture called by two names, *Kill the Golden Goose* and *Kill the Golden Ninja.* Along with hapkidoist Bong Soo Han, Parker kicked and punched his way into video. He was in *Buckstone County Prison* and *Seven.* You will also see him on old TV reruns of *The Courtship of Eddie's Father* and *I Love Lucy.*

Stardom is not limited to the movies and television. The events he held were often launching pads for many young martial artists. A win at the Internationals meant magazine and sometimes television coverage, along with offers to be paid to compete or demonstrate at other national events, or become part of a corporate-sponsored team and more. Being a part of the Ed Parker family was a good move for many competitors.

The Family Tree

Ed Parker published our family tree in *Infinite Insights into Kenpo, Volume 1.* The tree has become an important reference for instructors and students. Every legitimate teacher has, or had, a teacher. A written tree normally helps establish a lineage by providing a form of proof. Instructors of Ed Parker's Kenpo Karate can trace their lineage back to someone on the tree. It is clear-cut. For example, I have promoted many black belts since 1976. Each of them can produce a signed certificate showing his/her rank and the date and place of the promotion. The certificates are signed by me and are therefore verifiable by contacting me or checking my website's "belt tree" page at www.wedlakekenpotv.com/leewedlake. Certificates for students promoted before 1991 are signed by Ed Parker as well as me; later certificates have Parker's stamped signature. Since I am on the tree as a first-generation Parker student, my black belt can show direct lineage from Ed Parker to me to the teacher I promoted and straight to you, the student. It does not get much clearer than that. You know you are in an Ed Parker school.

I have been on many examination boards in the U.S. and Europe, and some practitioners have a certificate with my name as witness. However, although that means I was there, it does not mean I taught that person. If they are not on my family tree, they are not one of my directly promoted students.

Ed Parker's certificates have been copied and his signature forged by certain enterprising individuals who want to "prove" they are in the lineage for financial gain or prestige; however, this is rare, and the Internet makes contact with authentic instructors easier than ever. It is important to note that Ed Parker allowed many individuals to join the International Kenpo Karate Association (IKKA) in the mid-'80s who were not Parker Kenpo stylists. Along with ex-Tracy,[4] offshoot (spinoffs of Parker's school), and independent Kenpo people, there were even Okinawan style and Korean tae kwon do schools in the IKKA then. These people were to learn the Parker system as a requirement of membership. They were what we called "converts." Most made efforts to do this. Many did not, apparently just wanting to wear the patch or use the Parker name. Therefore, one can join a school that presents IKKA certification with the appropriate signatures but is not teaching the system. Caveat Emptor!

The Ed Parker IKKA Seniors

Every organization has its leaders, movers, and shakers. Before Mr. Parker's passing, the IKKA had a structure that included a president, an executive vice president, a vice president, and a secretary/treasurer. Ed Parker was the president; his wife, Leilani Parker, was the secretary/treasurer. The other posts were held by a variety of people before 1991. In the early '70s Dave Hebler (best known as one of Elvis Presley's bodyguards) was executive vice president, followed by Danny Rodarte. The late Tom Kelly of Wichita, Kansas, took over shortly after. He was called Sibok by many, which means "senior student" in a Chinese-style school. He was a seventh-degree black at the time. Richard "Huk" Planas took over in 1981 as executive vice president. He, too, was promoted to seventh. Larry Tatum was the vice president and also eventually moved up to seventh under Mr. Parker. He was running the Santa Monica, later to become

---

4 The Tracy brothers parted from Parker, started their own chain of schools, and proceeded to spread Kenpo in the U.S., perhaps more than Parker did. The Kenpo systems taught by the two lineages are similar in some respects and very different in others.

West Los Angeles, studio for Mr. Parker. Joe Palanzo was moved up to seventh in the mid-'80s, after the others, and he served as vice president until Mr. Parker died. Frank Trejo was managing the Pasadena, California, headquarters studio from 1977 until 1990. Ron Chapel of Los Angeles was close to Mr. Parker too. (If I had a question about someone and who he had trained with, these are the first people I would ask.)

Please note that nobody was promoted to eighth degree or higher by Ed Parker in his system. The aforementioned men went up in rank but by association or acceptance by their peers. After all, there was nobody left to promote them after Ed Parker passed away. There are those who possess(ed) certificates for higher levels but they were acknowledgments of rank, not promotions.

Is There Any Tenth Degree?

The feeling in my lineage, and some others, is that the rank of tenth belongs to Ed Parker. Nobody is really expecting to assume the rank out of respect for him. However, when there is no central source for promotion, as there was when Ed Parker was alive, there has to be another way to achieve tenth. To not use the rank would effectively make the system a nine-degree system, and it was set up to have ten. Someone had to go to tenth but it apparently got out of hand due to the aforementioned lack of a central source. As of this writing in 2013 there are more than seventy people claiming tenth. I wrote *Kenpo Karate 101* in 1999, and I stated then that nobody in our lineage at that time (Parker/Planas/Wedlake) was planning to take the rank of tenth degree. That changed when Richard Planas took the rank two or three years after the book was published. Mr. Planas and I split not long after, but not over his rank..

To be fair, some of these people are not really doing the Parker system anymore. Their systems look and/or work differently than Mr. Parker's—though they are definitely based on his system. Others have started their own systems and associations and promoted themselves. Still others are doing Parker Kenpo but have either assumed the rank or have been elevated by their association. The lines then get pretty blurry when someone wears the Parker patch and belt markings but practices an art that is really something loosely related to Parker's system. Therefore, it's difficult to pick out who's who in the zoo.

There is even debate on the titles involved, and that of Senior Grandmaster (SGM) was and is misused. The way Mr. Parker listed the ranks in his *Infinite Insights into Kenpo, Volume 2*, page 10, was that a tenth-degree practitioner is a Senior Master of the Arts (SMA). Mr. Parker is, and always will be, SGM Parker. Long-time Kenpo practitioner Dennis Conatser in Arizona uses the title for Parker of Founding Grandmaster (FGM), and it's a legitimate way to make the differentiation from those who use the wrong designation. At this writing there are a few senior ninth degrees who have chosen not to take the rank of tenth. It's not that they are not worthy.

How to Be a Good Student

Most students will accept without question what the instructor has them do. However, I believe the student is still obligated to be like a child and ask why, why, why. "Because" is not acceptable now, just as it was not a real answer when you were a child. When we are not sure, we should ask. And our instructor is obliged to provide explanations and demonstrations to suit. (Sometimes those demonstrations hurt!) A lesson only sticks when it is accepted by the subconscious; if your mind does not accept the technique, it will not become ingrained, it will not be yours. Then it will probably not express itself when you need it, because it is not a part of you to give. Therefore, thorough explanations are required along with conscientious practice to "get it."

It is understood by good instructors that human beings do not retain everything they are presented with at a given time. Students need not get upset when they cannot remember something; this is why questions are encouraged. Please note that many instructors do not allow questions and may say it is disrespectful. But good instructors know that if students do not understand something, they will not integrate that knowledge. So ask! Remember too that if an instructor does not cover all the requirements for a test during class, you are responsible for saying, "Hey, we didn't cover . . . "instead of waiting until test day and saying, "You never showed me that."

There will be things you reject. The instructor should expect that. After all, it is why there are so many different martial art styles. People just do not agree on how to approach the subject. Hard, soft, medium systems, more hands or more feet, grappling only, weapons, no weapons, heck, who needs karate, I've got a gun! However, I have found that we often tend to reject information just because we don't understand how it works. For example, I was a hot-shot third-degree black belt in 1982.1 had won many trophies in fighting and forms, did some full-contact karate, and had done okay in street fights. Huk Planas came to teach a seminar at my studio in Chicago and told me that I was doing a beginner technique wrong. Nobody wants to be told he is wrong— especially as a teacher, which I was. But I kept that information in the back of my mind, and thought it over. It took some time, but eventually I realized he was right. It happened to be a very important piece of information; it applied to everything else I did. My body had said, "No, he's wrong" because I had been doing it one way (incorrectly) for so long. But by not outright rejecting the information as incorrect and by taking the time to analyze it, I learned a principle that improved my abilities many times over.

Of course, I do not encourage people to change everything they do in a technique or form just because a visiting instructor says to. I say this because I teach around the world and see it all the time. I taught a seminar in Exeter, England, at the invitation of Jaki McVicar and Mervyn Ormand. My advanced seminar was a question-and-answer "troubleshooting" session on techniques. I demonstrated a technique and heard someone say, "Now we have to change it back. It's just like how we originally did it."

Maybe this class should have waited before making their first change. By the time of my trip there they had seen three versions of the technique, and two of the three matched. By comparing and contrasting present, alternate, and new methods, one can see the value of both and decide which one to use as the ideal. As a guest instructor I advise my class to consider first what I share with them, practice it, then integrate the information when they see fit. Their lead instructor is the last word as to how it's to be done in their school.

Physical Limitations and Previous Experience

If you are physically hurt for some reason, tell the instructors and they can modify or even delete movement.[5] You absolutely must inform your school about any limitations you have. It is a safety consideration. Years ago I had a student who would not do an outward block properly. I did what most any instructor would have done. I walked over, grabbed his arm, and moved it to where it needed to be. His whole body went with it, torqueing in the direction I turned his arm, as if I had put him in a wrist lock. This was a reaction I had never seen. He told me that he had broken his arm as a child and they had not set it correctly. Consequently, he could not do the block the "correct" way. Had he informed me or had I known to ask, I would not have had to find out that way.

Perhaps you did a movement another way in another school and it worked for you. Discuss that with the instructor and decide what to do about it. Sometimes it is better to leave it the way it is. Often it will be improved for you through physical correction and a more detailed explanation. Frequently, better understanding of the involved mechanics, timing, and application of the movement will convince you that the instructor really has a better way.

---

5 In a martial art class it would not be appropriate to just blurt out a refusal. A raised hand and a one-to-one conversation with the class lead or an assistant will be fine.

How to Practice

The teacher's job, especially in a commercial school where you are pay-ing for the service, is to cover the material in the syllabus that you will be required to know. Your job is to pay attention, ask questions, take notes, and practice. Practice is required! Very few of us can see something, retain it, and do it competently at any given time without practice. Almost everything we learn requires repetition to do well.[6]

The first step of practice is to go to class and learn the lesson on a basic level from the instructor, not another student. First impressions are the strongest, and your initial training will stay with you much longer than you think. You will probably feel inundated with information in the first few classes. This is normal and should be expected. An instructor expecting you to remember everything from every lesson is unrealistic. Review should be built into the classes. In this way, the feeling of having too much at once will begin to dissipate in a few classes or by the end of the first month of training.

Solo Practice

Try not to use class time as practice time. It is inefficient, and besides, class time is meant for introduction of new material and polishing of the things you were supposed to be practicing so you can move on. Progress is the name of the game. Every day you do not practice is a day farther from your goal. I practiced every day, and still do.

The actual amount of time you practice is to be determined by you. Start with 30 minutes a day and work up or down from there. You will

---

6 Much research has been done on the value of visualization versus actual physical repetition. I recommend visualization to everyone. It is very helpful to injured prac-titioners on the road to recovery to keep things fresh in their mind. Anyone fearful of physical attack should use visualization in concert with physical training. Think through attack scenarios in detail and always with a victorious outcome. Professional boxers watch films of their opponents to see what they do, shadowbox, and visualize their own reactions. It works for them, it will work for you. A key is that the visualiza-tion includes successful outcomes.

establish how long and when you will do it. Set a regimen of what you will practice. As you progress, the amount of material increases, and structuring your practice time accordingly becomes important. You may find that 15 minutes is enough to cover what you have learned in the first lessons. You will then need more time for the new material. It will take less time to go over the previous material since you should be more efficient because of regular practice.

Partner Practice

Ed Parker told me, "You've got to have a partner." Years ago our partners were called "dummies." They were not stupid; the name came from the mannequin-type dummy. You may still hear the phrase today, "Don't be a dumb dummy." It means if you are the attacker, you should work with your partner, reacting to the strikes, not covering up and shrinking or being like a stone statue. Some now call their partners "smarties."

In "ideal phase" practice, you move the way the technique is designed in order to help your partner get used to the reactions and positions. It is a form of "cooperative opposition." In "formulation" practice, go where they put you. It is still a good idea to keep the occasional check hand up, though.

There are two sides to every technique—I mean yours and the attacker's, not just right and left. You are supposed to know both sides. If everyone understands the technique, nobody gets hurt. The attacker is practicing the attack as the defender practices the defense. Being the defender is far from wasted time: use your time as defender to practice your breathing and learn how to absorb impact.

You both have to agree on how much force will be involved in the session—for example, "hard attack, hard response." Generally beginners should move slowly and without much force. Advanced people and instructors may look like they are killing each other, but they come up smiling. It takes practice. Pad up if you are sensitive to pain or you both want to go hard. Mouthguards and shin and forearm pads are a good investment.

Burnout

"Burnout" refers to the feeling that you have had enough and just do not want to continue. Often this feeling is normal and easily remedied. Learning plateaus are fixtures in the educational process. You will move along a steep learning curve and then your progress seems to slow significantly or even stop. The "curve" flattens out into a "plateau." This is how people learn. They absorb the information then need time to assimilate it. It is possible to learn so much that you can't do any of it well, and often frustration results.

When I was in flight school working on my commercial pilot license, I experienced this. I was working intensively on the license. I flew a lot and took the books with me wherever I went. Then, when I had all the required time in, all the dual instruction and required maneuvers, I could not fly within the mandatory parameters consistently. My instructor was disappointed, as was I.

What to do? I avoided the airport for a full week. I did not stop by to say hello, which was hard since I passed it twice a day and interesting people were always around. I did not fly or read the books. I did not think much about aviation. I was not thinking of quitting; I just needed a break. The next week I scheduled a review flight with another instructor; I passed the checkride with no problem. I am sure I would have failed had I tried to force it through that plateau.

Many studios have built-in time off when they shut down for a week in summer and at the end of the year. I recommend you take time off when you need it. Be sure to talk with your teachers to tell them what's up. Often this burnout feeling comes right before an exam, like mine did. We even called it the "pre-belt blues." You do not feel like you are learning anything because you are already loaded up and polishing for a test.

Taking a break is not the only way to deal with burnout. A pep talk from your teacher can help. Doubling your efforts works too. Pacing your lessons helps prevent the whole thing.

Our Self-Defense Techniques

Not all martial art systems are created equal. There is a significant difference in the emphases of the systems. Kenpo is one of the most self-defense-oriented of today's systems. Many people coming in the door do not know this and it is not their fault they do not. Since my initial books were written, other systems are now widely available that have the same emphasis, such as Israeli Krav Maga and Russian Systema. Know that these are military self-defense systems and that Parker Kenpo is a civilian self-defense system.

The core of our system lies in its self-defense techniques. Ed Parker had a reputation for phenomenal self-defense ability. He was well known as a street fighter in Hawaii. In a magazine article I read about Hawaiian Kenpo, the interviewee stated that he saw Ed Parker "stacking bodies" in a street fight at a drive-in restaurant. Understanding this, it is no surprise that we have numerous interesting self-defense techniques in our system.

The techniques serve many purposes. On the surface they are simply examples of methods to defend yourself against physical attack, teaching recognition of attack lines and application of basic principles. Kenpo people typically spend a great deal of time working on basics, principles, and the terminology associated with the techniques.[7] Techniques are composed of combinations of basics: the single, isolated movements such as blocks, kicks, etc. You gain knowledge of how to hit, when to hit, and where to hit. Or "tools, timing, targets." These are the important lessons learned in self-defense—along with what the late Joe Lewis said, which was "to make the other guy miss."

At a certain point, the time you have spent standing in a horse stance doing blocks, parries, punches, strikes, and finger techniques will pay off. All the elements you have been taught, such as setting your base, methods of execution, angles of delivery, timing, targets, breathing, and more, are

---

7 While terminology is important, note that some will spend so much time working on this aspect of technique that they cannot do a physical technique well but they can tell you in detail what it is and how they are going to do it. The lesson here is to set your priorities.

brought together in an explosive sequence. Now, in a simulated attack, you experience specific examples of what targets to hit, the anatomical weak points. You will see what position both you and your opponent must be in to accomplish that.

On another level, the techniques function very well as devices to teach students how to think analytically. Many of the techniques are called "what if" scenarios or "category completion" movements. Some techniques are designed to show alternatives to techniques already learned—that is, "what if" something changed in the course of executing the original, ideal phase of the technique?

The "category" idea becomes clear when you look at Ed Parker's written work. He liked lists of movements. You see it early in his second book *Secrets of Chinese Karate,* published in 1963. There, the first example you will encounter is on page 124: a list of punches. You will see more such lists in his later books. The system, as he arranged it with the help of Richard Planas and Tom Kelly in 1970, was intended to categorize motion; it was manifested most completely in his *Accumulative Journal,* also known as the Red Book. In Parker's system you will see the same sequences of movement performed on both the right and left sides for balanced development. You do not necessarily have to practice a technique right- and left-handed, as you will find most sequences done on the opposite side somewhere else in the system. The problem is that he obscured them and you have to look hard or have a guide point them out. The opposite-side mechanics are hard to find because Parker either separated them by putting them in other belt levels or disguised them. For example, the elbow sequence in Crossing Talon is done left-handed for an attack from the front. The right-handed mechanics are done for an attack from the rear in a technique called Crossed Twigs. Once you see it, it's obvious.

Knowing the basic self-defense techniques of the Parker system will get you out of most common attack situations. Learning the rest of the system gives you an excellent core system for interpreting or "reading" movement of all types. This makes you better able to decipher the body language of an attacker, even a practitioner of another martial arts system, and allows you to relate different applications of similar movements in other systems. You can look at karate or kung-fu techniques and say, "Hey, that's just . . ."

What's with All the Names and Their Code Words?

New students usually wonder and ask about the names of the techniques. In the Chinese martial arts you will often find movements and techniques with poetic or lyrical names that describe actions, objects, or concepts. For example, "Dragon whips his tail" refers to a type of spin kick. "Willow leaf palm" is a hand formation that looks like the long, thin willow leaf. "Return to mountain" refers to the idea of going back to basics (though it is also a physical technique).

Since Kenpo is a Chinese-based system, it is not surprising to find that techniques have similar names in this system. Ed Parker said that when he was a young man learning Kenpo from Professor Chow, some techniques had names, but not all. Some used numbers as names such as "basic four-count." He interacted extensively with kung-fu men in the Chinatown schools (*kwoons*) of Los Angeles and San Francisco. Having that influence, it just makes sense that he would name all his techniques; having names for techniques also made them easier to list. Parker said that the names made the intangible tangible and added an element of mystery and fun to the art.

Parker told me that he created names to give a mental image of what was happening, either what you were doing in defense of yourself, or what the attacker was attempting to do to you. Breaking down the names and knowing their codes usually helps you remember how the technique goes. For example, an instructor calls for the technique Checking the Storm. Ah-ha! you think. "Storm" refers to a club attack. The technique name tells me that I need only *check* the attack, not obstruct, grab, or trap it. Thinking about the name tells you which technique it is and reminds you what you need to do. It is a bit easier than having an instructor shout,

"Purple belt technique number 12!" When the instructor shouts, "Parting of the Snakes!" your look will not be nearly as blank. Of course, you cannot think about this sort of thing on the street. The names are a learning aid. You are not going to tell an assailant that you are going to do Dance of Death on him and expect that he will run, terror-stricken, down the street.

The code names in the Parker system are partly based on the old Chinese terminology that comes from the saying, "Make every fist a mace, every hand a sword, and every finger a spear." So, here they are.

Mace—fist

Sword—chop (In these pages and in my teaching, I tend to use "chop" and "handsword" interchangeably.)

Spear—finger thrust

Leaves—fingers

Twig—arm

Branch—leg (branches are larger than twigs)

Hammer—hammerfist

Pendulum—downward block

Feathers—hair

Salute—heel palm (This comes from the Fascist salute of the '30s and '40s. Parker was in his early teens during World War II when he saw this in photos.)

Hoof—foot

Wing—elbow

Talon—a claw-like grab; Eagle and Falcon techniques are related for this reason

Death—1) choke attack 2) the attacker would die as a result of your technique

Bear—bear hug attack

Ram—1) tackle 2) punch attack, from the old "Himalayan ram" punch term

Snakes—1) snake around a limb with yours 2) slang, "snaky" people

Storm—club attack

Lance—knife

Rod—gun (slang, rod is a street term: "packing a rod")

Destruction—usually refers to left side

Gift—handshake

Fans—parries

What's with All the Numbers?

Just when you thought it was safe with the names, there are numbers to deal with. The Kenpo forms have numbers instead of names, as well as a "short" or "long" designation. Therefore you will hear a request for Short Form One or Form Six, etc. Many systems have names for their forms or a name and number combination. Mr. Parker numbered the first four forms (Long and Short Ones and Twos) partly to illustrate their timing in the introduction of material to new students. The rest were just progressions. There are a few sets consisting of additional, related information, and they have names only.

Breathing and *Kiai*

The military uses the "Rule of Three." You can last three weeks without food, three days without water, and three minutes without air. Which one is most important?

There is a tremendous amount of information out there on breathing techniques. Some people recommend that you breathe in and out through the nose. Others say in through the nose and out through the mouth. Still more say in and out of the mouth or in through the mouth, out through the nose. Further variations describe whether or not your mouth should be open or your teeth clenched while breathing. I have even heard one person suggest that the skin is the primary organ for breathing. I discuss some of these different ideas in more detail below.

The first experience I had with this subject was in judo. I was told to breathe out when falling, which makes a lot of sense; it prevents the wind from being knocked out of you. I was also told to breathe as closely to normal as possible once on the ground. It is traumatic enough to get hit or thrown hard enough to go down, so you need to breathe normally in order to keep your presence of mind and defend yourself on the ground. ("Normal" breathing includes the heavier breathing associated with exerting effort.)

Judo was also where I was introduced to the *kiai*, the "spirit shout." I was taught two traditional sounds, *sa* and *hai*. I did not think about it then, since I was only about eleven or twelve years old. That is what they said to do, so that is what we did. Now I know that the *kiai* is a tool to bring mind and body together. It synchronizes the physical movements with the emotion and spirit directing those movements. You need to know how and why it is done and where in the body it comes from. The *kiai* provides these elements:

1. It solidifies the body, thus enabling you to take impact and shed it more easily than those untrained. It is interesting to see how a strike that would have dropped you as a beginner can be shrugged off after just a few months of training.
2. It lowers your center of gravity, solidifying your base.
3. It synchronizes mind, spirit, and body. (Ed Parker's definition of *chi* is combining mind and breath with proper body alignment.)
4. It can frighten your attacker. Imagine how you would feel being punched and kicked by a screaming person. When the *kiai* is sudden, it is startling, just as any loud, unexpected sound would be.

The *kiai* comes from deep inside your abdomen, not up in the throat like a shrieking child. You use your diaphragm muscle, the one that causes the lungs to inflate and deflate. It is attached around the bottom of the rib cage. Diaphragmatic breathing uses more of the lungs' capacity, enabling one to breathe more efficiently. As you draw more oxygen, you have more fuel for the body, thus you have more endurance. You flush toxins out of your system better. Ultimately you need less oxygen because you use what you get more efficiently. Familiarize yourself with the terms aerobic and anaerobic: "Aerobic" means "in the presence of oxygen" and refers to low-intensity exertion of a longer duration. "Anaerobic" refers to high-intensity exertion over a short time. Most fighting is anaerobic, since it is of short duration and explosive.

Ed Parker liked using the analogy of a teapot to describe the effect of the *kiai*. He said that if you took the top off the pot as it boiled, it stopped whistling since the pressure was dissipated. He believed one should breathe out sharply through the mouth to help focus the power generated in the movement to be emphasized. This explains why instructors differ as to when the *kiai* is done. I like to *kiai* during the first moves of a self-defense technique, since I feel they are the most important. I want to end the situation as quickly as possible, and if I focus everything immediately I can accomplish that. Others like to *kiai* at the finish of the technique.

Parker described something he called "incremental breathing." His idea was to breathe out in shorter, focused breaths on each movement. This was something many of Parker's students got "hooked" on; if you see them training, they sound similar to Ed Parker. He liked to use either a sharp "hmmm" or raspy "pock" sound, and he would sound like a machine gun—he almost never used the "hi-ya!" sound of the traditional type of *kiai*.

Taiji practitioners recommend keeping the tongue on the roof of the mouth at the soft palate and breathing in and out through the nose. This keeps the mouth from drying out, which happens when you breathe in and out through the mouth. In addition, it completes the body's energy circuit, the "microcosmic orbit." Boxers also breathe in and out through the nose. For practicality, this keeps the mouth closed so the jaw does not get broken easily by a punch. The fact that the mouth is open during the *kiai* and the Kenpo practitioner usually fights at close range is probably why Mr. Parker did not really *kiai* with an open mouth. The open-mouth *kiai*, I believe, should only be done when the opponent is at a complete disadvantage—where his intentional or unintentional moves cannot break your jaw. Therefore, I subscribe to Parker's "hmmm! pock!" school of thought. It is similar to the idea of the silent *kiai* taught by some schools. If your physical alignment and timing are right and you strike with the attitude of the *kiai* but without making a loud sound or any sound, I believe you get the same result.

Many Chinese systems use an impassive face during forms. They say you give away your intentions by contorting your face and yelling. Their practitioners do entire forms without a grimace, unnecessary eye shift, head turn, or sound. I used this method in forms competition for years and did well; but then, I have also done the opposite and done well.

Falling and Rolling Skills

If your art teaches you how to take someone down—be it with a throw, trip, takedown, sweep, leg pick, or anything else—you need to know how to fall. It is a safety consideration. I cannot tell you how many times in my career as a teacher of the arts I have had people come to me with stories about how knowing how to fall saved them from injury. We trip over things, fall off our bikes, and slip on ice. Knowing this skill can prevent muscle pulls or tears, ligament/tendon damage, fractures, breaks, abrasions, bone chips, concussions, and more.

In the judo school we spent a lot of time on *ukemi*, breakfalls. I am told that traditionally one spends six months learning to fall and roll before learning to throw.[8] You start as an *uke*, the "dummy" for the more advanced students, for a portion of the early months. In the beginning I learned to roll, fall sideways, backward, and forward, and do standing flips. We shoulder-rolled over our fellow students. In Kenpo we also do some falling and rolling work in the standard techniques. Personally, I don't think it is enough, so I put my judo knowledge to work in my own classes. My students learn the standard falls and rolls in the sequence I

---

8 In traditional Shaolin systems, students reputedly stood in a horse stance in their first six months of training as well, before learning forms and self-defense.

was taught in judo. The progression works well to overcome the fear of falling. My further explanation of why we need these skills follows. Keep in mind that these skills may be needed when you take a partner, opponent, or attacker down, not just when you are taken down.

If you fall and have the wind knocked out of you, your body reverts to something called "life-support breathing." You breathe in short gasps, which are enough to keep you from turning blue until normal breathing is restored. Falling skills reduce or eliminate the probability of that happening. Now you can fight to win instead of fighting for air.

The prescribed technique of tucking your chin as you fall will prevent your striking your head on the ground and all that that entails. The Russian martial art of Systema teaches the falls with one hand behind the head, and no slaps, a technique I teach as well. It further protects the skull and prevents injury to the neck. The first thing the body does when it is pushed hard enough to lose balance is that the head snaps forward or back. The direction depends on whether the push is from the front or back. This makes it more difficult to tuck the chin. The force involved in doing this increases the speed at which you fall, which then decreases available reaction time. This tuck-and-roll action must be automatic. Tucking the chin is accompanied by keeping the mouth closed. This action prevents chipped or broken teeth, or biting the tongue, if the back of the head does hit the floor. The forward movement of the head resulting from ground contact when falling with an open mouth can cause these injuries.

Keeping your hands up and away from the ground will help you avoid breaking a limb or limbs. Typically people will try to arrest their fall by putting their arms out in the direction of the fall. Bad timing often results in a locked-out arm that in turn damages bones and joints. In the years before airbags and seat belts, many a broken arm resulted when someone saw a car accident coming. The arms are extended in a futile attempt to keep the threat at bay by pushing or grabbing at the dashboard, and the impact then breaks them. There is simply no place for the force to go. When falling, just roll with it—do not lock your arms out to stop yourself. However, in some systems the hands are used to slap the ground. The slap spreads the force over a greater area (as does a roll), a major precept of the falling techniques. Now the question is, "Won't I hurt my hands?" Yes, you may bruise or take some skin off your palms—but that is a fair trade for a broken body part.

When I trained with Mike Sanders he told me a funny story about his Kenpo teacher, Mills Crenshaw. Crenshaw saw Mike, who was also a judo black belt, attempting to integrate throws into his Kenpo self-defense. His statement, according to Mike, was, "Mr. Sanders! The Japanese are a very industrious people. They will pick a man up and throw him down. However, we are basically lazy. We just hit him enough times, and he falls down by himself!"

Strong and Weak Sides

Kenpo, like many systems, is a strong-sided system. This means that almost all movements involve the right side doing the bulk of the work; since most people are right-handed, this is their strong side or power side. We use power-side forward and power-side back techniques: we may step forward with the power side and work from there, such as in our self-defense technique Five Swords, and we may also step back with the power side, assuming a position that the body feels more comfortable with in most instances. The power-side back position feels like a boxer's guard—the body knows it can hit hard from there. It is the same position you use to throw a ball or swing a racquet. However, there is a need to know how to work from both sides. Given a fight with rules, like in boxing or sport karate, you get to choose your guard position. On the street, taken by surprise, you take what you get until you can sort things out.

Most standard, ideal-phase techniques are taught one-sided, mostly using the strong side. There are a few reasons for this. The obvious one is that it is your stronger side. You are probably much more coordinated and powerful on that side. Therefore it makes a lot of sense to respond with it. The second reason is that your brain normally will not let you use the weak side under stress. Spontaneous action is usually going to default to the strong side. This is the reason for training—to get the unconscious response to express itself as effectively as possible.

However, sometimes in training you can fool your body into thinking that your weak side is your strong side. By learning the occasional standard technique on the weak side, it becomes less awkward. This is necessitated by certain situations in which an attacker ties up your strong side—for example, in Crossing Talon. When your options are reduced, you need to be reasonably effective with the weaker side. Mr. Parker taught the mechanics of both sides of the body in the standards, but with different attacks. (The standards are the sequences practiced— the standard curriculum of self-defense techniques, also known as "forms"; basics are the individual moves.) As mentioned earlier, Mr. Parker often put opposite-side mechanics in the forms so that practitioners would get both sides and ideally see the relationships. While he did say it is beneficial to practice moves on both sides, those who do not will gain nominal right/left proficiency just by learning the standards. I think you will find that most instructors can do most everything on both sides, and some in reverse. (There is an opposite *and* a reverse, you know.) A problem for some branches of Kenpo is learning the forms but not all the applications.

Attitude and Self-Defense

"The warrior lives for peace but is prepared for war."
—Anonymous

In martial arts, the ideal is that we never have to fight. The conventional wisdom is that we become so confident in our abilities that we are afraid for our opponent and therefore can walk away without having to fight. Subjugation of the ego is what we are striving for so that we do not have to physically dominate to satisfy that ego. (For a lifestyle that is supposed to do just that, you sometimes cannot believe how much ego there is in a room full of black belts!)

Even in resorting to hitting the opponent, we can use Ed Parker's idea of regulating. We may not have to hit the person as hard as we can. I tell my students that the only difference between a joint lock and a break is the amount of force. It is an example of regulation. Develop the ability to control your motion to be able to regulate power transfer with ease.

Training in verbal confrontation tactics is beneficial. After many stimulating conversations with a private student of mine, he related to me something he had picked up from another martial artist he knows. I really like this approach for dealing with a physically aggressive person. First, you stand with your hands up in a "passive" position, like talking with your hands. (We teach this regularly in our curriculum.) You then say in a loud, clear voice, "I don't want to fight, but if you force me to I will fight to win. Now back off!" This covers the bases. I learned an acronym, CLAP, that may help with this: make it Clear, Loud, As an order, with Pauses. You tell the opponent just what you intend to do and what he or she needs to do to prevent it without escalation. You are also indirectly telling the spectators, if any, that you do not want to fight; this could be handy when the police show up.

Another tactic I have used, one verified by police officers I've taught as very workable, is to speak softly. It tends to calm an attacker because it changes the mood of the confrontation. They have to quiet themselves to get your message. You really have to be intuitive to use this, but I have found it valuable.

Mr. Parker was a master strategist. He told me once that he would *not* say what most street fighters say when starting an altercation: "I'll kill you!" The psychology here is that people hear this all the time. Since they have heard it before and are still alive, this phrase really has little or no effect; there is no real threat associated with it, no slowing of the thought process to mull over the consequences of a fight. But if you instead say,

"I'll blind you," that is very different. I consider this an example of sophisticated simplicity in thought.

Flight or Fight, Posture or Submit

Most of us know the "flight" or "fight" reactions to dangerous situations. These are physiological reactions that occur under stress to prime the body to run or protect itself physically. Chemicals released into our system allow us to warm up the body in preparation. The phrase "turn fear into fuel" reflects this. In David Grossman's book *On Killing* he adds two more stages: "posture" and "submit." Posturing is composed of aggressive stance, speech, and action taken by the combatant(s) prior to any of the other three options. This could mean shaking a fist or making some other gesture, shouting, pointing, or standing chest to chest with an opponent: any of these could potentially end the altercation. As the saying goes, it is not the situation—it is how you react to it. If one option fails, we can resort to one of the remaining three options.

Here is a scenario. You have someone shouting at you and making obscene gestures. You could return the favor (posturing). You could ignore it and leave (flight). You could engage in verbal or physical fighting. Or you can submit. Grossman says submission is shown in animals by fawning or exposing a vital part to the victor. It is common and prevents unnecessary deaths. In humans, submitting could mean fawning as well, or it could mean simply facing the consequences of taking further verbal or physical abuse without fighting back.

Recognizing what your body is doing in any given situation goes a long way toward knowing how to handle the circumstances you face. Differentiating real and false threats is another avenue to pursue. An excellent book on this subject is Gavin De Becker's book *The Gift of Fear*. It is a must-read for any martial artist—in fact, read it twice. De Becker writes extensively about stalkers, those prone to domestic violence, murderers, and assassins. This makes it valuable for police, private investigators, and even corporate officers. It is all fascinating, and much can be gleaned for use by us, the martial artists. One should pay special attention to the chapters on "Promises to Kill" (subtitled "Understanding Threats"), "Imperfect Strangers," and "Intimate Enemies." These, I believe, will help mentally arm you against potential everyday threats. Check the Recommended Reading list in the back of my book for more resources on self-defense. Couple them with your training in Kenpo and you are well on your way to being able to defend yourself and loved ones effectively.

Weapons

"Detached reflection cannot be expected in the presence of the upraised knife."
—Supreme Court Justice Oliver Wendell Holmes

One question we often get, particularly at women's self-defense classes, is about what to do when weapons are involved. The question takes the form of "What do I do?" or "Can you show me how to take a weapon away from someone?" I liken this to a demolition class I took in body-guard school. We learned how to find and identify weapons and bombs. The instructor's final words to us were, "Don't **** with bombs." His advice is well taken. Weapons fall in the same category. Avoid them whenever you can. Then, when it is unavoidable, use the little knowledge you have to keep from getting seriously injured or killed.

Defense Against a Weapon

I believe a responsible instructor will not try to teach people who walk into his class with no experience how to disarm an attacker in one or two short lessons. It has been done, even successfully, but it's an exception rather than a rule. Confident self-defense takes experience and practice—maybe some luck as well. Weapons are force multipliers: they amplify the situation, introducing and heightening the damage potential. The attacker does not even have to really know how to use the weapon in many cases.

Almost anyone can swing a baseball bat hard enough to crack a skull or can puncture your skin with a knife.

"Divert, seize, control, and disarm" were Ed Parker's words to us. These are the principles for handling weapons in the martial system. First, divert the attack and make the opponent miss. How? MOVE! Run, dodge, turn, block, parry, fend him off with a folding chair, whatever it takes. Next, seize the weapon limb if possible or at least control it by grabbing, pinning, or pressing it. Finally, "disarm" comes in two varieties. One is to take the weapon away; the other is to hit the attacker hard enough to cause him to drop it.

Now, all this is very nice to know. However, there are two sides to every story. In karate schools people are taught to use weapons such as a staff or sword. In today's "fun karate" schools people swing around all kinds of reproductions of ancient weapons. These edged weapons are made of cheap aluminum and have no sharp edge for safety purposes. The blunt weapons are often made of nice wood or high-impact materials that come in different colors. My point is that most of these people do not really know the applications of the movements they do, and most certainly do not know how to defend against them. As I said, it is "fun karate." One of the beliefs Ed Parker instilled in me is this: what works for you can work against you, and if you want to know how to defend against it, you need to know how it works.

Kenpo schools include defense against the knife, gun, and club in their standard curriculum. These are common weapons. A good weapons instructor can show you how all this interrelates and the applications of those movements against other weapon types. I think immediately of the baseball bat and the chain or a broken bottle. Each weapon is slightly different. The differences can be in how they are held, used, built, or damage the body. Typically a baseball bat is swung with two hands while a tire iron is swung with one. A knife is used differently than a gun. A double-edged blade may cut differently than a kitchen knife. A broken bottle will certainly cause a different wound than a chain.

If it is any comfort, there is an advantage in facing someone with a weapon. The weapon often is displayed early on in hopes in intimidating. This can tell you, if you have the knowledge, which side it will come from and what the intent probably is. A man with a club in his right hand will not likely switch it to the left. If he does, you will see this easier than if he simply threw a combination punch.

Use of a Weapon

I mentioned that most karate schools teach some weapon skills. It is usually with the *nunchaku, sai, tonfa, bo,* or *kama,* which are Okinawan weapons. They were farm implements used by peasants to defend themselves from members of the Japanese military occupying their island. Today these "weapons" have almost no practical use in our society, but they are fun to learn to manipulate, provide good exercise, and have a long tradition behind them.

On the street, the most common of today's weapons are the knife and stick. You can find them or something like them almost anywhere, any time. A rolled-up newspaper can be a stick and a screwdriver a knife. The stick and knife are considered to be the weapons of Kenpo. You'll see them used in our Forms Seven and Eight. Our self-defense techniques teach you how to defend against them, but you should also seek instruction in their offensive use. I highly recommend taking instruction in the Filipino martial arts (FMA). Eskrima, kali, and arnis are all terms for the stick and blade arts of the Philippines. My good friend and workout partner, Al McLuckie, taught me the basics of the arts he trained in; *Cabales Serrada* and *Pekiti-Tirsia* were his major influences. We both worked with Danny Inosanto and Leo Gaje, well-known Filipino instructors. Al became my model. When I learn a technique, I think about how well it may work against him. He is lightning-fast and powerful. That mental template has been very useful in judging workability of movement.

One of the interesting facts about the Filipino arts is their approach to teaching. While most karate systems teach empty hands before weapons,

FMA often does the reverse. In karate they believe you should learn how to use your limbs first and how to coordinate your body. Then you can manipulate a weapon. The FMA people say you should use the weapon first. It exaggerates mistakes and forces you to feel the proper body mechanics. Once you can do weapons smoothly, you move to the empty hands. Ed Parker did say there is an opposite and reverse for every move, concept, principle, and definition.

The old adage about making sure you know how to use a weapon that you carry is cogent. It is a necessity to limit or eliminate the possibility of it being taken away and used on you. To expand on this point: If you pick up a knife with a vague idea of how to use it, it's not as useful as it could be. If you knew the differences between single- and double-edged, single piece or folders, knife-shape, etc., you would know how to apply the knife more effectively. You might know that a certain grip should be used to keep your hand from sliding forward and being cut. You may know that certain body targets are better for certain knives—some are hacking tools and others are slashing or thrusting. Being trained may help to keep you from being disarmed. If you drop the knife and want to keep your opponent from picking it up, stand on the grip so all he has left to grab is the blade. If it's a gun you managed to take away from the attacker, at least know enough not to pass your hand or other body part in front of the barrel.

Weapons have always been here and always will be. I believe you should familiarize yourself with them even if you do not like them— especially if you do not like them. You may not like guns, but if you know how they work, your chances may be better if you are ever faced with one.

2.

Salutations and the Foundations of Form

Forms have existed in martial arts for centuries. They are a way to preserve and pass on information; we have these forms and sets just as every culture has its folk tales. For cultures to survive, it is important that information is passed on to newer generations—whether through writings, oral tradition, or dance. In the Philippines, for example, the women and girls of the village preserved the dance-like movements of the arts of arnis, kali, and eskrima. Those movements held the secrets of the combative footwork of those deadly arts. Keeping these secrets locked into a dance rather than in a martial arts practice enabled the people to prevent the Spanish conquerors from knowing what they were doing and punishing the men for practice of a martial art. One example is the handkerchief dance, with the handkerchief substituting for a knife: such a dance could be performed in public with no fear of retribution. Those same movements with a stick and knife in hand would lead to punishment. A similar scenario was played out in South America with Brazilian Capoeira. The captors and masters would not allow the slaves to practice something that could be used against them, so the slaves disguised their martial movements in dance and a form of circle play.

Whether disguised as dance or codified as forms, physical sequences carry information about our martial arts forward through time for us to learn, perform, perfect, analyze, and teach. Someone saw the value of combining single techniques into cohesive sets to prevent the loss of one or all movements. Histories of Chinese martial art systems say that the originators watched various animals and duplicated their movements as closely as possible. They put the deer movements together, just as they did with snake, monkey, crane, tiger, bear, praying mantis, and others. This gave them an encyclopedia of knowledge and techniques to draw from. Today we have multiple encyclopedias—material from systems all over the world.

While a portion of modern martial art is probably very close to what was done a thousand years ago, it is likely that most of it has been refined and updated over time. No doubt, much has mutated purely from the process of being perceived and passed on by human beings. The learning and teaching of forms is like the child's game we call "telephone" here in the United States: Ten children line up, side by side. The first child tells the second one a simple sentence. That child whispers it into the ear of the next, who repeats the process. By the time the message gets to the last child, it most often is unrecognizable from the original. It can be the same way with forms. The further one gets from the source, the more change is possible. Add the influence of instructors who don't grasp the scope of the form and you may come out with something very different from the original—whether in sequence, concept, or purpose. This is a strong argument for finding qualified teachers who are as close to the source as possible. Lineage becomes important in this aspect. But while finding a teacher who was taught by the master or a senior student is often difficult, today there are more mechanisms to get the appropriate information. Seminars and the Internet are examples (caveat emptor on both!). They are no substitute for a qualified instructor, but they can put you on the right path.

Salutation Basics

A salutation is used at the start and finish of a form. The main purpose is to show respect. Even if you are practicing in an empty room, you still bow or salute to show respect for those who came before, to the originator of the form or system, and for your friends, family, teachers and/or mentor. In a demonstration, it also shows respect to the audience.

We have a variety of salutations in our system. A simple bow with hands at the sides and eyes up is the first salutation learned. Technically, in our system there is a difference between a bow and a salutation. A bow is to an inanimate object, like the studio itself. A salutation is to people. Whatever the technical difference, a bow shows respect in any case.

The salutation or meditation horse is taught next. This is the introduction to the hand-over-fist position and its symbolism.

The Hands and Arms

The open left hand is placed over the clenched right hand. The arms are at 45° downward angles. The angles are tested by sliding the right hand along the left forearm. No contact is lost when the arms are positioned correctly. If the wrist of the left hand is bent, the right hand drops away from the left, losing contact. The whole configuration should be no higher than your chin. The covering of right by left symbolizes the mind over the body. The clenched fist means three things: body, warrior, and weapon. The left open hand means mind, scholar, and shield. These are paired: mind/body, scholar/warrior, and shield/weapon.

With these hand symbols we show the relationship of the mind and the body. By placing the scholar over the warrior or the mind over the body (it is the same thing, really), we show it is the mind that is more important than the body—mind over matter. By placing a shield over the weapon we show that we come in peace, friendship, and respect. Another interpretation is that we shield the weapon, indicating that we do not display our full knowledge and keep our weapons hidden.

There is some discussion as to the exact position of the fingers. There are two major variations. The left hand can be wrapped over the right, the fingers and palm all in contact with the fist. The other position is the palm covering the knuckles while the fingers are extended in the chop position. (I saw Ed Parker personally, and in photos, do both.)

Hand wrapped.

Fingers straight.

Two more variations:

Angled open hand.

Hand angled and pushing.

The Horse Stance

The standard horse you were taught is used in this salutation. Starting from attention with toes and heels together, you step to the left. You should have been shown how to proportion the stance by turning both heels out 45°, then toes out 45°, and then make your feet parallel to create the horse. (See *Infinite Insights into Kenpo, Volume 2.*) The knees are bent forward over the insteps and out, making the shin bones vertical. In this salutation, the step out to the horse is made with the left foot only. The reason is that the left is the symbolically weak side; most people are right-handed, which becomes the strong side. We show that we are "casting off the weak" by moving the left foot. The philosophy behind this is that we practice martial arts to make ourselves stronger in some way. Perhaps it is to become physically, emotionally, or spiritually stronger. It may be to correct a perceived deficiency, such as a lack of knowledge of self-defense. Whatever it is, training will make us stronger and assist us in casting off this perceived weakness. The left step also physically represents the Chinese concept of

The attention and horse (meditation, salutation or formal horse) stances.

Yin and Yang, the idea that everything has an opposite—for our purposes, the opposites of weak and strong. In a group, everyone stepping with the left keeps you from running into each other as well.

The hands should make the hand-over-fist position as you form the horse stance. As your left foot stops and your weight settles, your hands should be in position. On the "close" command from the instructor, your feet and hands should be timed to move together. Arms normally move at approximately three times the speed of the legs, and since the hands have a further distance to travel—arcing up, out, and down to slap the legs at the sides—the timing is critical. The hands should be in a claw formation, which forces them to make contact heel-palm first. This is an illustration of the double-factor concept used in a claw strike (by hitting with the heel-palms followed by the fingers—see the Glossary for more on the double-factor concept).

The whole closing movement of the salutation is an elementary timing drill like the opening. In the steps, there should be no lag or lead of the head. These simple steps are an introduction and reinforcement of proper body alignment. By moving the left foot out and not lagging or leading, you learn to move your head out of the way of an incoming strike. All this is more formally explained when a beginner gets to the initial fighting stances and foot maneuvers. ("Lagging" means you move your foot or feet but leave your upper body still, creating improper alignment and likely getting hit since you did not increase distance. "Leading" means starting with your head and/or upper body and having your legs catch up. In other words, you stick your face out there first. When done here in the step to the horse, your head and body should remain aligned vertically, essentially becoming a smooth side-step as if an attack were coming from the front.)

About the Formal Salutation

This is also called the long or walking salutation. A version of it is illustrated and described in Ed Parker's *Infinite Insights into Kenpo, Volume 5.*

Ed Parker created this salutation as a combination of the old Shaolin and the modern-day Kenpo salutes. The first half, the walking part, is based on the Shaolin salute. The section done in horse stance, moving the hands only, is Kenpo. Parker explained that he did this to show that our Kenpo is a blend of old and new.

This salutation is seen at the beginning and end of the forms starting with Short Three. It is also done to start and end classes and seminars. Some schools teach it right away; others do not. Either way, students should be told the appropriate interpretations when it is taught. They should not be doing it (or anything else) without knowing what it means. "Appropriate interpretation" means the one your school uses, since each school teaches its own meaning for the salutation and may emphasize one interpretation over the others.

The first four forms were initially taught with the horse stance salutation, not the long salutation. The structure of those initial forms compared to the technique forms is significantly different, so it follows that the long salutation would signify that difference. The points of origin of the hands are different in the first four forms, too. The One and Two forms, starting in a horse salutation, have a high point of origin; this means the hands are at your shoulders or higher. Forms Three and above have low points of origin, since your hands are at your sides. I believe Parker did this to categorize the points of origin in the salutations. To elaborate: A high point of origin refers to having your hands up, such as in a guard or passive position—that is, as if talking with your hands. A low point of origin generally means your hands are down at your sides.

In the early 1980s this long salutation crept into the basics forms. The stated reason was that it gave the new student more motion. I maintain, due to discussion with Mr. Parker, that the moving of the salutation down to the basics forms was done for competition purposes. Many schools had students competing in tournament forms. Our short forms do not have the aesthetic appeal of some systems' forms, and so the salutation was added to provide some flavor to the simple forms. If you count the movements, you will see that the salutation has almost as many moves as all of one side of Short Form One. Without any difference between the salutations for the basics forms and the technique forms, we have lost some reference to point of origin (the effort to categorize high and low), and there is much repetitive motion. When one does the horse and the long salutations together (as is taught in some schools), gestures are repeated. The "hiding the secret" hand-over-fist position shows itself twice, as does the close. This is a break from the "economy of motion" concept: Ed Parker advocated logical, efficient movement. These additional movements defy that.

The salutations initially had a form number that would be indicated by a hand sign. The practitioner would hold up one hand and extend a finger or fingers from the other hand in front of this "background" to indicate the number of the form. (To make a background means to open one's hand, palm forward.) For example, Long One would be done with one hand in the handsword position (another name for the chop position), palm forward at your side. The index finger of the other hand would float just out of contact in front of the background hand. That would be read as a One.

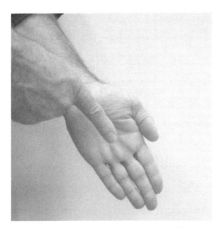

This is Long One, a low form, palm as backdrop, finger extended. Short One would have the finger folded.

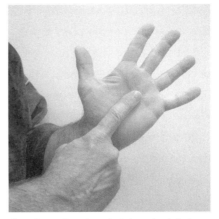

This indicates Form Six, a high form, hands higher than the symbol for One, fingers spread and one in contact to total six fingers.

The origin of these numbers stems from competition. In the early years of American karate competition, some tournaments prohibited competitors from saying their name or form in their presentation. The hand-gesture numbers were a way to get around that rule, so one could still show the audience what to expect.

In my travels I have met many people, seen many variations, and heard many explanations of the numbers. In the early '70s when I studied in an offshoot Kenpo school in Chicago, I heard from students there that the numbers were some sort of Hawaiian hand sign. When I finally met Ed Parker, I asked him about that. "That's really what they said?" he asked me, and laughed. (He then went on to tell me how the numbers originated in competition practice.) I think the details of the how and why of the salutation form numbers have given Kenpo people a lot of fuel for arguments; much time has been spent on determining whether you start on the left or right, for example. I recommend spending your time thinking about and discussing more important elements of the art.

Executing the Formal Salutation

Salutations are like sign language. You must be able to do the stances, gestures, and timing in a "readable" manner; an audience must be able to interpret what you "say" with your body. Each and every movement has meaning.

1. The salutation starts in an attention stance. The attention stance is done with the feet parallel and touching, knees bent, back straight and head up, with the hands at the sides.

2. Your right fist is extended forward first, followed by the left open hand—not simultaneously.

3. As this is done, the right foot is moved forward. When your weight settles, you are in a twist stance. Now the hands will be at your right shoulder in the left-over-right configuration.

    The interpretation of this configuration is "scholar over warrior" or "mind over body," as discussed earlier.

4. As the hands are pushed forward to a position in front of your heart, your left foot will step forward into a left cat stance.

    The cat stance is a ready position, a fighting stance. The hand position here means "come forward to fight." Typically Chinese systems use the cat stance in their salute (either as the salute or within the salute), while most other systems use the attention stance. A cat stance can be used to fight, while the attention stance cannot. The attention stance and bow show respect and trust. The cat stance shows respect and *guarded* trust. Striking movements are hidden in the Shaolin salutes, both empty-handed and with weapons. The hands being at chest level may also signify that one's heart is for mother China, but this interpretation is omitted today for obvious reasons.

5. Now, place the hands back to back but not necessarily touching and pull in a rolling action, as horizontally as possible. Rolling (the pulling motion of the arms) is done by rotating the hands palm-up and thumb-side out while drawing them back to your sides, as in a downward back-knuckle-type move—as if you were to smash the back of one hand into the palm of the other.

Take two steps back: the left foot moves back from the cat stance, followed by right foot back to end in attention stance, all while the hands are rolling. You will end in attention stance with your hands cocked in fists at your sides. All this constitutes the Shaolin-style salute.

Balancing the two forward steps with two steps back shows that the performance is one of demonstration, not challenge. It is widely accepted that one who steps forward twice but back only once is making a nonverbal challenge.

Typically one will hear the full interpretation of this salutation as "The scholar and warrior come forward to fight, back to back, to take their country back." We have to consider the history of the country this came from, as it enriches the meaning of this sequence of movements.

China's history goes back at least five thousand years, but one has only to look back a few centuries to get an idea of what events influenced these people. Much of China was once governed by European countries. It was the Boxer Rebellion that cast these foreign governments out. Watch the movie *55 Days at Peking,* and in the first five minutes you will begin to understand the Chinese side of the story and, therefore, the meaning of this aspect of the salutation. The symbolism of the rolling hands—"to take our country back from foreign domination"—becomes much clearer.

The second half of the salutation is derived from what Parker called modern-day Kenpo. He was referring to the twentieth century. Three hand positions are used: open hands, palms forward; hand over fist; and the prayer position. The crest of the Mitose system of Kenpo, called Kosho-Ryu, shows these hand positions.[9]

6. The first part of the salutation concludes with an attention stance. To start the second part, step to the left into a horse stance.

7. As you do this, circle the hands out, up, and overhead to end with the index fingers and thumbs touching, palms forward and away from the body. The timing is such that the feet and hands stop simultaneously. The end position makes a triangle of the empty space created by touching the fingers and thumbs together. This symbolizes being friendly and unarmed: "I have no weapons."

---

9 The Mitose system is related to the Parker system. James Mitose and Parker's teacher, Professor William K.S.Chow, worked together. The Mitose family did a Japanese version of a Chinese art, while Chow was doing a Chinese art taught to him by his father. (Parker said he did not know what the name of the system was, but that it was a White Crane type of system.) It is commonly related in our oral history that Mitose taught Chow, though Parker said they worked together and that Chow was not a student. See the written history in *Infinite Insights into Kenpo, Volumes 1* and *2,* for more information.

8. Now draw the hands down to the standard left-over-right position, as in the meditation horse stance. The interpretation here is "I hide my secret."

9. Continuing down and in toward the chest, the hands end in the prayer position, symbolizing that one is asking for forgiveness for being forced into having to use their skills.

10. The closing motion is identical to the salutation/meditation horse stance. The claws (heel-palms) are executed up and out, ending at the sides as the feet come together in an attention stance. This completes the long salutation.

This portion of the salutation reflects the ideology behind the Kenpo Creed, which establishes a moral viewpoint for the Kenpoist:

"I come to you with only Karate, empty hands. I have no weapons, but should I be forced to defend myself, my principles or my honor, should it be a matter of life or death, of right or wrong: then here are my weapons, Karate, my empty hands."
—ED PARKER, 1957

There has been some controversy about whether Ed Parker wrote this creed. Evidence points to the fact that he did, but it has been used by karate schools of all systems without attributing his authorship. Either way, the fact is that Ed Parker has shown the value of this creed in providing a moral compass for the martial artist.

Comparative Interpretations, Systems, and Variations

There are additional interpretations of the hand positions in the second section of the formal salutation that I will include here for informational and comparative purposes. The standard meaning of the triangle is that of being friendly and unarmed, since the palms are facing out. The negative space (the triangular empty space that the palms make) is involved also. The points of the triangle can refer to "heaven, earth, and man" in many systems. Some kung-fu systems have used this hand symbol to show their affiliation with the Triads, Chinese organized-crime societies. The forms of many Japanese and Okinawan karate systems incorporate a modified form of the triangle as part of their salutation. The hands are often overlapped, so there is a very small opening of negative space, and they are held up over the head. In this high position the triangle symbolizes reflection of thought, or having a clear, receptive mind, like the moon shining on the water.

The hand over fist in Shorei-Ryu karate—an Okinawan system based on a Chinese art—means "I can control my karate." I think that is an excellent meaning. In Shorei-Ryu, the gesture is performed with more movement but the end position is the same. (By "more movement" I mean using a bigger movement by doing large circles from outside to inside to bring the hands into that configuration.) Often one will see the three positions (open hand, hand over fist, and prayer position) done rapidly at the same height, right in front of the chest. It is interesting how the similarity of these elements can show the historical connection of our arts.[10]

The Chinese systems have many variations on the Shaolin salutation. An interesting one is to hold the right fist with the little finger out. Done

---

10 *Shorei* is the Okinawan translation of the name "Shaolin," so their name would loosely be translated as "Shaolin school." Martial art histories tell of Chinese sailors teaching their arts in Okinawa, so it is no wonder that elements of their salutations survived. Mitose's Kosho-Ryu also came through Okinawa before going to Japan and, eventually, Hawaii. Kosho-Ryu Kempo translates as "The old pine tree system." The Chinese ideogram for Shaolin is two pine trees, the "young forest"—showing another relationship between the systems.

during demonstration or competition, this is meant to be a message to others in the same system. It says, "I'm leaving something out on purpose."

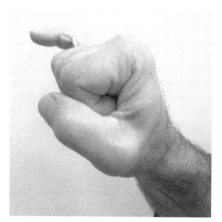

Other schools do not merge the scholar and warrior hand formations. That signifies the historical chaos of the time that the system solidified and the fact that the people did not yet have the unity they needed to throw the invaders out of China.

Schools that salute from the left side are few and are called "renegade schools." Their history states that they come from renegade monks who sided with those who took the Shaolin temple and burned it. (The temple was repeatedly burned over time starting in the fourteenth century. The reference here is to the burning by troops of the Qing government in 1641.) Kenpo is based on the traditional Shaolin, so we salute from the right. It is a common mistake to salute from the left at the end of Long Form Five. The salutation is one thing we do not do from the left for category completion, as it is historically incorrect. Another story is that a follower of Daruma wanted to show his commitment to the Way (*Tao*) by cutting off his left arm. The right side was thus used to remind practitioners of that commitment.

Some forms of Kenpo use two other hand formations, which are also correct. They are the full-contact and no-holds-barred salutes.

The full-contact salute is done with two closed fists.

The no-holds-barred salute is done with two hand-sword or chop formations.

As with other variations of the salutation, these come from the days when challenges were common. That is not so unbelievable when one considers that the same thing happened here with bare-knuckle boxing. Fighting for a living has been a way of existence in some cultures for years. (It still has appeal here in the West. We make movies about it.)

There are offshoot Kenpo systems with other interpretations of the Parker salutation, mostly because they have varied the movement within or romanticized it. Some schools circle the legs out in the second section as they step out to the horse stance. They say they are "clearing their robes." (Shaolin monks had long robes that they needed to get out of the way in combat.) Parker's *Infinite Insights into Kenpo, Volume 2*, describes just such a maneuver—but it is not in the context of the salutation. It is a historical note concerning stepping into a horse stance. When I was in one of those offshoot schools as a beginner, they taught some forms circling with one foot first and other forms with the other foot circling first. It confused many students and gave instructors something to hang over their heads, since you could fail a test for circling the wrong foot first.

The raising of the hands over the head was also thought to be related to the monks. It was said that the sleeves of your robe would fall away from your arms, displaying the brands on your arms, indicating your school. I discount this for three reasons. First, the second half of the salutation—when the arms are raised overhead—is not Chinese; it is from the Okinawan variation. Second, it was the early '70s, when the TV series *Kung Fu* was popular; I think we were told that just to keep us in on the fad. Third . . . well, we do not wear robes.

Self-Defense Applications of the Salutation

All the systems have self-defense application for the movements in the first part of the salutation. The interpretations of the movements are as varied as the systems. I was first enlightened on this by master Wai-Lun Choi in Chicago. Choi was originally from Beijing. He won the Southeast Asia full-contact kung-fu tournament in 1973. He ran the first *kwoon* (school) in Chicago's Chinatown that was open to non-Chinese, and I studied there as an eighteen-year-old brown belt. He showed me how he thought my salutation was applied. Choi had me grab his right wrist with my right hand and employed a common reversal with that arm as he kicked my shin and struck with his left hand. Ed Parker demonstrated several applications of the salutation's movements as well. Knowing what I know now, I realize that Choi simply "read" what I was doing.

In all the years of watching Parker Kenpo people do their art, I have seen only one man do anything close to what would be practical application. He was competing in the black belt self-defense division of the European International Championship held in Jersey, Channel Islands, by Graham Lelliott in 1998. That man, from Ireland, worked the foot and hand movements of the salutation into the close of his self-defense routine. For example, he used the right front crossover as a sweep kick to the head and the step to the cat as a kick. Although there is application hidden in one of our forms, it is our job to find other ways to interpret what we learn. I was pleased to see that idea in action.

The Purpose of Forms

In our system forms act as a dictionary, an encyclopedia, or an appendix—that is, they define, describe, and preserve information. A dictionary will give one or more definitions of a word. If you were to look up "Kenpo," the dictionary would tell you the correct spelling and pronunciation, and might even have a phrase incorporating its use. But this is basic knowledge, without much context. An encyclopedia provides more in-depth knowledge. Under an entry for "Kenpo" in an encyclopedia, you might find a description of its origins, history, outstanding qualities, and philosophy. There would be much more about the subject of Kenpo, not simply a definition of the word. Additional or related information is found in an appendix; the annual appendix to the *Encyclopedia Britannica* updated information from the previous volumes. Some things change or new information is discovered (this especially applied in the past after many copies of a book were printed). The appendix fills this void.

In Kenpo, the first four forms act as dictionaries. They provide basic information and exercises. A brief "definition" of movement is illustrated. Repetition of some movements creates the exercise component and some context. The rest of the forms are the encyclopedia forms, the knowledge-in-depth; they elaborate on how to apply the basic movements, and the concepts are developed further. The related sets are like the appendix, pointing out other facets a student should be aware of such as finger formations or kicking. Sets are defined as "additional, related information"—basically a form containing supplementary information (the Finger Set is an example). The Western Chinese often use "set" and "form" interchangeably, but in our system it's a form with related information. "Standards" are the set patterns taught with their widely used interpretations, so "standards" and "sets" are also somewhat interchangeable terms.

The forms are a wonderful tool for developing many physical qualities. By practicing forms correctly one will see improvement in the following:

Speed

Power

Balance

Endurance (breathing)

Timing

Strength

Rhythm

Flexibility

Body alignment (posture)

Cardio-vascular fitness

Finding physical, emotional, and spiritual centers

Numerous mental benefits can be derived from forms practice as well. Exercise releases endorphins, chemicals in the brain that promote a feeling of well-being in most people. The mind and body connection is experienced in a well-executed form. Below are some of the benefits. (These will be discussed in later sections.)

Mental visualization

Mental speed

Perception of things internal and external

A consciousness of balancing right and left brain

A vehicle for the analysis of why the forms are designed as they are (this is the bulk of technical knowledge)

An awareness of how the upper and lower body work together

An awareness of how the limbs move in relation to the torso

Finding your center

A History of Kenpo Forms

According to Dan Inosanto, two of the first forms in our system are based on forms Parker learned from Professor William Kwai Sun Chow. Short

Form One and Short Form Two are taken directly from the Hawaiian Kenpo that Ed Parker learned as a teenager. Later he would develop the Long Form versions of these two base forms. Mr. Parker personally confirmed that information with me.

There is a significant difference in the structure of the first four forms when compared to the rest. Parker labeled them "basic definitions." Forms One and Two (short and long=four forms) are called basics forms, while Short Form Three initiates the self-defense application forms/techniques that continue through Form Eight. Mr. Parker trained his students first in the fundamentals, then the self-defense—the forms reflect that thinking.

Parker's "Web of Knowledge" is involved in the sequencing of the forms. As mentioned earlier, Kenpo techniques are divided into three broad categories: dead, semi-live, and live. Dead attacks are classified as grabs. Semi-live are pushes, since they can become a grab or a strike and also remain a push. Live attacks are punches, kicks, or their combinations and weapon attacks. These categories were used to sequence the techniques in each belt rank; their original order generally ran grab, push, and punch—or dead, semi-live, and live. Short Form Three (a.k.a. "Short Three"), as the first self-defense form, is for dead attacks. Long Three adds push defenses to the grabs. Forms Four, Five, and Six are all for live attacks. Ed Parker was a logical and consistent man.

These forms were developed over many years. We know that Form Six existed as early as the '60s: it is listed as a requirement for testing on the old IKKA test result form used at the Salt Lake City school run by Mills Crenshaw. (My teacher, Mike Sanders, studied there and I have the promotion form from his brown-belt test. It's reproduced later in this book—see the "Additional Observations" section at the end of Chapter 5.)

There are forms taught in offshoot Kenpo schools around the world that are not Parker Kenpo forms. Some of these include Book Set/Panther Set, Tiger and the Crane (which are Hung Gar kung-fu forms), T'am T'ui, Hoon Chow, Hourglass, and Mass Attack. One reason these forms were added in some schools was that an instructor needed more material to keep the students paying. If the instructor ran out of things to teach, the students would quit, so more forms were added—the longer, the better. If he taught them with a heavy front-end load, the students were kept from the black belt longer, and were less of a threat (as far as exceeding the teacher's skill and maybe leaving to start their own competing school). Some studios' curricula integrated Kajukenbo forms, too. These showed similar movement and application but different rules of motion from Parker Kenpo. These forms should not be passed off as Parker Kenpo forms.

The following list summarizes the Parker forms and sets, along with others he prescribed that were created by his students and integrated into the curriculum.

The core Parker forms include:

Short/Long One
Short/Long Two
Short/Long Three
Form Four
Form Five
Form Six

In addition to the forms there are sets (i.e., forms with related information), which include:

Star Block (also called Blocking Set)
Finger Set
Two-Man Set (also called Black Belt Set)
Coordination Set
Kicking Set

There are further additions to the sets and forms of American Kenpo. Many of these were created by and added to the system by individuals other than or with Mr. Parker. He approved their use yet did not require everyone to learn and teach them. Why he did that is fuel for heated discussion. Those sets and forms are:

Striking Set (now One and Two)

Kicking Set Two

Coordination Set Two

Finger Set Two (also called Moving Finger Set, although the Moving
Finger Set as originally intended was never completed)

Stance Set One (originated at the Santa Monica school)

Stance Set Two

Staff Set (created by Chuck Sullivan from a longer traditional form)

Form Seven

Form Eight

There are people who have further versions of these, like Staff Set
Two. Others claim to have an Elbow Set or Parry Set. There is a Nunchaku
Set listed in *Infinite Insights into Kenpo, Volume 5*, though Ed Parker never
developed or required a Nunchaku Set.

Thesis Forms: The Parker Kenpo system is one of the few that requires
students to create a form. These are known as thesis forms (also called
creation forms or personal forms). When I was coming up in the ranks
it would cause an uproar at tournaments among traditionalists when
someone said they had either modified or created a form. "Who are you
to change a traditional *kata*?" they would say. "What gives you the right
to create a form? Are you putting yourself on the same level as the masters?" It was interesting to see how upset they would get. I thought,
someone had to create the forms sometime, somewhere—so what was
so wrong with a person being creative? I later found that the Parker
schools encouraged this process. Please see Chapter 10 on thesis forms
for more information.

Learning Forms

The worst thing you can do is to practice with no goal or no idea of what
the day's practice session is focused on. Each and every session should be
designed to accomplish development of at least one of the benefits listed

in Chapter 1. If you want to broaden your knowledge base and improve your skills, forms will help.

Instructors should preface form instruction with a brief explanation of what the forms are and what they do. In short, they should tell you why you need to know and do the form you will practice. The general characteristics of forms have already been listed. The specific themes and sub-themes of each form will be discussed as we get to them.

With few exceptions, forms are solo practice. You learn them in a classroom from someone who takes you step by step though the sequence. Ideally that person has shown you the form in a building-block fashion. We have a saying: "If you want the students to learn a lot, show them a little. If you want them to learn a little, show them a lot." I have found that small pieces, done slowly, promote effective learning. You are then expected to practice that sequence, both in the classroom and at home. Once you're able to perform an acceptable semblance of that section of the form, the instructor will give you more.

Typically, you will learn the form facing a reference direction. Most classes start and end facing the same direction. It is easier to learn when the pattern is familiar, with your walls and other reference points always being the same. But when you go home you have to pick new points. In itself this is not hard at all. It is when we start putting angles in and changing sides that it gets more complex.

The practice of forms is an exercise in moving oneself through time and space. It is normal to get lost in doing a form. This presents itself noticeably the first time an instructor asks you to turn to the opposite direction and run the form. You have been practicing in one direction and can do a fair job. Now, when turned 180°, chances are you will not even be able to finish the form. This confusion does not last long—if you practice facing the other directions. These changes in perspective cause a change in perception and reaction. This exercise is a form of mental gymnastics; you are forced to think about what it is you are doing. My taiji teacher, Tom Baeli, calls this a right-brain, left-brain exercise. You have to reduce everything familiar down to its essence and rebuild it in different ways. You cannot just run through the form by memory while thinking about something else. This exercise of facing multiple directions should be practiced with all your forms.

When you were young and learning to ride a bicycle, chances are you did not just jump on a two-wheeler and ride away. Mom or Dad bought you some training wheels. One day they took them off and launched you on your way. You fell down at times, but if you never gave up, you now have the skill to ride a bicycle for life. Martial arts and forms are the same. If you have the drive, some "training wheels," and a good teacher, you will have these skills for life. Do not expect yourself to be able to simply see the forms and do it like the black belts. It will take time and effort. Like your mother and father, your instructors will help you along the way. The first steps will be slow. That is fine, and we expect it. The instruction you receive and the tips in this book will help you.

How to Practice Forms

To illustrate a point about practice, Ed Parker used an analogy of practicing the piano. One person could sit there and bang on the keys for an hour while the other performed the prescribed drills. Both students practiced for an hour, but one was "at it" while the other was just "in it." The "at it" person would likely get better more rapidly by paying attention to detail. Be an "at it" person in your forms practice. Forms practice without focus can be the worst kind of "grinding it out" exercise. It is even worse when you do not know why you are doing it. Take a facet you want to improve on and make it the focus of your workout today. Plan your session around that idea. Rotate these ideas for greater mental stimulation and more rounded workouts; this keeps the forms from becoming stale drills.

Eliminate Extra Steps

Extra steps are small, unnecessary foot movements. Terms such as "floating" and "breaking the heel" are used to describe these mistakes. They are stuttered movements within your foot maneuvers. Often a student will move the foot two or three times in a maneuver when once is enough. When moving forward in a step-through maneuver, an extra step shows itself when the front foot moves first, usually by pointing the toes forward in the direction you want to go. (A step-through is known by many names in the martial arts and refers to doing a step forward or back, changing from one lead side to the other.)

Point of origin.

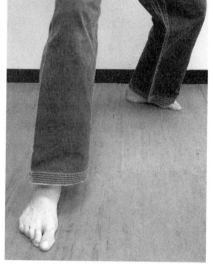

Extra initial move, foot turns out first.

This extra move happens because most Kenpo stances are done with the front foot turned in on a 45° angle. This is counted as one movement. Then the step-through occurs. The rear foot coming forward is the second movement. We now have 50% more movement than we need. A final adjustment of the first foot may occur, making our step-through have three foot movements instead of one.

A step-through reverse will do the same. It involves "breaking the heel." Typically the student lifts the back heel first, then sets it down again to do the maneuver. The step-through reverse can involve four steps as a result. The heel comes up, then down. That is two moves. Then the front foot slides back for the actual step-through. That is three moves. Then the front foot adjusts itself inward to the 45° angle, which is move number four.

Correct heel position.

The "broken" heel (wrong position).

"So what?" is an attitude many people have. Sure, someone who floats their feet may still be able to generate considerable power. But it is the small percentage of gains in power from correcting details that allows smaller people to generate almost as much power as larger people. Here are reasons to delete these extra steps.

Rule number one in our system is *Establish Your Base.* In this instance, by floating your feet and breaking your heel you are unnecessarily shifting your base. Your root, your connection with the earth, is lessened. Smaller surface areas are involved, and balance is unnecessarily affected. Breaking your heel actually causes your weight to shift forward before you retreat. It is a form of reverse motion, since you went forward to go back. This is wasted motion.

Moving the front foot first, as in my example of a step-through forward, also telegraphs your intent to move forward. An experienced fighter takes in a big picture of the opponent. A dropped shoulder, widened eyes, or the small movement of a foot is often enough to indicate that you are about to launch an attack. An inexperienced fighter may be so nervous that anything you do is enough to send them moving away out of reach.

Finally, adding extra steps just plain looks sloppy. Forms are precision sequences. A clean form strips away extraneous movement. It looks laser-sharp and crisp with strong, balanced moves. If you want to look better than your competition—whether that means your classmates, other competitors, or your old self—get rid of the extra steps. In the end you will be technically better, more powerful, and have better-looking form.

Practice in Slow Motion

In taiji the idea is to move slowly while practicing in order to feel every body movement and position. As a teenager beginning Kenpo, I remember wondering how these taiji people could expect to fight when they practiced moving so slowly. As I came to know, being able to do anything quickly comes from practicing it slowly. Taiji practitioners hold every posture and perform every transition in slow motion to familiarize the body with where it needs to be. In training, they will learn a posture and hold it as long as they can. Incorrect alignment often corrects itself. For example, if your arm is held too high, the muscles will tire quickly and the arm will descend to the natural position. In transitions, one can actually feel the individual muscle groups working.

This practice method is valuable to anyone in any system or discipline. When I was in bodyguard school, I learned that the martial artists of the handgun world preach the same sermon as we do: "Draw fast and shoot slow." The motto of the United States Practical Shooters Association is *Diligentia Vis Celeritas* or "Accuracy, Power, and Speed." By doing the actions of drawing, aiming, and firing repetitively in slow motion, one learns to do it the same way every time. The result is fast, smooth, and accurate movement. You can develop martial arts ability in an identical manner.

As an up-and-coming competitor on the tournament circuit in Chicago, I saw many high-quality black belts perform. One excellent and well-known karate practitioner who won regularly was Ben Peacock, a student of the highly regarded martial artist Jimmy Jones. Peacock and a Chinese man named George Ling Hu tied for first place in black-belt forms on several occasions. It was classic competition—hard-style karate versus soft-style kung-fu. They seesawed back and forth for first place. I made it a point to talk with these two men to see what they could tell me about how to get as good as they were.

Hu was not communicative. The one thing I remember best about my contact with him was a comment he made after watching me compete. He said, "You move like a woman." Being a young brown belt from the South Side of Chicago, you would have expected me to bristle. But my experience in the Chinese community, through study in a Chinatown *kwoon*, had taught me that this was a compliment. It meant I had flexibility and grace of movement.

Peacock was much more informative and told me his practice method, which was to take every move of the form and hold it for five seconds. This gave his body time to feel the position and recognize it later when the speed was increased. Once the movements were correct he increased the speed of one technique at a time. Then he would speed up sections. Next, he put the sections together and had the whole form. He would not go past a move at speed unless it was right. I used this method immediately, and in the years after I learned and applied those tips, I reached the National Top Ten and became an international instructor. I teach it to my students today, though I have formalized the practice a bit more now. Drawing on my experience as a pilot, I use a checklist.

The "Pilot's Checklist" for Forms Practice

Pilots use a checklist to help ensure that critical items are not missed. I use this concept to check my body position while employing Peacock's method. I start at the bottom of the feet, checking foot position. I have found that if you "put your mind in your feet" (or any other body part), you get a different sense of what is really going on. Pressure on your soles or tension in the ankles will reveal information about weight distribution and alignment.

Good form, feet parallel.

Poor form due to foot position, toes out.

Move up to the knees and check their alignment in the appropriate planes. Be cognizant of undue pressure or incorrect position and adjust accordingly. Your knees have to last you the rest of your life.

The hip and pelvic alignment is next. In Kenpo the hips are level and the tailbone tucked. It is another facet of anchoring. You can settle more efficiently and develop power and stability this way, and the alignment allows the chi to flow. It looks better than sticking your buttocks out, anyway.

The spine should be straight and the shoulders relaxed, not hunched.[11] Hunching and rolling the upper back into a curve limits mobility and cuts kicking height. Proper stretching of the pectoral muscles will help curb any tendency toward this posture, sometimes called "banana back."

Good form, back straight.   "Banana back."

Your elbow position and hand formation should be appropriate for what you are doing. In forms competition, there can be tenths of a point between first and second place. It may be the position of your little finger in a chop or an inward heel-palm / elbow sandwich that drops your overall score. In the real world, who really cares if your little finger is out a little, as long as it does not get jammed or broken? But it is things like this—or a foot that creeps out of parallel—that hurt your competition score. Once again, put your mind in your hand and really feel where everything is.

---

11 Remember that straight is not synonymous with vertical; you can have a straight spine with your body on a diagonal. Look at sportbike motorcycle riders. Non-riders look at them and ask how they can ride those crotch-rockets bent over. But they are not really bent over: they have a straight spine and the "bend" is at the hip joints. It is an entirely different feeling from being bent over.

Finally, consider the position of your head and eyes. Normally your head is upright and aligned with the spine. This promotes chi flow and efficient breathing. If you look carefully at still photos of martial poses, you will see many tilted heads and misaligned hips. Breathing, balance, posture, power delivery, and chi flow are all affected. Your eyes should be focused wherever the action is to be. As in other Chinese arts, the eyes should be approximately half to two-thirds open. It is a yin/yang thing. A yin and yang symbol represents opposites in balance, with each having a little bit of the other. Therefore, you would not want your eyes fully open or fully closed. The eyes open wide and dilate during the *kiai* or a similar intense stage. In some *qigong* exercises, the eyes are opened to almost bulging, to enhance development of the warrior spirit.

If you use this mental checklist you will have a powerful tool for internalizing your art. I check things off from the ground up since we root ourselves in the earth; without a solid base, as Ed Parker prescribed in his basics priority, all else is reduced in terms of effectiveness. Forms consist of basics, so practice the individual basic moves the same way. It works for the techniques also—they are just short forms.

Suggested ground-up checklist:

Feet—properly positioned for the stance you are using

Knees—bent as required

Hips—aligned correctly for the stance being used, pelvis tucked

Spine—straight

Elbows—anchored

Hands—formed correctly

Shoulders—aligned with the hips

Head—up, suspended, eyes focused

Check breathing

Practice for Power

Spending time practicing in slow motion will help you improve power. Proper alignment promotes development of body momentum in any or all of the three axes of height, width, and depth. Feeling each movement internally will give you an awareness of which dimension(s) you are working in.

It is absolutely more difficult to move slowly than quickly, and even more so when you are also trying to imagine yourself moving fast and hard. Yet moving in slow motion will allow you to feel the contraction of muscle groups, timing of breathing, and settling of the weight. Once you have this "feel" you can speed it up and easily generate the power you want. Power is a combination of mind, breath, and body. Mindful slow-motion practice will help with all three. The initial instruction given to students is primarily external. It is focused on alignment, speed, and muscle contraction. After this is done somewhat correctly they are told to hit with an "attitude." That is the mental dimension. An internalized practice method involves the mental facet more since more thought goes into the totality of the movement.

This is not to say that practicing for external speed and power is wrong or does not work. In fact, this sort of practice is a useful stepping stone. The beginner student's practice will focus on the hard, external movements. But students will soften in method, not in impact, as they progress. One of my first instructors, Mike Sanders, told me that we start with hard, karate-like movements to begin to appreciate how much power one can develop. In Kenpo, blocking (hard) progresses to parrying and avoiding movements (soft). The soft complements the hard, enabling the Kenpo practitioner to have full use of both tools. Breathe out, settle, contract the muscles, and hit hard on every major move.

Practice for Speed

I will have new students do Short Form One in several ways. First we do it slowly, to ensure that everyone in class is doing it the same way. Next we do it with low stances, as low as possible without contorting the body. It's not technically correct for Kenpo, but it is a good exercise and strength builder. I then have them do it with as much torque as possible. Then we do it faster. Finally, we put it all together: as low a stance as possible with maximum power and speed. Now the question is, what happens? The students find that they cannot do it quickly and still get into the stances properly to generate the power. The lesson is that the lower body dictates the speed of the upper body. Students can only do a form as rapidly as they can do it right. "Right" includes being in a stance that provides balance, protection, power, and mobility. When they go too fast, there is just not enough time to settle—therefore there is no base, which means diminished power. This drill illustrates the importance of coordinating the timing of the upper and lower body.

Doing fast repetitions of a form is like doing wind sprints. It is good for building endurance, but it is not good for building precision movement. Moving too quickly tends to make one sloppy. It is far better to move slowly, developing accuracy and consistency. Only then should you increase the speed of the movements, pushing the envelope to see just how fast you can do it right.

Practice for Timing

Martial arts training is a science of how, where, and when to hit. *How* is training for self-defense (how your natural weapons are formed by your body parts). *Where* refers to the anatomical weak points of the body. *When* is the timing.

While bigger people can generate power just by their size and strength, for most people it is difficult to develop power without having the right timing. Even if you know "how" and "where" to deliver a strike, if your "when" is off, that strike will not be efficient or powerful. Doing the previously mentioned speed and power drills will improve your ability to time your motions properly. Timing will come with some guidance. The drills will develop timing. Supervision and guidance will show in improved results when practicing with a partner.

Developing Visualization

Instructors tend to teach things the same way every time. It is when a student does not grasp the concept that a good instructor looks for ways to get the idea across in a different manner. A problem with always teaching things the same way is that we may give an impression that the example we use is the only application for a move. It is very easy to show the first block in Short Form One as being a good defense against a right punch. It gives a student a mental handle and quickly illustrates how the block is used. Yet the student may not understand that the same block can be used against a left punch, a right or left grab, a push, or a kick. This is where visualization drills can help.

"Visualization" may not be the best word to describe this. "Partner exercises" might be a more appropriate term for a major part of the drills. The Japanese martial artists say *bunkai,* which is the translation, interpretation, or application of the form movements. I use the term "visualization" here because seeing the physical interpretations of a form movement on a person lends itself well to understanding. By physically placing an attacker's body in position, one can see how the movement in the form works on a body. This in turn helps students visualize what their movements are doing; learning the techniques should tell them why. Now the mind's eye can see what is happening through the form.

There is an adage in martial arts about three performance levels of forms. In the first level, one just does the movements. In the second level, the practitioner "sees" the attacker. In the highest level, the audience "sees" the attacker. The third level is what we strive for—a high-quality performance in which this pantomime of battle is clear to all who watch it. A master of mime duplicates motion so well that a viewer's mind fills in the blanks. We "see" what is not there. Your forms should do the same.

Watch students learning a new form. You will often see them rolling their eyes up as if they were trying to picture something, like when someone is trying to find the words to describe something to you. It is because they are trying to visualize the movement in that same manner. Some people will do a new sequence with their eyes closed. They are closing off input from one sense (vision) to enhance the input from another (kinesthesia or touch). This elimination of one or more senses can be a valuable tool for some, enabling a fuller experience of movement through time and space.

Practice with Partners

This includes the visualization and application drills as well as two-man sets and synchronization exercises. Two-man sets are prearranged sparring forms. We have one two-man set in our system.

First moves of the Two-Man Set.

The idea with the two-person set is to be able to adjust your distance depending on the size of your partner. Under ideal conditions, both of you would be the same size and weight; this will mean that your drill will work the way you were taught—and it looks good, since the body proportions are the same. Working with partners of varying sizes forces you to adapt your footwork. This then applies to self-defense and sparring. With prearranged sparring, since both know what the other is going to do, the chance of injury is reduced (as compared to "real-world" self-defense situations).

You can also practice "team forms." Get one or more partners and see how closely you can synchronize your movement. This is more difficult than it looks. You will find that you want to use vision to cue your movements. Your sense of hearing and even your sense of energy fields will become sharpened. There will be times during the form when you have your back to your partner and have to listen for or even "feel" for their movement. Try it!

These drills are limited only by your imagination. Start with the standard of standing side by side. Decide what your cue to move will be. Then run the form and see what happens. Make your corrections and adjustments as you go. Then try having one person do the left side as the other does the right side, mirror-imaging each other. Try back-to-back and offset positions. Add more people and try squares and diamonds. Work those facing both inward and outward. These are all great physical exercises. Children in particular will benefit from the cooperation skills demanded. There is a strange and wonderful feeling produced when one sees a group working in concert, even more so when it is a sizable group. Most people will realize that it takes a good deal of work and practice to make such a presentation. It is a great feeling to be part of this as either participant or spectator.

In order to educate the public when doing a demonstration that includes forms, I used to do a variation of the side-by-side idea. We had three team members. One of us would do the form at demonstration speed. Then we would do it again: this time the solo practitioner would do the form technique by technique, and after each technique, the pair would perform the application. In this way the spectators could see what each movement was intended to do, and they were able to have more of an appreciation for the karate form—it was no longer just people waving their arms and legs around in a spectacular manner.

Practicing for Competition and Demonstration

Forms competition has some aspects worth discussing. Like a belt exam, you have a panel of judges critiquing your performance. They may or may not be Kenpo stylists. By extension, they may or may not have any idea what you are doing. Therefore, all of them should be using some baseline criteria for evaluating a form.

In general, all judges will look for balance, stance, focus, power, speed, formation of natural weapons, body alignment, timing, continuity, consistency, confidence, and intensity. If they are truly qualified judges, intimately familiar with the system and/or form being demonstrated, they should then grade on how that particular form is being done. Is it the standard? Has it been modified? Is it just being presented poorly? These will all be considered.

When you have selected a tournament to enter, time your practice sessions over weeks or months so that you peak in that target time frame. It is possible to over-train or peak too soon so that your performance is not optimal. It will take some experimentation on your part to find out what it takes for you to accomplish this. The body needs recovery time in any exercise regimen, so you need to consider that and probably not do a fast, explosive form workout every day. Earlier in this chapter I wrote about practicing in slow motion, and that would be a good tool to use on the days between the hard and fast competition-speed workouts. Plan to take a day off sometime as well because your body will need rest.

Use a mirror to check your body positions, but remember that looking in the mirror may change your body position, particularly your head, and you'll have to consider that. Making a video of your performance is a good option, as is having a coach or teammate watch and make suggestions.

Don't forget that diet is important to the athlete and also that nerves may take a toll. New competitors often lose the first few times out until they get used to the pressure of competition. A good coach will try to recreate the feel of a tournament in the school with a mock competition, drills, or by having you do the form alone while a class observes, which can make you nervous. I recommend going to watch a tournament first to see what it's like, but just diving right in works for some of us. Watch other competitors and see if they have an approach that may help you, such as how they address the judges or enter the ring. Make sure you have a clean, regulation uniform, too. That counts in your score, whether it's in the rule book or not.

Forms were not originally designed for competition. In today's world, you have to overcome ill-qualified judges, system prejudice, and favoritism. By the latter I mean that judges tend to favor their own system since they are familiar with it and know how to grade the performances. When faced with an unfamiliar sequence, some judges are unable to use the default parameters I mentioned above, those being stance, speed, etc. A technically strong performance overcomes much of this prejudice and often favoritism.

As a former international competitor, I took note of some things I saw other first-class competitors do and worked them into my presentation. I initially lowered all my stances to look like the hard-stylists from the Japanese and Okinawan schools. I did that because the majority, if not all, the judges were from those systems and I felt it would make my form look more familiar and understandable to them. It would not be technically correct for our system, but this was for competition. I added the *kiai*, a tactic many Kenpo people use, and I changed the timing sometimes to make the form look more karate-like. I'd add facial expressions to go with the *kiai*. Over time, as I started to win, I began to raise the stances and use the Kenpo flow. Ed Parker talked about tailoring techniques—I tailored my presentation to fit the event. It worked quite well, and I ultimately was the first Kenpo stylist to make the National Top Ten in men's black-belt forms.

Leave the Standards Alone!

I strongly believe in keeping the standard forms in their original format. There are sound principles embedded in the forms, and changes frequently alter or lose them. In my experience, changes in forms are most often made by people who did not learn them correctly or were not taught correctly. If the principles were explained and absorbed, the changes made would never have appeared.

As a former competitor, I understand well the reasons for alterations in timing, stance, speed, and even sequence. However, any altered forms should be presented to the student as such and very clearly so. Previous masters of many systems invested time, energy, and their genius in the creation of those forms. They did this to preserve the information for us, like a time capsule. It is a disservice to students and disrespectful to those instructors to present these altered forms as original work. Over the years I have taught Kenpo in my school and around the world in seminars, and I live by this creed: Give credit where credit is due!

Ed Parker developed a unique system and preserved it in his forms. I learned mutated versions of it as a beginner, and it was only later that I found there were many pieces missing. The system is like a jigsaw puzzle: There is a big picture but you need all the pieces to complete it. Without the guidance of Huk Planas and Ed Parker, I would never have been able to put the pieces together.

3.

The Basics Forms:
Short & Long Form One and Short & Long Form Two

Huk Planas calls these "Basics and Exercise forms" though in truth all forms involve exercise (repetition and physical exertion). But the first four forms have an emphasis on fundamental movement while later forms offer applications of the movements for self-defense. Many Kenpo practitioners refer to these first four beginning forms as the "lower forms" and the subsequent ones as "higher forms."

Short Form One

Kenpo forms can be compared to an inverted pyramid, and Short Form One is the small yet indispensable base that everything else is built on. In Short Form One we introduce the four directions and basic, hard-style blocks. Single-beat timing of the upper and lower body while retreating is the key theme.

This form was first shown step by step in Ed Parker's *Basic Booklet* and was repeated in *Infinite Insights into Kenpo, Volume 5*. The *Infinite Insights* books and the *Accumulative Journal* list what the forms teach. I would like to expand on those ideas a bit and offer some others.

In my lineage, I have broken down into levels what it is that we expect students to know about the form. There are four items we expect every yellow-belt candidate to know: we ask them what the order of the blocks is, where the power comes from, what we call the footwork pattern, and what the form's theme is. These are important for the student to know because they act like a roadmap, telling you how to get from A to B. If the student understands that the basic footwork and blocking order is the same in the first four forms, it should be easier to remember. Therefore, we expect a student to be able to tell us the following about Short Form One:

> The blocking order is Inward, Vertical Outward, Upward, and Downward.
> The power comes from torque, the primary principle used in the One Forms.
> The footwork is called a cross, or plus, since it faces the four walls.
> The theme of the form is retreat.

These components remain unchanged when applied to the left side; it is the same in Long Form One.

If you understand that you will add new information with every new form, you will see that in each form the sequence of blocks is the same, yet there is always something added. In Short and Long Form Two, for example, the basic footwork remains the same as in One, but the other four angles are integrated. Short Form Two introduces the power principles of *back-up mass* (body weight moving in line with the strike) and *gravitational marriage* (back-up mass on downward planes, thus changing height and adding the power of gravity to a move; both terms were created by Parker). The themes change and sub-themes are added. Yet the framework of understanding is erected with Short Form One, the small but powerful base of our inverted-pyramid image.

Higher-level students will be expected to know more about the form. Items such as major/minor blocks, types of torque, differences in points of origin, and methods of execution will be discussed. At the black-belt level a student should be able to elaborate on the relationships of the forms to each other and to the self-defense techniques found in the forms.

Footwork

All martial arts work on eight basic angles. This is the furthest one can reduce the possibilities of attack angles: there are potentially 360 angles of attack, but it would be impractical to attempt to teach defenses against a punch from all these angles. For our purposes, introductions of angle changes in form involve 90° changes first. The 45° changes are next. In forms those angles are the ones we primarily utilize. The orbital switches (45° or greater) and the orbital adjustments (less than 45°) are considered in the techniques on multiple planes.

Parker Kenpo uses the first four directions of 12:00, 3:00, 6:00, and 9:00 in Short One. Alternately you could use compass points: North, South, East, and West. When you draw this pattern on the floor it makes a cross. This is the pattern we expect students to identify, and it will be used again in Short One, left side, and Long One. The Two forms begin with these four directions, and then the corners are added to total eight. One of our general rules is that you finish a pattern before starting a new one. This is a good example of that.

The advanced student would know that the footwork pattern is really an "L" shape. Consider that there is a center point of the pattern. You never cross that center point to truly trace a cross with your maneuvers. It is really caused by the two types of cover step within the form. A 180° cover is done between the outward and upward blocks. 90° covers appear between the inward and outward blocks and the upward and downward blocks. The covers are in accord with the theme of retreating. (Parker Kenpo classifies three types of cover step.)

Timing

The timing of the first four forms (Short and Long One and Two) is reflected in how they are designated: they have numbers instead of names. The One forms are single-beat timing forms. They essentially do one thing at a time. The Two forms are two-in-one forms. Most movements in these forms do two things at once. This line of thinking does not carry past the Two forms. Yes, you can do three things at once, but you'll run out of limbs at Form Four.

The timing is affected by the footwork: remember, your lower body dictates the speed of the upper body. This is why Short One should be done with step-through foot maneuvers. The step-through changes your distance from the opponent in relation to the rotation of the body. Many people substitute a twist-through maneuver. The twist-through first changes distance and then rotates the body. That is a different kind of timing, which is demonstrated in Long Two. The twist-through is a good tool for helping a student set their base and rotate with great power, but it is not the appropriate footwork for Short One.

Power Principles

The fact that your body is three-dimensional dictates that there be three methods of generating power. Ed Parker elaborated on dimensional zone theory, noting that there is a power principle for each of the zones of width, depth, and height. By changing width we develop torque. Changes in depth generate "back-up mass," and drops in height use "marriage of gravity" (gravitational marriage).[12]

Torque and back-up mass are in everything. When you shuffle forward to punch, your body and arm rotate but your primary source of body momentum is back-up mass. Simply punching from a forward bow torque is the main principle but by leaning forward, you have also engaged back-up mass. You can see that more than one zone and power method may be used at a given time. When we say we are using a power principle, we are generally referring to the main principle of a particular move or form.

---

12 I do not agree with the term "reverse gravitational marriage." It fits the definition of back-up mass. That definition states that when body weight moves in line with a strike, back-up mass is being used. If your body weight is moving upward with your strike, I call it back-up mass, not reverse gravitational marriage. (Is it safe to say that would be "gravitational divorce"?)

Short Form One uses torque as the primary power principle. We ask the student to recognize and be able to define torque. The mechanical definition of torque is "twisting force."

There are two types of torque, direct-rotation and counter-rotation. Direct-rotation torque turns your hips in the same direction as your block or strike. Counter-rotation turns your hips in the opposite direction of your movement. Short Form One has instances of both. It even shows the same block using both types. Once I introduce this idea to my students, we run the form by the numbers and say the type of torque being used each time. This exercise really drives the idea home.

The Blocking Order

The four cardinal directions are covered with the blocking sequence of Short Form One. Since inward blocks have no minor blocks, they are the first. Your hands are up in the salutation horse stance, so your first block is a right hammering inward block. We start with the right hand since we are a strong-sided system. The first four forms all start with a right hammering inward block. The left, being chambered at the hip, becomes a thrusting inward block.

You need to know how to do an inward block in order to do the minor moves between the vertical outward blocks—another reason why inward blocks are taught first. Vertical outward blocks are included in Short Form One primarily because we want to preserve them as part of the system. In Kenpo we use them as checks, not as blocks. Yet many systems do use them as blocks, so we have them in the form to complete the category of motion. Since we work on opposites and reverses, inward then outward makes sense, as do the upward and downward blocks that follow.

The Theme: Retreat

I teach the theme of Short Form One as "retreat." Every step in the form moves the student away from the incoming attack. This is based on instinct. Most of the population will back up or recoil when attacked; it makes good sense to take advantage of that response. Stepping back increases distance and response time. It aids in dissipating force in the event you are struck. These are the guiding principles Ed Parker stressed when teaching the yellow-belt techniques. You establish your base while moving away from the attacker, disturbing his balance in the process. Overall it is a safer way for the new practitioner to move.

Short Form One: Detail of the Form Sections

Note: I have not attempted to illustrate every move and sequence discussed in these pages. The first three forms are illustrated step by step in the Ed Parker books if you want to see images for them.

Every block in this form should be done as hard as possible. This will promote a feel for external, muscular, opposing force. (Later sets and forms will show how to ride the incoming force instead of opposing.) The purpose here is to strike the opponent as hard as possible to deflect an attack. By one definition, a block opposes force with force, or against a weapon in flight, without intent to hurt. While we may not be trying to hurt the opponent, we do need to generate maximum power to ensure the attack is moved aside. Remember too that we are moving ourselves as well, using footwork to help make sure we do not get hit.

1. The first section of Short Form One includes the inward blocks. Begin in a salutation horse stance.
2. From the salutation horse, slide your left foot directly back to a right neutral bow stance with a simultaneous right hammering inward block.

     An important lesson is given here: when we step back, we step directly. A common mistake is to slide the left foot into the right and then back to the neutral, "squaring" the step. This does nothing to give you distance away from an incoming opponent or make you a narrow target. By stepping directly, without lag or lead, you gain distance and narrow your width. By sliding the feet, you are able to keep contact with the ground for superior balance, a smaller margin for error, and greater power delivery. Unless you intend to kick, sweep, step over something, or avoid a leg attack, there is no need to pick your foot up. This is one of the general rules of Kenpo governing footwork.

The hands are already up in the hand-over-fist position of the salutation horse, which dictates that the first block is a right hammering inward block. The left hand comes down as you block with the right. The left hand chambers at your side, which contributes to maximum opposite force. Opposite force is another example of yin/yang—in this case it is push and pull. One hand pushes forward as the other contributes by pulling back just as hard and fast. Also called "action/reaction" by some.

3. Since the left arm comes from this chambered position, the next block has to be delivered as a thrusting inward block.

This first section serves to set the categories of "hammering" and "thrusting" methods. The "anchoring" inward blocks (the third type) are found in the Star Block Set (see Chapter 9) and Form Four.

4. The second section of Short Form One introduces vertical outward blocks, as well as the need to cross your body with minor block movements. Inward blocks have no minors; outward, upward, and downward blocks do. In theory, we could make our first 90° cover step to 3:00 and face 9:00, while doing the left vertical outward block, right from its point of origin. The trouble is, we would not have enough travel with the left arm to have much effect. Instead, cock your left hand at your left hip to prepare it, and cover your face with your right hand as a minor inward block during the transition step. Now we have the travel and protection throughout the cover to make it effective. This is an example of a direct rotation powering the block. *Note:* Momentum is not the same as travel. It is a result of travel. Travel is the distance the weapon moves before it hits the target. Too little travel=too little momentum. A baseball player cocks his arm way back to gain travel, which results in speed and distance.

5. The second vertical outward block is done as a counter-rotating movement.

   Both these blocks should be done as vertically as possible, not on an angle as in some hard systems. There are several reasons for this. The main one is that in Kenpo, we do not use this as a block. We use it as a check. As mentioned earlier, it is included in the form to preserve the motion in our system. Our primary outward block motion is the extended outward block. We teach that to beginners in the Star Block Set so they have it right away, even before Short One.

6. The third section commences with a right 180° cover and right inward block.

7. That move finishes with a left upward block, followed by the step back to the right side.

   The cover, as we know, helps us move away from a threat we cannot see. These blocks come up the centerline, through what I call the "intersection." By doing this we can change to any other block with economy of motion when necessary. Therefore, the blocks should be done in the standard method, that is, with the new hand in front and extending and retracting on your centerline. Ed Parker taught this way in order to enable us to strike with a downward elbow as a facet of the retraction of the block.

8. The fourth and final section starts with the opposite 90° cover step. We did one with the right foot between the inward and outward blocks; now we do it with the left foot. Our minor block is now an inside-downward palm-up block. This almost mirrors the inward to outward cover we did in the high zone—one of three horizontal zones used in Kenpo, the high zone extending from the top of the head to the solar plexus. (I say "almost" because to perfectly mirror it, the outward cover would have to be an extended outward cover, i.e., a checking or guarding hand that "floats," usually the rear hand. This is another Parker definition for "cover.") To check the angle of the block, it should be parallel to your thigh, the edge of your fist 90° to your stance.

9. Finally, we will step up to where we started in a salutation horse stance with our left foot. No extra steps with the right foot, please.

10. Perform the hand-over-fist salute and close with the left foot. If you choose to do the left side as well, do not close but instead start the other side with a left hammering inward block.

Long Form One: Some Background

As mentioned earlier, each form builds on the previous form's information. While the footwork pattern, blocking order, and power principles from Short One remain constant in Long One, many additions are made. Where Short One used torque to power the front hand, we now use it to power the back hand as well. The forward bow and cat stances are added. Three new blocks are incorporated at the end of the long form. The addition of the use of the rear hand as a major move is conspicuous. Use of the "highlight" or "stand-out" move is introduced as well; understanding this will answer many questions for the uninformed. The cat stance, a left outward elbow, and one step forward are stand-out moves.

The cat stance freezes the transition from stance to stance to illustrate proper weight distribution in a step-through foot maneuver. Done properly, it eliminates the need for extra steps and unnecessary shifting of weight. The left heel should be firmly planted without breaking away from the ground at any time. This, along with the single-beat timing theme, is the reason we use the cat.

The left outward elbow between the outward and upward blocks is a highlight of reverse motion.

When a movement is done alone like this, the purpose is to draw attention to it. Reversing the motion of the left punch prior to it would make a back elbow. Reversing the direction results in this

Right cat stance, side view.

These two moves, a punch and outward elbow block, reverse their line.

elbow. People like to work this into a self-defense technique. It works but it is not the idea here since these are basics and exercise forms, not self-defense forms.

A step forward with your right foot into the first downward block is another stand-out move.

Both Long and Short One have a right downward block as the first downward. The difference is that one steps forward, the other back.

Simply put, it says you can step forward or back to block. It acts as a signpost to the theme of advancing in Short Form Two. You will find a fully matched set of right and left downward blocks stepping both forward and back in the first four forms. The Two forms show the advancing and retreating left downward blocks.

Transition, front view.   Completed move.

The final horse stance facing 12:00 is called an *isolation.* The isolation concept is designed to draw attention to your hands and arms by eliminating leg movement. In this form, the isolation serves to demonstrate the two inside-downward and the push-down blocks. In this case the isolation says "here are three more ways to block and we will apply them in a subsequent form." We did the four basic blocks in Short One and added follow-ups to them in Long One. We will do the three additional blocks and their follow-ups in Long Two. This demonstrates the consistency and progression of ideas in the forms.

The use of rear hand blocking as a major appears for the first time in the second half of the Long One form. The general rule of using the rear hand with a forward bow is seemingly broken since we don't use a forward bow in the second half of the form. There are two reasons for this. One is that it teaches you to use your upper body like a forward bow when your lower body is frozen in position. This would be useful when sitting. The other reason is that when you block, the attacker is coming to you. When you punch, you go to them. A forward bow is not necessary when blocking with the rear hand.

Long Form One: Detail of the Form Sections

Begin the right side of the form as you did in Short One, with a right hammering inward block. Once settled in your right neutral bow, shift to a forward bow and punch with a left straight thrust punch, triangulated with your center of mass, around the level of your solar plexus, with the wrist straight on your punching arm and elbow slightly bent. Chamber your right hand at your right ribs. The front knee should be no farther forward than your front toes. Your back leg should be locked, heel planted on the floor. Your shoulders will be level and your back straight.

When learning and practicing, make any adjustments now, as continuity and consistency are important and always will be. These positions will be repeated throughout the first half of the form. Instructors will be looking for that consistency for two reasons: 1) power transfer is affected by form, and 2) consistency affects how your form looks aesthetically.

Now is where the first "stand-out" movement is inserted, which is the right 45° cat stance shown in the photo in the previous section (a couple of pages above). Transitioning back into the left neutral bow with the right and left inward blocks will cover your centerline as you retreat and settle with the left thrusting inward block. Deliver the right straight punch as a mirror image of the first punch. This completes the inward block section.

The outward block section starts just as it does in Short One. Everything else follows the same pattern, having the punches inserted after the vertical outward blocks. Some important points to watch here are that you are consistent with the major/minor delivery of the blocks (with the new hand always in front), and that the other hand is fully chambered, palm-up.

In between the outward block and upward block sections, there is another highlight. It is the single outward elbow in the form. It is executed with a cover step of the right foot. There are three foot movements here coupled with three hand movements. The elbow is with the cover, the shift to a left neutral with the left upward block, and the shift to a left forward bow with the right straight punch.

The upward block section follows the same consistent pattern of the first two sections, which is: block, punch, block, block, punch. Once again the new hand is in front and the stances coincide with the respective movements. In other words, don't settle then block or vice versa.

The third highlight now occurs during the transition to the downward blocks. This is the only time you step forward to meet an attack in this form, by stepping toward 6:00 with your right foot and delivering the right downward block. Like a "coming attraction," this is to show that the next form will be an advancing form. You then continue as before, using the majors and minors, punching in between the major blocks.

You have reached the halfway mark of the form when you execute the second punch in the downward section. The second half of the form is simply the left side of Short One, since it starts with a left inward block.

You will use your back hand now without the forward bow normally associated with the use of the rear hand for the two reasons previously stated. Therefore, in the second half of the form, your upper body shifts like a forward bow but your feet do not move while in place.

Execute, in place, three thrusting inward blocks, starting and ending with your left, then step-through reverse and execute three more starting with the right. Do a left 90° cover step and three vertical outwards, starting with the right, facing 9:00. Step-through reverse and do three more. Cover step now with your left foot to face 3:00 and execute the series of upward blocks, starting with the right hand from the right neutral, then stepping-through in reverse to complete the next three, all facing 3:00. Now step with your right foot to 6:00 into a left neutral bow facing 12:00, using another 90° cover step. This is consistent with the theme of retreating we have used throughout the form, with the exception of the one step forward with a downward block used at the start of the downward-block section. Execute the three downward blocks (using inside-downward palm-up blocks as minors) starting with your left. Step-through reverse and execute the three last downwards from your right neutral bow.

The horse stance isolation follows by stepping forward into the square horse with your left foot and facing 12:00. As you step up, deliver a left inside downward block, palm-down, finishing as you settle into the horse. Maintain the horse and execute two more of these blocks, first right, then left, to total three blocks. These three blocks are low point-of-origin blocks. They travel all the way across the body at the same distance from the body as when you throw a downward outward block.

The next three blocks are inside downward, palm-up blocks, starting with your right. These are high point-of-origin blocks. Therefore they chamber high like an inward block. These travel about two-thirds or three-quarters of the way across the body because your muscle structure will not let them go any further effectively.

Both sets of inside-downwards should be done cleanly. Nothing looks worse than windmilling these blocks without chambering the hands or having any regard for the timing involved. Follow with three push-down blocks in a left-right-left sequence. This block is like a heel-palm strike down your centerline on the vertical plane. As such, your fingers should be pulled back to protect them, and the heel of your hand should be directly on your centerline. The hand should be slightly rotated in toward you and the elbow bent. You will probably end with the hand approximately at your belt level. Reaching below that usually results in leading with the fingers, which can result in spraining or breaking them in actual use.

You now deliver a series of eight punches, starting with the right hand. The first six are straight thrust punches, of which two are directed straight ahead to 12:00, then two to 10:30 and 1:30, and two more to the sides, 9:00 and 3:00. Complete the isolation with two uppercuts, right then left. As each punch is thrown in this series, the other hand should be cocked at your ribs, palm-up. Many students miss the rotation of the hand back to the palm-up position as they chamber. This contributes to a loss of power since they are taking the torque out of the punch, and it looks really sloppy. It has a tendency to make one's elbows wing out when the arm is not rotated and chambered, giving the impression of flailing. It is not a pretty sight. Forms are precise movement drills, so work the details.

In closing the isolation, bring your right hand up into your left palm for the salutation as if throwing a third uppercut. You are now in the left-hand-over-right-fist salutation position (see Chapter 2). Close the form by bringing the left to the right as you did in Short One, or continue by working the mirror-image left side.

Like Short One, this and all forms can be done on both sides. This is a good coordination builder and promotes mental stimulation. Unlike Short One, over time Long One moved around the belt levels as a requirement. It was taught to beginners at first. The sequence was Short One, Long One, Short Two, Long Two. Later it became a blue-belt requirement. The sequence then was Short One, Short Two, Long One, Long Two. Then it went back to orange belt. There is logic to both sequences. I feel the Ones/ Twos sequence should be taught instead of One/Two/One/Two.

Short Form Two

Although Short Two is a beginner form, it is difficult. The positional use of the cat stance and use of the 45° angles add a dimension that seems to throw students off. This basic form has a lot of information in it and is well worth looking into in depth.

Footwork

The corner angles are added to the footwork in this form. However, they will not be traveled on until Long Form Two, which gives us the full eight basic angles (directions) of attack and defense. You should realize that although you face the front corners, you don't travel those lines. You stay behind the 3:00–9:00 line you established in the outward block section of the form. Like Long One's isolation, in which you punch 10:30 and 1:30, not until you travel on those lines will you complete the pattern. When asking for directions, someone may point in a direction but you won't get there until you travel. Eight is the minimum number of directions we can use to effectively recognize movement directions. A circle has 360 degrees, yet it would not be efficient to have techniques against a right punch on every one of those degrees. The eight cardinal points are sufficient.

We refer to the eight directions as a star pattern. Since this is a new pattern (having only explored the cross pattern thus far), we apply one of the general rules that states we finish a pattern before starting a new one. We will work the four walls we did in the One forms and then add the corners. The back corners will be first (in Short Two), then the front corners (in Long Two). This will be a constant up through Long Form Three.

Advancing

This is the first of the advancing forms. Advancing, timing, and power are themes of Form Two. Like the One forms, we start with a right hammering inward block in a right neutral bow stance. We step forward to the stance, now showing another way to get into the right neutral bow. Using the idea of categorization of movements, we now see that it's possible to make a stance by stepping either forward or back. This idea is transferred to the self-defense techniques. We may teach a technique stepping forward as a standard, yet reality may force us to step back. Either way, we still get the desired stance, a right neutral bow.

Cover hand.

Since we are stepping in, we bring in the cover hand. There is more concern for the back-up weapon, as we are closing the gap between ourselves and the opponent. This is the reason behind checking with the rear hand on the first move, unlike Long Two.

We don't cover in Long Two because the idea has been presented in Short Two, and we are back to working full range of motion. The check hand covers the middle zone of defense. If the front hand is too high, it may be checked, which can possibly cause it to trap the rear hand.

Timing

The Two forms get their number designation from a change of timing compared to the One forms. We call them the "two-in-one" forms because we start doing two major moves at once. The second section of the form illustrates this. The steps to 3:00 and 9:00 are done with an outward block and a straight punch. The components are the same as in Short Form One but the timing is now simultaneous instead of sequential. The third section, the upward block and middle-knuckle strike, uses simultaneous action in opposite directions—up and down.

Power Principles

New ideas and principles are added with every new form learned. The power principle of torque is found in virtually everything we do. It makes sense that it is the focus of development in the first forms. Back-up mass and gravitational marriage round out the methods of generating power. These two are added to torque in Short Form Two. The first two movements of blocking and chopping are torque movements. The next two of blocking with the punch are back-up mass techniques. The third section shows how to use back-up mass on the vertical plane, a marriage of gravity. With this we now have the three major methods of generating power categorized in the forms.

The second half of the form shows how to combine the power methods in sequence. The downward block/heel-palm section uses torque (the block) followed by back-up mass (the heel-palm). The block and half-fist section reverses that by doing the extended outward block with back-up mass and the strike with torque. The idea presented here is one of getting you to think of opposite and reverse as related to use of power. The simple rearrangement of the methods of generating power is an example.

Much of what is shown in forms constitutes signposts only. The movements are designed to remind you of movement and application or to get you to think beyond what is immediately present. If you think about the power principles and how to combine them, logic will tell you when to apply what. These three principles can be used individually and in various combinations along with borrowed force. Examples include:

Torque—Back-up mass
Torque—Gravitational marriage
Back-up mass—Torque
Back-up mass—Gravitational marriage
Gravitational marriage—Back-up mass
Gravitational marriage—Torque
Torque—Back-up mass—Gravitational marriage
Torque—Gravitational marriage—Back-up mass
Back-up mass—Torque—Gravitational marriage
Back-up mass—Gravitational marriage—Torque

Gravitational marriage—Torque—Back-up mass
Gravitational marriage—Back-up mass—Torque
Borrowed force

This shows that we have at least sixteen ways or combinations to use the body momentum. The self-defense techniques contain these combinations and are easily found now that you know how to look for them. For example, Dance of Death and Thundering Hammer use torque, back-up mass, and gravitational marriage in that order. Lone Kimono uses torque, gravitational marriage, and borrowed force. You get the idea.

Additional Stances

The wide kneel stance is added to your repertoire in this form. The 45° cat stance is emphasized. It appears not only on the cross pattern but on the angles. This essentially says you can use a 45° cat on a 45° angle, just like we do the neutral bows on the angles. With angle changes come perspective changes. While we point the toes at the corner to do a neutral bow facing a wall, we must point the toes at a wall when working toward the corners. This is obvious in this form, and it recurs throughout subsequent forms.

New Hand Formations

Four additional hand formations are introduced here in Short Form Two. The closed fist, used as a punch, was the only offensive weapon utilized in Long One. Short Two adds the chop, middle-knuckle, heel-palm, and half-fist strikes. Given the need for categorizing knowledge of other ways to strike, these strikes are included in the form. A more in-depth look should be taken at this point.

It is not just that we have more ways to strike, it is the context in which they are used. The opening movement of a closed-hand inward block then changing to an open-hand strike is significant. It demonstrates a theme in the form. Instead of being locked into doing everything with a closed fist, as in Long One, we will now explore other possibilities and combinations.

Looking at the sections of the form, we see the closed-hand/open-hand combination twice. It appears first in the block/chop section and again in the downward block/heel-palm section. We are seeing this combination done with the same hand and with alternate hands. This is not only to use those combinations but to improve our coordination. This, along with the third and last sections, familiarizes us with the dominant hand.

The Dominant Hand

To illustrate the dominant hand I use an analogy to the child's game of rubbing your stomach and patting your head. It is somewhat difficult for most people to do. The tendency is to either pat your head and your stomach or rub your head and your stomach. If your right hand is your dominant hand and it is patting your head, chances are your left will want to do the same. The dominant hand will cause the other hand to "follow" it.

The third section of the form—in which one drops to a wide kneel stance with the upward block and downward middle-knuckle strike—is an example of dominant hand in action. Instructors will tell you that most new students will form both hands into a middle-knuckle fist. The same thing happens at the end of the form where one does a half-fist strike with an extended outward block. Either the block looks like a half-fist or the half-fist becomes a full fist. It takes training to get the hands to work more independently of each other. Although Short Two is a beginner-level form, it can be quite a challenge. With all the new ideas and coordination exercises it contains, I consider it to be one of the more difficult forms to master.

Short Form Two: Detail of the Form Sections

The first section of the form contains the inward blocks, as in the previous One forms. Step forward with your right foot into a right neutral bow with a right hammering inward block. Settle your stance as you block, not as you chop. Too many students rush the subsequent chop and deliver it as they settle, diminishing the effect of the block. Block solidly in the neutral bow, then deliver the chop. The pattern established by the One forms continues—that is, a right hammering inward block, then a left thrusting inward.

This is the only basic form in which you cover with the rear hand. This was discussed previously in this chapter (see "Advancing"). The right outward chop is frozen in place as you step forward. This is called "walking up" to the hand, which puts it in the cover position for the second side with no excess motion.

The chop may be done either in a neutral bow or a high wide kneel. In a real-world situation, one would not chop without some form of height, width, or depth change to power the strike. Often this chop is done with no movement except that of the arm. You can do that in the form simply to demonstrate the torqueing of the limb, or you can add a small drop to the high wide kneel to get some power on it. If you use a forward bow for it, like in Five Swords, it changes your body position to that in Long Two and that's not what we are after here. The emphasis is on striking now with the front hand as compared to the back hand in the last form.

The second section uses the outward block, consistent with the previous forms. Draw back to a left 45° cat stance from the second chop. If your neutral bow was correct, you will have minimum movement—that is, only the left foot moves. Should you have to adjust your right foot to get the correct alignment of the cat, you probably had your right foot off the 45° line of the neutral bow. That comes from "creep," the tendency to let your stance go toe-out. You must discipline yourself early to get your stances right in order to eliminate this problem. It will just get worse if you let it go. Your hands will simultaneously cock on your right hip, palms facing each other, left hand over right. This will ensure full travel of the next movement. The cat stance is included here as a transition, in place of a natural stance.

Step toward 9:00 with your left foot, which is logical since it is the light one, and settle into a left neutral bow on the 9:00 toe/heel line. As you settle, your left hand will execute the left vertical outward block as your right delivers a straight thrust punch. Mirror this move by sliding your right foot into a right cat facing 12:00, cocking your hands on your left hip, and then stepping to 3:00 into a right neutral bow with a right outward, left punch combination.

At this point we often see students step to the wrong angle with the front foot—10:00 instead of 9:00, for example. They will then move the back foot to correct the alignment instead of the front foot, which was the one that was moved to the wrong place. Correct the foot that made the mistake! If you do it the other way, you train yourself to make additional unnecessary foot movements. This hinders economy of motion, reduces power and stability, and looks sloppy. It also changes the form, building in elements not originally intended. This gets passed on to the next generation of students.

Section three starts by sliding your left foot into a 45° cat toward 12:00, then immediately back toward 5:00 in a V-step transition, keeping your hands stacked left over right. Pivot counter-clockwise to face 6:00, dropping into a left wide kneel stance. As you drop, your left hand executes an upward block as your right simultaneously strikes vertically downward, formed as a middle-knuckle fist. The block and strike are done at the same time, in opposite directions. In the previous section, the block and strike are also simultaneous, but moving forward and using back-up mass on the punch and torque on the block. This section shows marriage of gravity, which, as we know, is vertical back-up mass. (Back-up mass is body weight moving in line with the strike.)

The middle-knuckle strike moves in an arc from vertical to horizontal and back to vertical. It is another test question built into the form, since it is the reverse of the previous move. Some people like to change the timing here, slowing the strike and managing to eliminate the two-in-one timing that this form was designed to show on the vertical plane. Others like to extend the arc downward and add an underhand hammerfist-like strike.

The second side is done by making a V-step with your right foot. Bring your right foot into your left in a reverse cat transition, then slide it to 1:00. This establishes your base so you can now turn to face 12:00 in a right wide kneel stance. Your hands travel in an overlapping figure eight, ending in the right upward block, left middle-knuckle fist position.

Section four begins with a left step to 4:30 into a left neutral bow stance as your hands do a right inside downward block palm-up, left downward block combination. This is the first of the 45° angles worked in the form footwork. Since you are now facing a corner in your neutral bow stance, your toes will face the rear wall (6:00). This may be confusing at first. When you face a wall, your feet point at the corners. Therefore if you face the corner, you feet face the wall. This will hold true for the rest of the form.

Step-through forward with your right foot on the same line to 4:30 with a right straight heel-palm at chin height as you settle in a right neutral bow stance. Your left open hand should now be covering your right ribcage, and your feet are now facing 3:00. As you do the step-through, you should be careful not to extra-step by turning your left foot outward first. Make this a standard step-through maneuver.

Slide your right foot through a cat stance transition and into a right neutral bow stance facing 7:30 as you execute a left inside downward palm-up minor block followed by a right downward block, timed with the completion of the step. Your feet point toward 6:00. Step-through to 7:30 with your left foot and deliver a left straight heel-palm, right hand covering your ribcage.

What we have shown here is how to connect the power principles. We used torque in the One forms and introduced back-up mass and gravitational marriage in the first half of Short Two. Now we begin to demonstrate the combinations by using torque immediately followed by back-up mass, separating the principles.

Section five requires a 180° turn to face 1:30. This is performed by pivoting your left foot 90° inward toward 12:00 and sliding your right foot back into a right 45° cat stance, ending facing 1:30. Draw your left hand in toward your left shoulder by dropping your left elbow. This will ensure that you execute a thrusting inward block instead of a type of circling inward, which does not exist in the Parker system. We do not do that because it breaks the principles of line of sight, angle of execution, and economy of motion, among others. Do it like you are going to slap your own face, but move it out of the way at the last second by turning it and facing 1:30.

As all this is happening, your right hand and arm have no significant movement to make. Since the right hand was in the cover position at the left ribcage on the previous move, when you turn it will be in the cocked position for its next blocking movement. The end configuration of this cat stance has the shoulders squared to 1:30, the left hand in the inward block position in front of the right shoulder (at the edge of the zone of defense), and the right arm cocked under the pectorals.

Slide the right foot forward, back to its point of origin, into a right neutral bow stance to 1:30 as you deliver a right extended outward block. Note: This is sometimes seen/done/taught as an "extended upward," a kind of hybrid upward/extended outward block. Since the pattern of inward/outward/upward/downward blocks has been established, you need the extended outward block to be added to the progression now. Otherwise, you won't see it until Form Four. Your left hand is chambered at mid-chest in a half-fist formation, your forearm resting just under your left pectoral. This is an introduction to natural positions. You have to be taught to chamber your hands at your ribs. This position recurs in the second section of Long Two.

Immediately fire the left whipping half-fist to the throat, transitioning in and out of a right forward bow stance. Your right extended outward acts as a check, remaining in place as you strike; return your left hand to point of origin at the chest. This section gives an example of how to reverse the power principles, using back-up mass for the extended outward, and torque for the half-fist.

The second side of this section is done by sliding the left foot forward to a left 45° cat stance facing 10:30, while executing a right hammering inward block. Your left hand adjusts slightly across your body to set up for the left extended outward block to follow. You will note that the method of execution of the blocks has been reversed here—that is, we do a thrust then a hammer. We normally start with a hammer, then do a thrust, as in the beginning of all the basics forms.

Slide your left foot forward into a left neutral bow stance as you deliver the left extended outward block, facing 10:30. Deliver the right half-fist in the same manner as the first side, transitioning in and out of the forward bow stance. This step completes the establishing of the eight basic footwork angles.

Keeping your left foot where it is, step forward with your right foot into a salutation horse facing 12:00. Close with the left foot and then bow as in the previous forms. You should end very close to where you started.

Long Form Two

Long Form Two is the last of the basics forms. It follows the rules and patterns set up in the previous forms. The footwork will complete the walls-then-corners pattern set in Short Two. The blocks are the standard sequence of inward, outward, upward, and downward. We are still advancing and using two-in-one timing. Following the principle that we always add new information in every new form, we will find much added to the patterns of the hands and feet and categories of motion.

Footwork

Not only will we advance with two-in-one timing, we will retreat with it in the last half of this form. The inside downward palm-up blocks and inward overhead elbows are done with twist-through maneuvers, which promote this type of timing. The twist-through differs from a step-through. Twist-through maneuvers rotate, then gain or lose distance, or vice versa. Step-through maneuvers gain or lose distance with rotation *simultaneously* not sequentially. In other words, a step-through gives rotation with distance, while a twist-through gives rotation then distance or distance then rotation. Their two-in-one timing is a reason why the twist-through foot maneuvers are saved for use in Long Two. It makes the theme of the form more cohesive—this theme is advancing and retreating with two-in-one timing, not just advancing as in Short Two.

The twist-through foot maneuver never made the basics list because of the rush to complete the original manuals and requirements lists. It stands out as a maneuver in this form and demonstrates the only way to utilize both hands fully and efficiently from this maneuver. The twist-through has applications in both directions, forward and back, in this form.

Front and rear crossover maneuvers are added to our list of new items. What is commonly called a crossover is actually a crossover-step out. These are related to the twist-through done in Long Form Two. In this form we have the front, rear, and in-place (rotating) twist stances. Therefore we augment the categories of twist stances and their complementary foot maneuvers.

Timing

Two "beats" are generally added to the base motions established in Short Two. For example, the first section of both Short and Long Two is like the self-defense technique Five Swords. Short Two starts with two moves: block/chop. Long Two starts with four moves: block/chop/poke/spearhand. This pattern continues in Long Form Four. In that form, Five Swords is six moves: block/chop/poke/spearhand/chop/chop. The addition of two more counts or beats per version is obvious. Ed Parker's idea of the inverted pyramid of information is now more evident.

Hand and Arm Strikes

The new hand strikes are the vertical punch, chopping knuckle punch, hammerfist, claw, vertical two-finger poke, vertical back-knuckle punch, and vertical inward forearm strike. Elbow strikes now included are inward, outward, upward, inward overhead, and outward overhead. Outward elbows are actually introduced in Long One, between the outward and upward block sections. They are shown at the end of Long Two after a sandwiching heel-palm/elbow.

The addition of these strikes and punches expands our knowledge of angles of delivery and methods of execution. We see hammering claws, snapping punches, thrusting eye pokes, looping elbows, and roundhouse heel-palms.

Kicks

No previous form has kicks. Although Kenpo is a hand system, it is unusual in most martial arts to wait so long to start kicking in forms. Mr. Parker believed that a student should develop a strong base beneath their blocks, strikes, and punches before starting to kick. Kicking inherently reduces stability. It therefore makes sense to develop the base with the different hand combinations throughout the first forms, then start kicking.

Two kicks are introduced in Long Form Two, the side and front kicks. Side kicks are done in the second section of the form, front kicks in the fourth. The side kicks are snapping kicks. They match the method of execution of the jab, which is done at the same time to show the relationship of hand to foot. There is a hidden kick in the fifth section. It is a thrusting sweep kick inserted in the front crossover to the uppercut/upward block, which is actually a strike.

Isolation

The isolation in this form consists of the last two simultaneous elbow strikes, those being the left upward and right back elbows. It is commonly thought that the isolation is all four elbow strikes at the end. This leads to confusion and sets the student off on a path of thinking that is almost guaranteed to prevent figuring out what the isolation actually means.

This isolation acts as a test question. Instructors give students guidance as to how the isolations function. If students understand this, they can decipher their meaning. If they do not, they will continue, as many others have, to grind along just doing movement without much meaning. The Russian philosopher Gurdjieff said there is a difference between knowledge and understanding. Knowledge is knowing of information, understanding is realizing its application. Some Filipino systems relate this to a monkey playing ball with a coconut. It just uses the coconut for a ball, not realizing there is something good to eat and drink inside.

Long Form Two: Detail of the Form Sections

This form starts like the previous three forms, with a right hammering inward block. To add use of the front hand as shown in Short Two to that of the back hand as shown in Long One, you execute a Five Swords-type of technique. This shows how you can now use both the front and rear hands after the inward block. Remember, we always add new information with each new form.

You start by stepping forward from the horse salutation into a right neutral bow with the right inward block as you set your base. Your rear (left) hand does not check; it is chambered. Now slice through and diagonally down to the right across the neck and body with a right slicing chop as you pivot in place to a right forward bow with a right straight heel-palm to the chin (or straight finger thrust to the eyes), chambering the open right hand. The timing of the body shift from the neutral bow into the forward bow is, again, two-in-one. The first half of the shift powers the right hand, and the second half the left hand. This is done smoothly, delivering the two strikes in one count. The right chop should not be done by itself, since there is nothing powering it when done in that manner. Immediately shift back into a right neutral bow with a right vertical finger thrust (spearhand) to solar plexus level, left hand chambered. The spearhand is essentially an undeveloped natural weapon. Very few people use this in self-defense, since it requires striking generally harder targets, like the torso, and you are likely to hurt yourself if it is improperly formed. Yes, there are people who use it to break boards or run their hands through watermelons, but that is not your average practitioner. It is in the form to preserve it. Most people would use a vertical punch or uppercut in its place.

Continue to the second side, as in Short Two, by stepping through forward to a left neutral bow with a left thrusting inward block. Once again, take care not to extra-step by turning the front foot out early. Complete the section by slicing out with the left handsword, striking with the right palm or finger thrust in a forward bow, and then pivoting back into the left neutral bow with the vertical finger thrust. The hands do not cover like they did in Short Two; they chamber instead. The main reason for this is that you want full range of motion, like you did in Long One. You want to be able to feel what the maximum power is that you can generate from these positions. You will need, and want, to condense that travel later, while retaining the same amount of power.

Going into section two, you slide back into a left 45° cat, with the hands stacked at the right hip, just as in Short Two. Once again, your feet should have automatically taken the 45° position if your left neutral bow was correct. Step off toward 9:00 into a left neutral bow with the left vertical outward block, right straight punch combination. Now throw a left straight punch from the outward block as your right pulls back just under your right pectoral, at your chest. This continues the "natural positions" introduced at the end of Short Two. Shoot your right straight punch horizontally from that position as your left hand cocks like a jab, fist diagonally up and elbow down by the hip. The left fist is positioned as a jab and thrown as a vertical snap punch. Simultaneously, you will execute a left snapping side knife-edge kick.

This should be done without any leaning of the body, either forward or backward. The first photo below shows no lean; the second illustrates the incorrect posture. Just as a jab is thrown without telegraphing, the kick can be thrown in the same manner.

Without leaning.

Too much leaning.

Therefore, it will be low, about shin height. This combination of the kick and punch shows the relationship of the jabbing foot and hand. It also illustrates the first one of the punch/kick combinations in the form. If you look hard enough, you will see this (the front hand/foot combination), then the (opposite) front hand/rear foot combinations, and finally the rear hand/rear foot combinations.

As you throw the jab and kick, your rear hand will be in that natural chamber position. You then plant the left foot, slide into the right 45° cat with the hands chambered at the left hip, and continue with the opposite side of the section, ending in a right neutral bow.

Section three starts with you sliding into another left 45° cat, hands chambered, then back toward 5:30 with the left foot so that you can establish a base and turn counter-clockwise to face 6:00 in a left neutral bow. As you settle in the neutral bow, execute a "universal" block, left hand doing a downward block and the right an inward block, simultaneously. Here again we have the two-in-one timing showing, but this time with two blocks. In the previous section we had a block and a punch.

The section before that, we had two strikes. We now see the category completion inherent in the forms, i.e., strike/strike, block/strike, block/block. It is one of the reasons the universal shows up out of sequence. The three previous forms followed the basic order of inward, outward, upward, downward. Now we have inward, outward, universal, then upward, downward (and then the inside downward and push-down). It is another example of a "stand-out" move. It is so obvious, you have to ask why it is there. It is there to show the category and also to show orbital switching, which becomes apparent with the very next move.

Shifting in place to a left forward bow, you execute a left upward block as your right hand simultaneously delivers an underhand hammerfist to the groin. These two actions are completed as the stance change occurs, so that your front hand is up in the block position and your rear hand down and out with the strike. Immediately return to the left neutral bow as you drop your left arm and hand into a hammering claw, at face height, and deliver a right outward back-knuckle to the jaw hinge, using two-in-one timing. Your hands are now on a vertical 12–6 line, right hand on top, elbows down, at this point. Continue this section by doing a double back-knuckle, rolling the left hand into an outward back-knuckle, right hand checking, followed by a right outward back-knuckle, left hand checking. These are done at jaw-hinge height and show the complementary angles of the jaw line to illustrate contouring. These two sections could be used against a kick-punch combination. However, you should experiment with a variety of attacks to see the varied applications.

Move your right foot in and toward your left foot, making a V step, and finish the second line of the V by stepping to a right neutral bow facing 12:00. Your arms will make the opposite universal block, left hand on top. Shift into a right forward bow with the upward/hammerfist position, and continue by shifting back into the neutral bow with a right claw, left back-knuckle position, followed by right then left back-knuckles.

The fourth section of the form is started by stepping toward 10:30 with your right foot, as your right hand blocks the low zone with an inside downward palm-up block (minor). As you settle into a left neutral bow facing 4:30, your major block, the left downward, is completed. This step is a complement to the first step to a downward block in Short One. It completes the set of forward and retreating steps with a downward block. In Short One and Long Two, you step away on the first downward block. In Short One, it is with a right downward; in Long Two it is with a left downward. Therefore, both "sides" (hands) have been used. The idea of stepping in with the block (advancing) is shown with the first downward in Long One, using the right hand, and in Short Two, using the left hand, also on the first downward block. Ed Parker cleverly placed this information about how to step forward and back, using right and left, in mismatched pairs, in different forms. Yet now it is obvious when you see it.

The two-in-one timing concept comes into use again as your left downward block flows directly into an inverted roundhouse back-knuckle at head height. Typically this sequence is demonstrated against a right front kick coming from 4:30. The block would hit the inside of the leg and continue right up to the temple. Shift immediately to a left forward bow with a right straight thrust punch to solar-plexus height, chambering the left hand at your left ribs. Follow with a simultaneous left straight snapping punch and right front snap kick. The kick is at groin height, and the punch at face height. Keep the punch on your centerline and not too high. Snap the kick; do not let it hang, which defeats the purpose of this move and the next one, and it just looks sloppy. Plant the kicking leg to 4:30, toes pointing straight to the same angle. Now turn it hard into a right side horse. You will be in the side horse to 4:30, but your centerline will face 1:30. Remember once again that, just like Short Two, your toes will face the walls when using neutral bows on the diagonal lines, and toes will face corners when using the cross lines, as they did in the One forms and at the beginning of the Two forms. In this instance, your toes will be facing the 1:30 corner because we are using a side horse. The purpose here is to use the rotation of the right knee with the stance change off the kick to buckle the inside of the opponent's right leg. Simultaneously, you are punching the solar plexus with your right hand, left hand chambered at the left ribs. This whole section is loaded with two-in-one timing from beginning to end.

The opposite side of the section is done by stepping forward toward 7:30 with your right, just like in Short Two. Don't forget to keep the left inside downward block as a minor during the transition step, which is done by pulling the right leg in and through the right cat stance, and ending with the right downward block. Continue with the right inverted roundhouse back-knuckle, the left straight punch, kick-punch, and side horse with a left vertical punch, ending toward 7:30. This is the halfway point of the form.

Section five follows the same line as in Short Two. You will now go back up the line you created in the previous section, heading from 7:30 to 1:30.

From your left side horse, execute a left front crossover maneuver by crossing your left foot in front of your right in a transitional twist stance and step out with your right, planting to 1:30 in a right neutral bow. As your left foot crosses, your left hand strikes the bridge of the nose with the fore-knuckles of the hand. Your right hand should be chambered at your right ribs to prevent its being checked in real application, and for proper line-of-sight alignment for the next move. The left crossover is a thrusting sweep kick in application, done as the left hand strikes. This section has always been considered an offensive technique, and it works well as such. It is the only aggressive move in the forms, providing a little food for thought and a clue to the offensive techniques that may derive from the forms. With the step-out, your right hand strikes in uppercut fashion under the chin and continues to form the upward-block position, typically striking under the chin with your forearm to open the throat line and brace the opponent for the subsequent eye pokes, as you settle in the right neutral bow. Poke the right eye with your left vertical two-finger poke, leaving the right arm in place as you do, crossing over your arm at the wrist. Follow with a right then left poke of the same type. When executing the right poke, line it up next to but not crossing behind your left. With your palms now facing each other, fire the pokes "pom-pom gun" fashion. You will end with your left poke slightly ahead of your right, by about a hand length.

The crossover/punch combination can be done with or without an accent on the crossover sweep. This section is an introduction to the front twist and crossover maneuver, as it has not been previously included in a form. The strike itself will be seen as either a full-fist fore-knuckle strike, like knocking on a door, or like an overhand half-fist. The uppercut/step-out shows how to use an uppercut stepping forward, compared to stepping back, as it is used two sections later. The two-in-one timing is again obvious, as is the footwork line direction and final position in its similarity to Short Two.

From the final position on the right side, crossover toward 10:30 with your right leg and do the same combination, using the right hand to strike with as you crossover and finish with a left neutral bow/upward block. Start and end the poke series with the right hand.

Section six is done by dropping back along the same line you just came up. Slide your left foot back into a rear twist stance as your left hand executes an inside downward block, palm up. Your right hand chambers.

Remind yourself to keep the spine straight and vertical so there is no "jet lag," lagging the head behind the lower body.

The body is vertical.   The body is "lagging."

This gives you an example of frictional pull used on a block that is being done like a parry, and directional harmony. Pivot immediately into a right neutral bow to 10:30 with a right vertical snap punch at waist height, left hand chambered. This sequence would be used against a right front kick, so that the punch would hit the short ribs or kidney, as you would be working the opponent from behind. This section introduces the rear twist, so we now have both front and rear twist added to our category of stances. We also now have the front crossover and rear twist-through added to the foot maneuvers category. A further note about this section is that we break sequence here in the downward blocks. In Long One, when we show the three additional blocks in the isolation, we do palm-down, then palm-up and push-down. In Long Two, we do palm-up, then palm-down and push-down. This is because when we come out of the eye pokes, our hands and arms are not in the appropriate point of origin to do a palm-down block. Use this type of thinking to uncover more reasons for sequencing in all your forms.

The opposite side is done by staying on the same line and retreating to 4:30 with your right foot and blocking with the right hand. Pivot out and deliver a left vertical snap punch from a left neutral facing 10:30, right hand chambered. This particular "technique" shows how to block and strike using both hands while changing your stance from one side to the other. The next sequence shows how to use one hand to do the same job, utilizing a necessary timing change.

Section seven requires that you change angles by 90°. You completed the footwork angle sequence as in Short Two when you did the last of the finger pokes. Then you start reversing the lines. Ed Parker said there is an opposite and a reverse for everything.

From your left neutral bow, step back to 7:30 with your right foot, as your left punching hand becomes an inside downward palm-down block. Settle into a left neutral facing 1:30 as your left hand continues its motion, using two-in-one timing, to strike under the chin in snapping vertical back-knuckle fashion. It's like the uppercut in section five, but moving and settling back. Your right hand chambers. This could also be an outward back-knuckle instead of vertical, but I like the vertical to keep the uppercut forward/uppercut back set of moves.

Continue back down that line, the 1:30–7:30, with a left step-through reverse and a right inside downward palm-down block. Flow with the block into the right vertical back-knuckle as you settle in the right neutral bow facing 1:30, left hand chambered.

Section eight now works forward, up the same line you just established facing 1:30. It has three identical sections that use the push-down block, our final block in Long One, and the rotating twist stance, the third type of twist.

From the right neutral bow, pivot hard into a forward bow with a left push-down block, right hand chambered. Transition into a right front rotating twist stance to bring your left shoulder into alignment for the next move. Do not bounce during the transition. Step-through forward, out of the twist, with your left foot to 1:30 as your left arm does a left outward overhead elbow and hammering claw, ending in a left neutral bow. Repeat on the opposite side by pivoting to a left forward bow with a right push-down block, right step-through to 1:30, and right overhead elbow and claw. Repeat the first side once more to end facing 1:30 in a left neutral bow with the left claw.

This section points out the timing change from the step-through maneuver to the twist-through maneuver. To repeat, a step-through gives rotation with distance, while a twist-through gives rotation then distance or distance then rotation. This and the next section show the twist-through forward and reverse. The outward overhead elbows use double factoring (two-in-one timing), since they elbow and claw. They also show the out-ward overhead path of travel, while the inward overheads will be shown shortly afterward. In addition, your footwork has traveled a "long line," something that will be significant in forms to come.

Now in a left neutral bow with your left claw up, shift in place to a left forward bow with a right straight thrust punch, left hand chambered. Immediately shift back into the neutral bow with a left inside vertical forearm strike, which should look like an inward block. This shows the reverse sequence of the block and punch used in Long One. Long One blocks, then punches; Long Two punches, then blocks. The idea here is that you punch and the opponent blocks it and comes in, so you use the block-type action after the punch to either block or strike.

This last section of the form travels back down the long line and into an isolation horse. From the left inward block, twist-through reverse with your left foot back to 7:30. Unwind into a right neutral bow facing 1:30 with a right inward overhead elbow. Your left hand can do one of two actions at this time. It can chamber or it may be used to show a grab or hook to the opponent's incoming head during an attempted tackle from which you pull him into the elbow.

Duplicate the action on the opposite side by doing a right twist-through reverse and a left inward overhead elbow, right hand chambering or grabbing. Show the gravitational marriage in this technique by dropping your weight with the elbows. You should be facing 1:30 in a left neutral bow.

You now step back with your left foot into a square horse, facing 12:00. As your left foot stops and you settle into your stance, your right inward elbow and left heel-palm execute an elbow sandwich. The heel of your left hand should make contact with your right elbow, not your fingers. This is important to show the proper formation of the elbow sandwich, a weapon not previously shown. Ideally your left hand should be a hand-sword formation, for a clean move, both in execution and in looks. Letting the fingers be limp and unformed promotes sloppy-looking form and does not work well in application.

Slide the left over, to the right and on top of the right arm, as your right arm draws under and to the left. This action cocks both arms for the next move, as well as provides follow-through for the elbow sandwich. Drive both arms out into twin outward elbows, fists closed, palms down. The actual isolation occurs now, as you deliver a right back elbow with a left upward elbow.

Your hands should be closed, although relaxed until the time of impact. Be aware of "false
travel." It is easy to create an impression of travel
with the weapon, even when it is not really moving much. To prevent it, keep your compact unit
(which is the elbow pinched to the biceps, created when you did the outward elbow) and
throw from there. Do not let the hands lead.

Bring your right hand up and your left hand
down into the hand-over-fist salutation in the

Ending isolation.

horse. Close by bringing your left foot to the
right, as you did in each form so far. Bow. This completes Long Form
Two. You will see that you have ended in a position back and to the
left of where you started. It is not necessary to end in the same spot, as
some people think. You should not, in this form, because of the footwork lines.

In Closing

You will notice that we did not prescribe a particular attack for most of
the form "techniques." Some have an attack to help demonstrate application of a sequence. Most do not because they are basics and exercise,
which accurately describes what they do. An embryonic basic such as an
inward block could be used to block, strike as a hammer or rake, or be an
inward forearm strike. I think that would be more accurately described as
an inward motion, thus removing a prejudice as to what the movement
is. In this manner, one sees that the first blocks in Short One could easily
be against a punch, a kick, a grab, or a push attempt. It is the method and
angle of execution that are important. The multiple applications are up
to you. There are common attacks utilized to get the student to use the
appropriate timing and power, so you will see the first block used against
a right and so on. Many of us saw Ed Parker do Short One grabbing with

his rear hand and using the blocking hand to break the arm. He was showing us some of the many possibilities of application.

It is your responsibility to research these possibilities, regardless of your rank and time in grade. Do not wait for someone to spoon-feed you the answers, or it may never happen. After more than forty years in Kenpo, I still find more information in the forms. You will not figure out the whole picture without knowing the forms completely and correctly, and by having the guidance of knowledgeable instructors. I was fortunate to have those people available in the persons of Ed Parker and Huk Planas.

4.

The Intermediate Forms:
Short Form Three
and Long Form Three

Short Form Three

Short Form Three is the first form to use actual self-defense techniques from the system's syllabus, most of them in full. The theme of this form is "dead" attacks (grabs only). Recall that the three attack categories established by Ed Parker are dead, semi-live, and live. Dead attacks are grabs, semi-live are pushes, and live are punches, kicks, and weapons. His Web of Knowledge initially broke attacks down in that order of priority, so the forms followed the same sequence. Long Form Three includes the dead and semi-live attacks, and Form Four contains the live attacks.

One should look for the relationships among the techniques in any form. The overarching relationship or theme here is that the techniques, as I have stated, aim to defend against grabs of several types. The Web of Knowledge differentiates between grabs, holds, hugs, locks, and chokes, among other attacks. This form addresses all of the above under the broad label of "grabs."

As an underlying relationship, most of the thirteen techniques utilize dual movement, shown immediately in the first technique with the U-punch. Due to the multiple types of elbow strikes and forward bow stances, some people call this the "elbow set" or the "forward bow set." I never heard Mr. Parker refer to it that way. Regardless, it is mainly the defense against grabs and the opposites and reverses within these particular techniques that give this form an important place in our system.

Technique Sequence

Destructive Twins   Grip of Death

Crashing Wings   Locked Wing

Twirling Wings   Crossed Twigs

Circling Wing   Wings of Silk

Crossing Talon   Conquering Shield

Scraping Hoof   Striking Serpent's Head

Fatal Cross

Students of variants of the Parker system may not recognize these names or may see similarities in them like "Silk Wing" instead of "Wings of Silk." Most will recognize the sequence, though the angles will typically be different, and there are reasons for that. Suffice to say that the information I now give you will apply anyway, if you do the technique similarly. Perhaps my explanations will clarify reasons for given angles, etc., and make the form more meaningful.

Opening and Closing

The form is opened and closed with the long salutation described in Chapter 2, "Executing the Formal Salutation." I have observed that many people add extraneous and/or superfluous movements to the salutation and may detract from its meanings.

An aesthetic balance is gained by doing the salute at the beginning and end; however, it should not be done between execution of a form on the right and left sides, where a simple close separates the sides of the form. The Three forms should be started with the hands down at attention, not from the salutation horse. Why? Because the salutation horse shows the high point of origin of the hands, and the other position, the close and attention stance of the long salutation, shows the low point of origin. The basics forms (One and Two) use the high, and the technique forms use the low.

Destructive Twins

This technique, Destructive Twins, gets its name from the opening U- or horseshoe punch—the twin punches to the groin and face. It is a defense against a two-handed front choke or pulling lapel grab. The right foot steps in between the opponent's feet with the pull (which uses borrowed force and the principle of purposeful compliance). You settle into a right neutral bow stance. The effect of the twin punches is that the opponent's body does not know where to go. The head-shot makes the body arch back, bringing the torso forward as the head goes back. The groin shot makes the body bend forward, moving the midsection back. The end result is that the body is confused and stays where it is, essentially frozen in place.

The next step with the right foot is to the outside of the opponent's left foot to check and to gain leverage for the hand movements that go with it. The high left hand now drops heavily onto the opponent's right arm to clear it, and snakes through under the opponent's left arm. Simultaneously the right arm is executing an inward block (strike, actually) above the left elbow. The left arm, which was snaking under, now takes the place of the right at the opponent's left elbow to check it, looking like a vertical outward block. These hand movements are synchronized with the right step to the outside and end in a right forward bow stance, right hand chambered. It is common to see this part of the technique done without the snake-through movement. Usually people do this by merely moving their left arm around and under to get the vertical outward position. This leaves no check in place to prevent the opponent from using the right hand in retaliation.

Deliver a left four-finger thrust to the eyes from the vertical outward position. This will cause the opponent to bring his hands to his eyes to protect them. This gives you a handle to grab at the wrist.

Now sink into a horse stance facing 10:30 and deliver a right straight thrust punch to the opponent's left ribcage. The left hand is pulling in and down to your left hip to ensure angle of cancellation.

There are several points of interest in this technique. The U-punch continues the two-in-one timing we were introduced to in Short Form Two. The inward-outward combination used to clear the arms off is followed by a punch. This is the minor-major block-punch sequence we did so much of in Long Form One, but with the punching hand forward instead of back. The finger strike is an insert to allow us to pull this off. Yet it neatly fits the category started in Long Form One, and continued in Long Two and here. That category would be inward-outward block combinations.

I have also observed that some of the hard-style systems start their third form with a U-punch as well. What do you think?

Crashing Wings

Slide the right foot back from the horse stance to a 45° cat stance facing 12:00 while executing twin eye flicks to load your arms for the double downward elbow drop into Crashing Wings. The elbows are anchored as the right foot steps out to 3:00 and the weight is dropped into a square horse stance to break the rear bear hug.

Continue by sliding the left foot to the right in a reverse cat stance (high reverse close kneel) and stacking the hands at the right hip, left hand over right. The left foot continues to travel on a diagonal to 8:00, creating a left reverse bow stance. This is the first instance of the "7" footwork pattern. You will see this again in the next form, Long Three.

Pivot hard to the left into a left neutral bow on the 8:00 line, delivering a left outward and upward elbow to the chin while cocking the right arm high, in the hammering inward block fashion. Continue to pivot to the left into a forward bow stance and finish this technique with a right chopping hammerfist to the groin. The right arm should be left extended in the hammerfist position over the left knee. In application this lockout (keep the elbow bent, though) acts as a check to prevent the falling opponent's legs from unintentionally coming up to the defender's face. The left hand is chambered at the left hip, as in the technique. As it chambers it helps pull the opponent over the leg and control where he falls, which should be with his head to about 1:30.

As a side note, people often fall over with their opponent when they do this technique. The solution is to lean and lock hard into the forward bow stance. When you turn and don't lean enough, the rotation serves to help you go down. You have enough problems with the attacker hanging on, so don't compound it with poor technique and then have to go into grappling on the ground—and that's if you don't manage to get hurt on the way down. With limbs tangling in the process of falling and trying to extricate yourselves, it is easy to fall on an ankle or hit your head.

Twirling Wings

Twirling Wings is a defense for an extended rear two-hand choke or a single or double collar or shoulder grab. If a single grab, it usually targets the right shoulder or is centered at the collar. The standard technique is against a left grab or two-hand choke.

Starting from the forward bow stance created in the last move of the previous technique, slide the right foot into a right reverse cat while stacking the hands on the left hip this time, right over left. The right foot continues to step to 3:00, momentarily settling in a modified rear twist stance. This pattern inverts the previous "7" pattern used in Crashing Wings.

From the modified twist, pivot into a right forward bow facing 3:00 with a simultaneous right vertical outward block (a striking check, really, like Destructive Twins) and left inward elbow strike. This continues to utilize the two-in-one timing introduced with the first technique.

Slide the left foot through and forward to 1:30 as the hands stack again at the left hip, right over left, and settle in a right reverse bow stance to set up the next technique.

Circling Wing

This gets its name, Circling Wing, from the movement of the elbows. While pivoting from the right reverse bow into a right forward bow facing 7:30, the right arm will track up, over, and down, as in an outward overhead elbow. This breaks the close two-handed choke by driving down on the radial nerve in the opponent's right forearm, and traps that arm under it by chambering to the right ribcage. In keeping with the two-in-one timing, a left finger thrust to the eyes is delivered at the completion of the forward bow stance. I've always felt this technique was Five Swords done to the rear.

Pivot in place back to the right neutral bow or side horse with a right upward elbow to the chin. The left hand is checking the opponent's right arm down in a sliding manner. This is necessary because they are trying to cover their eyes as they did in Destructive Twins. The sliding check prevents their hindering your elbow shot.

Immediately shift back to the right reverse bow with a right back hammerfist to the groin. The left hand is positioned high at your right shoulder in the cover position. It bears mention that the right arm needs to travel in, down, and across the body to ensure proper power transfer for the hammerfist. It is common for practitioners to drop it immediately from the upward elbow position almost vertically down. This, of course, creates a down line of force when what is needed is a more horizontal line of force to crush the testicles. Mr. Parker impressed on me that the timing of this strike is one of bringing the hammering hand almost to the opposite thigh, creating the travel and the appropriate line. The stance change then provides the necessary counter-rotation torque and maximizes effectiveness.

This and Twirling Wings are meant to work as alternatives to one another. If you start one and the opponent pulls or pushes, you should

be able to change to the other. If you started to step and turn back to do Twirling Wings and the opponent stiffens up to resist you, as often happens, step out and forward to do Circling Wing. It changes your line from horizontal to vertical, usually too fast for them to change their alignment to compensate. The muscles they were using to stop your rotation on the horizontal are not the ones they need to stop your vertical down line, and vice versa. This is a principle we use everywhere in the process of changing from one technique to another (this changing is also known as "grafting").

Crossing Talon

This version of Crossing Talon starts with placing the left hand on the right wrist to indicate a pin of the opponent's grabbing hand at the fingers. This occurs while shifting, in place, from the previous right reverse bow to a right neutral bow on the 7:30 line. This movement highlights the pin, in that there is no stepping or counter-grabbing with it. It illustrates that the technique is varied from the free version because of range. In the free version in Long Form Three the step is forward, as it would be if we faced straight on while being grabbed. In this form, Short Three, the opponent is grabbing from the side. This necessitates a longer step, a full step-through versus a step-forward, than the other version.

Follow with the left step-through forward to 7:30 into a left neutral bow while showing the counter-grab with your right hand. Make sure the rotating right hand is outside of the left; it should not come inside or over. If one were to try this on a person, it would not work since the left hand would be in the way. At the completion of the step-through, the right hand will be at the right hip and the left arm will be striking or pressing down on the elbow on your centerline.

Deliver a left outward elbow to the temple with some body lean into the strike. Be careful not to break your waist in the process. Delete the heel-palm and claw rip normally used in the application and follow-up with the left inward overhead elbow to the spine between the shoulder blades. Drop down into the elbow for the gravitational marriage. The right hand has maintained its controlling position at the hip throughout.

In my opinion, nothing looks worse than someone doing the form "all arms." I see this all the time and it seems to manifest here in this technique most visibly. The hands are moving 100 mph and the lower body is stock-still. No shift, no drop. We have been emphasizing body mechanics all along; let's not throw them out the window now. In taiji, practitioners are classified as being either turtles or fish. A turtle swims by just using its limbs. A fish swims by using its whole body. Be a fish.

Scraping Hoof

The previous technique used gravitational marriage. This one, Scraping Hoof, reverses the line to throw energy upward to thwart an attempt at a full nelson.

Slide or "cheat" the left foot in from the left neutral bow used in the last technique to a little narrower stance. Simultaneously arch the back to deliver a head butt to the rear and thrust both fists toward the ground, palm-in. The thrust aborts the grab and traps the opponent's arms.

The contraction of the body's muscles provides a "shock" type of power. I compare it to what Bruce Lee used to demonstrate with his one-inch punch.

The rule on the adjustment or "cheat" step is "cheat weak, kick strong." This is a right-handed technique in this form, dictating a left cheat and right stomp. The opposite side would cheat right and kick left. The interesting thing about this technique is that its ideal phase application is essentially ambidextrous because we kick with each leg to learn both sides. The opening move has to change with a change of sides. It is taught with the right kick first because most people are right-handed. A left-handed person would have to cheat right and kick left. Yet both, in the ideal phase, would kick with the strong leg first, then the weak.

Now shift weight to the left leg, creating a rear bow stance. This makes an "angle of disturbance" (an angle that disrupts balance without doing damage) and aligns the right foot for a back scoop kick to the opponent's left inner knee. Make use of the recoil to fire a right-side knife-edge kick into the supporting right inner knee. Now, as Sir Isaac Newton reportedly said, "What goes up, must come down." Drop the right knife-edge down heavily, scraping the right shin, and finish with a stomp to the right instep. The right foot will be parallel to the left in a horse stance instead of the normal "T" position across the instep as in the application. This angle of the foot is done "for the sake of the form."

When a movement is done "for the sake of the form" it refers to something done to smooth the flow of movement. In this case it eliminates having to realign the foot from the 90° toe-out position to the horse stance. The horse stance here symbolizes the face-on natural position we start so many self-defense techniques from. One will find this concept in subsequent forms.

Fatal Cross

Fatal Cross never made it into the technique requirement lists in the original system. It is taught for a two-handed front belt grab, or a low push. I teach it for the belt grab to stay aligned with the dead-attack theme of the form. It works well for the push too.

Clear the attacking arms off by doing twin shape-of-the-crane frictional pulls, as in the technique Hooking Wings. As you do so, step straight forward to 10:30 with the right foot. As the right foot stops, settling into a right neutral bow stance, deliver twin middle-knuckle uppercut strikes to the diaphragm. They hit just at the bottom of the ribcage on opposite sides of the solar plexus, about halfway to the bottom of the curve of the ribs. This causes the opponent to bend forward, and this is where the front head butt would occur. This head butt is hidden, and matches the back head butt in the previous technique. Take into account that if you don't do the head butt, the opponent will—accidentally or intentionally. It is common in Chinese martial arts to couple head butts with uppercut techniques. However, this usage is obscure as far as teaching Kenpo goes. It seems to be one of those things left to be taught to or figured out by the student, but isn't.

Immediately follow the middle-knuckles with a scissoring back-knuckle strike. The right wrist crosses over the left as the strikes are executed, striking the jaw hinges in a snapping action. The right-over-left configuration is important for the same reason it is specified in the Finger Set's scissor eye pokes. That is, the left hand is used to check down immediately without interference from the positioning of the right for the finger whip. These same eye pokes recur right after the scissor back-knuckles here in Fatal Cross. Now the hands are set for the high and low lines in the next technique.

Use some "body english" on the scissor strikes. Back-up mass was the key on the middle-knuckles, and it should be used on the following strikes as well. Without the step it is necessary to rock forward somewhat in your stance to generate power. Try to avoid merely throwing the hands and arms alone. It makes the movements look empty. You're not a turtle, right?

Grip of Death

The opposite side of the standard technique against a side headlock, the Grip of Death is now done on the same 10:30 line created by the step forward in the previous technique. From the right neutral bow, step forward to 10:30 with the left foot into a close kneel stance. This is often done with a horse stance instead, the reason being that the technique was originally done in a horse. A look at Ed Parker's first book, *Kenpo Karate, the Law of the Fist and Empty Hand,* will show that was how he did it around 1960 when this was published. It is also seen in the old Iron-man 8mm movies he sold back then. Sometime after that era he apparently rethought what he was doing and changed the technique to the close kneel to check off the possible counter to the groin. His rethinking of the system in that decade was made obvious when the codified 1970 version of the Parker system appeared in the *Accumulative Journal.* I call it a quantum leap from what one sees in that first book to what is in Volume 5 of his *Infinite Insights into Kenpo* series. Therefore, I do that particular move in a close kneel. I have seen it both ways and Mr. Parker was not definitive with me on it as it pertained to the form.

While settling into the stance (whichever one you prefer), strike the right kidney with the right hand (the high line) and the groin with the left (the low line). This is called an offset sandwich. The strikes sandwich the opponent but are not in directly opposing lines to one another. Sandwiching was a favored Parker technique, and he used it in many ways. In this form it is shown as well as implied. What I think is interesting is that this technique not only follows the two-in-one theme of the form but gets the same reaction as the very first technique, in a different way. I refer to the fact that the opponent's body will not know which way to go when struck and tends to stay in place.

Slide your right hand up the back, over the head, and down the face to the philtrum, that area between the nose and the upper lip. Anchor your elbow and pull down and back, using the body fulcrum to break the opponent's waist backward as the stance changes to a horse. Sliding the hand is important, as one cannot always see where one needs to go. After all, the person has his hand around your neck; you turned your head into his ribs and tucked your chin. The hand will contour the body to find the appropriate target, eliminating the need to grope around trying to find it. Breaking the opponent's waist is absolutely essential. This controls height, width, and depth. It puts the attacker in a precarious position, unable to get the bracing angles needed to retaliate. Many people do not consider this in the execution of the technique; they slur the timing and lack emphasis of the cancellation angle.

Immediately pivot into a right forward bow with a left straight heel-palm to the chin. The timing is such that the opponent's head is brought down and given a place to rest in order to accept the palm strike. Commonly, the timing is done incorrectly, with the pull down and heel-palm done together. This actually moves the head back away from the strike, reducing its effectiveness. It should be "pull, then strike"—not "pull with strike."

There are two ways to finish this technique to flow into the next. Some people place the right hand palm-down in the horizontal check position with the heel-palm, as it is done in the technique. Others wrap the right hand around to the back, hammerlock fashion, to represent the entry to the next technique. Either one is acceptable.

It is important to remember that the standard Grip of Death technique is most effective in application when you step diagonally forward to 10:30

with your right foot, when you start facing 12:00. It goes with the attack and keeps the line to the groin open. If you don't step that way you are resisting the pull they apply on you to bring you down into the headlock, and that may injure you more by causing undue pressure on your neck. By stepping to 12:00 you won't get the groin shot line either. Go with the flow.

Locked Wing

The Locked Wing technique is a defense against a rear hammerlock on your right arm. After performing the left straight heel-palm from the forward bow in the previous technique, spin left with the left foot to 4:30 with a left outward elbow in a left neutral bow stance. Your right arm is behind your back in the hammerlock position. Continue the action of the left arm counter-clockwise and around into a forearm break in a right forward bow stance facing 10:30; the right arm does not change position. Do a right step-through reverse to 4:30, settling in a left forward bow stance still facing 10:30 as the left arm locks back for the trap in the uppercut or "make a muscle" position. Keep the left arm in place as the right arm starts back, up, and over for an overhead heel-palm strike, timed with the right knee strike to create an offset sandwich to the back of the neck and chest. Note the comparison of the offset sandwich of this technique with the offset sandwich of the previous technique. The timing is such that when the right arm gets high on the front 45° line, the right knee is fired to maximize effect.

Momentum will take you forward into a right neutral bow stance on the same 10:30 line. This works the "long line" that overlays the one created at the end of Long Form Two. This is very transitional, and the hands flow through the rear wrist grab position necessary for the next technique.

It seems to me that the angle going into Locked Wing is where the biggest difference lies in the way the form is done in many Kenpo systems. The angles are 90° off, with most people stepping to 7:30 to do this move. I speculate that if they are doing the applications it would be easier and "make more sense" to do it that way, meaning that an attacker would have better access to the arm for the hammerlock from that angle. One can also recover from that angle easily enough to do the rest of the form on the original angles, or very close to them. In the broader scheme of things, the angle as I have described and do it makes the most sense, as it does two things. First, it sets up the long line I mentioned. This line is complementary to that in the previous form, Long Form Two, and balances the lines when one considers the forms layout as a whole, i.e., Forms One through Six. Second, the spinning step recreates an entry often used to put someone in a hammerlock, the front entry. Therefore I do the form this way, as I learned it at the Pasadena school, instead of how I originally learned it with the other angles.

Crossed Twigs

Crossed Twigs gets its name from the position the attacker ends in, with arms crossed. The transition from Locked Wing with the right foot forward continues along the same line facing 10:30. A step with the left foot along that line into a left forward bow (technically a right reverse bow) as the hands make twin shape-of-the-crane formations indicates the same angle-off step and

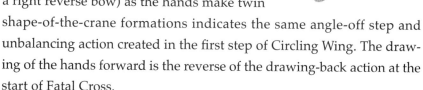

unbalancing action created in the first step of Circling Wing. The drawing of the hands forward is the reverse of the drawing-back action at the start of Fatal Cross.

Pivot immediately to the right with a right outward elbow to the jaw hinge in a right neutral bow stance. Follow with a strong downward pull with the right arm as the left is now positioned, hammerlock-like, across your back. This shows how you can "lock" yourself versus how the opponent locks you in the previous technique, Locked Wing.

A right inward overhead elbow to the spine between the shoulder blades follows the downward pull. Now the left hand is brought around to match the position of the right hand, palms in. Execute a left knee kick to the right ribcage as both hands strike down in twin heel-palms, sandwiching the kidneys. Return the left foot to its point of origin for the next technique.

Notice that the mechanics of this technique are opposite those of Crossing Talon in that they both have outward elbows followed by inward overhead elbows. In application, both have a follow-up knee strike, but the knee is left out of Crossing Talon for good reason. Remember to use the body lean and drop as in Crossing Talon.

Wings of Silk

A yoke-grab (also known as a chicken wing) triggers Wings of Silk. The elbows are "wings" and they slide out of the opponent's arms as smoothly as silk.

Now in a horse stance facing 1:30, simultaneously execute a left stomp on the opponent's left instep with a left-hand inverted crab pinch to the femoral nerve. This nerve can be attacked at either the crest of the hip or in the inguinal crease. The crab pinch formation must be strong and use the muscles of the hand, not just the fingers. The pinch causes the opponent's body to break at the waist, disturbing their leverage and limiting their ability to control your movement. The stomp causes sickening pain that occupies the mind. This stomp is done to the opposite side as the stomp from Scraping Hoof, which gives us the mechanics of right and left sides to practice.

Taking advantage of the opponent's broken-waist position that brings him down a bit, one can use borrowed force to enhance the next moves. Deliver a right back scoop kick to the groin as the opponent drops down. A right obscure back elbow may also be used to strike the chin simultaneously. Done correctly, both left-side strikes work together, immediately followed by the right-side strikes. Attempting to do all of them simultaneously may create diminished effect. Range, travel, power, and lines of delivery may be affected due to bad timing. Better to deliver both left strikes, then the right(s) for maximum effect. After all, this is a continuation of the two-in-one timing introduced in Long Form Two. It is not a four-in-one move. Also, be sure to deliver the right back scoop kick up and back to the groin. Too often the scoop gets thrown almost 90° off and would miss the target entirely, largely due to excess speed.

The right foot is placed down and across your body as if stepping on your left toes to 10:30, following the established line. Arms remain in place, the left clamping the opponent's left in place, the right now in transit. This movement starts a spin to the left.

To finish the spin the right foot now continues on the line and the body turns counter-clockwise to your left. Settle into a square horse stance facing 1:30 as the right arm executes an uppercut forearm break to snap the opponent's left arm at the elbow. Your left hand shows an anchored grabbing check at the left hip like Crossing Talon. The comparisons of anchoring with one and breaking from the top or bottom are obvious. The right and left uppercut breaks and their lines are shown in this technique and Locked Wing.

Another comparison exists between this, Crashing Wings, and Scraping Hoof. It is the degree of encirclement or extension of the attacking arms. If the opponent were to attempt the bear hug that triggers Crashing Wings and you moved forward to make him miss, he might get only your arms and clamp down, thus causing you to react with Wings of Silk. If you are "too slow" to react to his bear-hug attempt, he may continue his grab upward and form a full nelson, so you do Scraping Hoof. At least, that's how I see it.

Conquering Shield

Now, on the 1:30 line, execute the technique Conquering Shield, a defense against a front left stiff-arm lapel grab. I nicknamed it "up-down, up-down" because that's what it does.

From the square horse, pin with the left hand, simultaneously firing a right front snap kick with a right inward vertical forearm strike. The front kick strikes the opponent's right inner knee as the right arm breaks the left arm at the elbow. This is a continuation of the two-in-one timing idea. Now it is hand/foot striking forward while the last technique was hand/foot striking to the rear.

In Kenpo we rarely float our weight upward. This technique is an exception and is an example of another way to utilize marriage of gravity. The front kick-strike combination allows one to drive weight forward and up so that one can fully utilize the drop back down into a right neutral bow with a downward elbow to the opponent's offending arm. This brings the opponent in, hurts the arm, and loads the next strike.

Immediately drive a right upward elbow into the chin. Follow by striking down on the vertical line created in the previous move, with a right downward hammering claw to the face. The left hand is in a covering position high in the mid-zone. As in all techniques, the body should move with the strikes. In this case one moves the body up and down to enhance the strikes instead of just moving the arm. In many schools a

high wide kneel is substituted for the neutral bow to emphasize the drops and lifts. Show the torque on the hammering claw, and ensure its formation is correct, i.e., it should have the "iron ring" look and feel to it.

Striking Serpent's Head

The last technique of the form is Striking Serpent's Head, a defense against a front bear hug, arms free (your arms, of course).

Execute a right step-through reverse straight back to 7:30 from the current point of origin facing 1:30 into a left neutral bow stance, still facing 1:30. With the settle your left arm should be delivering an inverted back-knuckle strike to the opponent's left temple, or the mastoids if their head is turned the opposite way. The right hand is in the chamber.

Show a grab to the hair with the left hand, the same hand that did the inverted strike. This grab is the exact opposite of the body fulcrum used in the peel-back in Grip of Death, done earlier in the form. After the anchoring pull-down, fire a right half-fist strike to the throat on a diagonally downward angle toward the bracing forearm. This is done with a shift to a left forward bow stance and back to the neutral bow stance as the right hand re-chambers.

The point of contention on this technique is the angle at which it is supposed to be done. Many schools teach it as stepping back on the 12:00–6:00 line so the technique is done facing 12:00. I believe it should be done on the 1:30 line to get the angle in the form; otherwise it is missing. (We step to 1:30 going into Circling Wing, but that technique is actually done facing 7:30.)

The left hand stays where it is as the right foot comes forward to the square horse position. The right hand comes along with the step and punches into the open left, ending in the salutation horse position facing 12:00.

Close left to right and perform the formal salutation as it was done at the opening of the form. If the left side of the form is to follow, execute the close only, and go into the opposite side of Destructive Twins and continue with the left side of the form.

Relating the Techniques

Grab Defenses

Five techniques are actual grab defenses. They are Destructive Twins (which also works for a choke), Crossing Talon, Fatal Cross, Crossed Twigs, and Conquering Shield. These are lapel, belt, shoulder, and wrist grabs. A closer look shows the attack types as being either one- or two-handed. Further differentiation discloses front, side, and rear angles of attack, high and low, and pushing or pulling on the part of the opponent.

Locks and Chokes

Twirling Wings and Circling Wing are normally taught for rear chokes, although Twirling Wings is sometimes taught for a shoulder or collar grab. Locked Wing is for a hammerlock. Wings of Silk is for a rear two-arm lock, and Grip of Death is for a headlock. A closer look shows that the rear chokes are for far and close attacks. We have seen how the lines blur between attack categories when we discuss relationships, and that's a good thing, an example being Destructive Twins. It may open your eyes to understand how Mr. Parker looked at the attacks and their defenses.

Hugs and Holds

Crashing Wings and Striking Serpent's Head are for bear hugs (arms-free responses to both front and rear attacks). Scraping Hoof is for a full nelson. Why no pinned version? And the full nelson falls in here because of the amount of body contact, making it a type of bear hug that either didn't quite close or passed the point it could, so it continued up to the head.

This initially gives us the base information we need to start to compare the techniques. I encourage my students to look at what is in the form and ask, "Why these techniques?" We are taught more than one technique for a lapel grab, choke, or bear hug. Why did Ed Parker choose these particular sequences for perpetuation in the forms? The following discussion should help make sense of all that.

By Category

Looking at the form as a whole, we saw that the techniques are all for responding to grabs, i.e., dead attacks. Then we looked at the types of grabs: lapel, choke, wrist, etc. Next we saw the angles of entry, the attacks coming from the front, side, and back. We also saw that the grabs are either one- or two-handed, and static, pushing, or pulling. By cross-relating the movements, we will now look further into the mechanics of the techniques to discover more about the weapons used, footwork, entry angles, and more.

Dual Movement

Double-factoring was emphasized in Long Form Two. Short Form Three was created to continue that line of thought, and it does so immediately in the first move. We step forward, just as in Long Two, but punch with both hands. The second technique opens with two downward elbows, the third with a striking check and elbow; the full-nelson defense starts with two over-the-shoulder punches; and the next technique is totally two-handed. The following moves use sandwiching hammerfists and sandwiching knees/heel-palms. The second-to-last uses a forearm break with a front kick to show the simultaneous high and low lines. There are more dual movements along the way. No doubt this is an important concept in the Parker precepts of self-defense.

Introduction of New Weapons

Each form provides new information, and weapon formation is certainly part of that. This form gives us the overhead punch, four-finger eye poke, two-finger eye flick, downward elbow, foot stomp, twin middle-knuckle, scissoring back-knuckle and eye poke, knee sandwich, crab pinch, back scoop kick, forearm break, head butt, and inverted hooking back-knuckle.

The overhead punch is done with the uppercut strike in the first movement of the form. We call it a U-punch when done together. The top punch itself is an overhead punch to the nose. This first movement sets the tone for most of the rest of the form in that simultaneous action is highlighted.

The four-finger eye poke is also used in the first technique. Long Form Two showed us the four-finger poke with the fingers together and the two-finger vertical poke. Here we have an example of the four-finger poke with the fingers spread for margin of error. It is essential that the fingers be bent sufficiently to protect them, but straight enough to get penetration.

The two-finger eye flick opens the second technique. Here its purpose is to show us how to use economy of motion. We can use the extension of the arms previously used solely for loading the downward elbow sweeps as strikes. It is referred to as a "filler" movement. The interpretation varies as to application. Some use it as a method of lifting eyeglasses out of the way with the fingers to get at the eyes with the thumbs; others may use the fingers to move the eyelid and then thumb the eyes. Both work. The key idea in the context of the form is to economize movement by using the same lines forward and in reverse—no slicing or hooking, which changes the lines.

The aforementioned elbows in this technique are downward elbows. In the previous form either inward overhead or outward overhead elbows were used. This is the first time we use a purely downward elbow strike. It is notable that we use them simultaneously, in keeping with the two-in-one timing theme established in Long Two and carried through here.

Foot stomps are used in two techniques in the form. They match sides; that is, you will do one with your right foot and one with your left. You should be familiar with the definition of a stomp: a stomp has no supporting leg while a stomp kick does. In other words, if you drop your stomping foot and both feet rest on the ground, it is a stomp. If you retract the stomping foot so that you are standing on one leg, it is a stomp kick.

The middle-knuckle strike formation introduced in Short Form Two is carried forward to this form and beyond. Here it is done in pairs, like some other strikes in the form. In this case we use them in an uppercut fashion to the diaphragm. It is the first time we do them with the proper lines for the angle of delivery and bracing angles.

Scissoring back-knuckles follow the twin middle-knuckles. This formation takes advantage of borrowed force and borrowed reach, provides margin for error, and matches the angles of the jaw to aid in striking the jaw hinges. The two-fingered snapping scissor pokes that immediately follow are the same as in the Finger Set. However, one should really execute twin outward finger slices from the scissor position to take full advantage of the position, with follow-up in mind.

Knee sandwiches appear for the first time in this form. Related to the sandwich of hand and elbow introduced at the end of Long Two, we now sandwich a target with the hand and the knee. The two obvious knee sandwiches are the one-hand, one-knee sandwich and the two-hands, one-knee version. The missing sandwich is left out intentionally. That is the opposite-hand, opposite-knee version. We would thus have three types of knee sandwich:

> a right knee with a right heel-palm,
> a right knee with a left heel-palm,
> a right knee with both heel-palms.

These would also be done on the opposite sides in the other side of the form.

The "7" Pattern

A footwork pattern we use for takedowns is called a "7" pattern since it looks like the number drawn on the ground.

Crashing Wings shows the first use of it. In both Short Form Three and Long Form Three the pattern appears. It is shown both sides, "upside-down," and in reverse as well. The reverse pattern points out that two of our standard self-defense techniques, Dominating Circles and Tripping Arrow, are interchangeable in their takedowns. Although the exact reversal is shown and the other application (Tripping Arrow) is missing, it follows the Parker pattern of information being conspicuous by its absence.

Additional Observations

The entries are similar to Circling Wing and Thrusting Wedge (the latter appears next, in Long Form Three). One steps in, the other away to administer the eye strikes, followed by the upward elbows.

Scraping Hoof is done in application with kicks on both sides. Normally only one side would be necessary, as is demonstrated in the extension technique. If the one set of strong-sided kicks is not enough, maybe another set of the same would work instead of going to your weak side. Or possibly switching to the hands would be a better option, an idea found in Long Form Three when Scraping Hoof is grafted with Repeated Devastation. Obviously the weak-side kicks are taught to students when they learn the technique to help strengthen their abilities and increase coordination. Other answers are that lefties need their side done, too, or that maybe it is not possible to do the right side due to weight shift or injury.

Working the knees is illustrated in Crossed Twigs and Blinding Sacrifice. The examples show use of the rear knee and front knee strikes. Rear knees have more travel and probably hit harder. A front knee would be like a jab—fast and effective. The main difference is the weight distribution. Another consideration is what follow-up lines are available after using one or the other. Take a look at how the step-through knee in Locked Wing fits into this. Play with doing techniques that teach a rear knee and switch it to a front knee and vice versa. See what works and why.

Practice with Opponents

This form should absolutely be practiced with opponents. Obviously it is another opportunity to work your self-defense techniques on a body. It may be used to introduce multiple-attacker defenses. "Accidents" may unveil how the transitions can be used. As my taiji teacher Tom Baeli said,

"The information is really in the transitions." Doing it with partners will enhance understanding of the form and its purpose. As I point out in the previous chapter, doing forms with partners prevents it from becoming an empty exercise, and when it is empty, it is frustrating and almost fruitless. A lack of understanding will affect performance.

It is a student's obligation to know and understand the attacks as well as the defense. It readily becomes apparent when one watches a group practicing the forms with attackers whether they know the angles, attacks, responses, etc. Working as a group helps bring everyone up to speed. Speaking of speed, start slowly, and then build up to a realistic tempo. Years ago at the International Karate Championships in Long Beach, Kenpo fifth-degree (at that time) Sandy Sandoval did a brilliant demonstration of the form application. He did, as I remember, Short Three, first slowly to show the applications, then at full speed. It looked like a mass attack, which it was, really, and it was over in seconds. I was impressed. Since Ed Parker had created the form, he gets credit for the choreography. Mr. Sandoval gets credit for his speed, power, and accuracy. The students he had with him get credit for making him look good. I frequently use that demo as a mental model.

Long Form Three

In many offshoot schools Short Three and Long Three are taught for the same belt rank. I originally learned it in that somewhat confusing way. The Parker system separates them, and the two forms (short and long) are learned at successive ranks. I have found an attitude in many studios that forms are just "stuff to be learned to get a belt because that's what they do in karate." With that mentality, it makes no difference at what level one learns a form. This does not mean someone can't learn the sequence and make it look good. I have seen lots of trophy-winning forms that make no sense. All I'm trying to say is that it is more beneficial to learn and understand the forms, their meaning, and proper body mechanics of the applications, and that it is easier in this case to do that at different belt levels.

"Dead" and "Semi-Live" Attacks

This form integrates "semi-live" attacks with "dead" attacks. Ed Parker said and wrote that the forward momentum of a push required better timing to handle than a grab, and you have even less time to act when it's a punch coming at you. A push is the area between grabbing and punching, kicking or striking. Since he labeled punches as "live" attacks, pushes are "semi-live." Form Four deals with live attacks. You will see shortly the relationships between the techniques in Long Three, and later, how they relate to Four and higher. Interchangeability of technique applications is important, and always has been. Keep in mind that while certain attacks are specified for certain techniques, one can always apply the technique for similar attacks or attack lines. That is part of the research process that any truly serious student will go through in order to understand how the system works and what it means.

Technique Sequence

Long Form Three follows this sequence, with most being done both sides. There are more isolations, both short and long, simple and sophisticated, and everything starts with the strong (right) side. As in Short Three, the salutation is done at the start and finish.

Destructive Twins
Crashing Wings/Dominating Circles
Isolation
Parting Wings
Glancing Spear
The Halfway Isolation
Crossing Talon
Thrusting Wedge

Blinding Sacrifice

Wings of Silk

Scraping Hoof / Repeated Devastation

Desperate Falcons

Close and do the full salutation.

Destructive Twins

Destructive Twins is executed the same way as in Short Three, with an isolation added after the punch and before going to the other side of the technique. Wrist grab escapes are shown in the isolation using different fulcrums, lines, and circles to free yourself. Frictional pull is introduced in isolation for the first time, followed immediately by a straight punch. The punch is interesting because it is done with no torque. It uses borrowed force and back-up mass to work. That is a stand-out idea right off.

One of the often-asked questions is about the transition from the first side of the technique to the other. Is it feet-together, like a switch, or is it a horse? I learned it both ways, and Ed Parker did it with a horse, as did my other mentors in the Parker system. That horse stance is important—it reappears throughout the form, acting as a central point and a break between techniques.

The "Two-Horse" Form: That first horse stance is the first of the two horses. The second horse is created after you travel down the 12:00–6:00 line doing Glancing Spear and step out into the horse for the isolation. It is as if the second is a mirror of the first. If you looked down on the form from above, you would see one horse being worked at the beginning or front-end, and another being worked further back.

Crashing Wings/Dominating Circles

Crashing Wings is the response to a rear bear hug, arms free, and Dominating Circles is used against a front offset, cross-shoulder grab. Do Crashing Wings and Dominating Circles on one side, then an isolation, and then the same two techniques on the opposite side.

From the horse stance, step out to the right into a wider, deeper horse as you execute twin four-finger thrusts to the eyes. As you settle into the horse your elbows should drop into the twin downward elbow position you created in Short Three to open Crashing Wings. The finger thrusts are a filler movement, just as in Short Three. This time they are thrusts instead of finger flicks. The first technique, Destructive Twins, uses a single four-finger thrust. The present technique uses a double four-finger thrust for category completion. Some Chinese systems will execute that four-finger thrust inverted, though I have never seen a twin inverted thrust to the eyes, just a single. I mention this because to have true category completion you have to run the whole category and eliminate the non-useful and useless moves. (The two terms are not the same. There are moves that have absolutely no use and others we choose not to use in a given situation but might elsewhere.) Think about how the Finger Set starts. We do straight, vertical, and palm-up thrusts to show what we consider to be the workable lines and hand positions. There are no inverted finger thrusts to the eyes and no inverted vertical finger thrusts, palms-out. I have seen that and can't think of a good reason to do it. I can think of a reason, but not a good reason. All that said, I think that's why Ed Parker used the double four-finger thrust there.

The deeper horse accents the principles of marriage of gravity and angles of cancellation. Continue the technique as in Short Three with the reverse cat and step around into the elbow and hammerfist. Pivot into a training horse stance facing 10:30 to punctuate the techniques and start the form Dominating Circles.

You will now reverse the lines and "7" pattern you created while doing Crashing Wings. From the horse stance, move your left leg back up the line and into a horse stance facing 12:00. Your left leg is actually lifted off the ground, tracing the lines at a height instead of sliding along the surface. This is done without raising your body up, thus preventing a rise in your center of gravity, which in turn helps prevent your being taken down in the course of the technique. Dominating Circles is a dead-hand technique—a perpetual-control type, stand-up grappling technique. When the bridge between you and the opponent is built, the connection is made and either one of you can sense what the other is doing or even intending to do. Try not to let your head rise above its present level. You can, however, and there is an insert that allows you to get away with a rise and drop as in Conquering Shield. Keep the bend in your support knee, or even increase it a bit to prevent the rise and increase stability. Visualize your leg going around and behind your opponent's leg. Then drop heavily into the horse stance to buckle the opponent.

At the same time loop your left arm from the chamber into an outward overhead elbow. Time the elbow anchor with the drop into the horse. Your leg and arm are really doing the same thing, which is outward and overhead drops, using anchoring and gravitational marriage. This arm motion goes outside, over, and down on the opponent's arm to trap it under your left arm. Your head and eyes should be aligned with where the opponent would be, and you are in a horse facing 12:00. You have completed the reverse "7" footwork and returned to the first horse.

You now pivot toward 3:00 into what looks like a right forward bow with a left straight heel-palm at head height. Your right hand will check low, at about kidney height. I say it looks like a forward bow because it is not really a forward bow. I call it the "phony bow." As you know, you need a toe-heel line to properly execute a forward bow. Since you have started in a horse you don't have that and can't really do a forward bow without an adjustment step. That step is not added to the form, and a neutral bow is not substituted for the horse, as either would add unnecessary movement. Being trained in the Parker system, one would know the application and understand it. To more completely understand that sequence one needs to know the Tripping Arrow technique as well. It illustrates the interchangeability of Dominating Circles with Tripping Arrow.

Immediately pivot back into the horse facing 12:00, hands chambered, to finish that side of the two techniques.

O   O⬅O   *Isolation*

Bring your right foot slightly in, creating a "high" horse stance, still facing 12:00. This is sometimes referred to as a cheat step. A helpful reminder for which foot to step with is "right out, right in—left out, left in." You step out with the right to start the first side of Crashing Wings, then cheat the right foot in at the end of Dominating Circles. Do the opposite on the other side. The cheat helps keep you from getting too wide and unable to move with ease while setting up the next move, which is the left side of Crashing Wings. It also indicates a hooking-type foot sweep.

Now that you are stable in your high horse, thrust both fists down in front of you, indicating a double wrist grab. Roll both hands up and out into twin vertical back-knuckle snap punches at head height. This movement is used to break out of the double grab and strike the face. It is in harmony with the theme of the form and helps complete categories of motion used in defense of the variety of wrist grab attacks and counters found in the form.

Second Side: Your hands have been retracted to a position just in front of your chest, about pectoral height, which is a natural position.

Remember, those natural positions are first indicated at the end of Short Form Two. Now fire the twin finger thrusts to the eyes and step out to the left, dropping your weight in the opening elbows of Crashing Wings. Continue the pattern left-handed, mirroring what you did on the opposite side, up and through Dominating Circles into the high horse. Pay attention to the mechanics on the left side and ensure they match the right as best you can. It is common to see people mis-time the elbow in Crashing Wings, or even leave it out. I believe it is because most of us are right-handed and we have practiced that other side for so long.

Now we are back in the isolation horse. Cheat in, then thrust the hands down again and execute the same double wrist breakout and punches.

Now it's time for a test question: Mr. Parker or someone he termed an "authorized instructor" gave  you the keys to answer this somewhere along the way in your training. You can't do what you don't know. I was once told, "You don't know what you don't know." How true. So, the next isolation acts as a test to help you correlate concepts.

From those punches drop your hands to your waist, palm-in and one crossed over the other at the wrists. It seems that right-handed people will naturally put the right on top, and left-handed people, the left. I don't remember being told specifically that one had to be on top. This is an ambidextrous application. Therefore, I would say the dominant hand should probably go on top, as it very likely would in a stress situation. Your brain will not normally default to your weak side in response to a threat. Roll your hands palm-up and out, sliding them across your waist to your hips. Your fingers will now point down and your wrists will be bent.

Mr. Parker asked us to figure this out on our own. Sure, he told some people. I think that was because some were not homegrown instructors. Most of us were from another lineage and were coming home to learn it the right way. We were indeed fortunate since we may not have been instructed in the Parker methodology and thinking from the start, and some components were missed or misunderstood. So we were sometimes

given the answer to a test question. Yet we still had to figure out the relationships in context of the form. If one did not, it was just another technique. Ed Parker believed that if you had to "pull teeth" to get answers
you wouldn't be so quick to give the information away. With all that in
mind, as Tom Cruise said in *Top Gun,* "I could tell you, but then I'd have
to kill you."

Parting Wings

Step back to 6:00 into a modified
left neutral bow and execute Parting Wings, a defense against a two-
hand front shoulder push. Ensure
that your hands come up the middle from your energy center (*hara* or
t'an tien); in this case with your right
over or in front of your left into the
twin blocks, looking at your palms you should see your left palm.

As in the technique, pivot to a forward bow and deliver a right punching chop to the left ribs below the pectoral as the left hand crosses over
to the right side.

The left hand is now cocked for its thrusting outward chop to the
throat with a pivot back into a left neutral bow. The right hand is chambered at the right ribs for the vertical middle-knuckle strike to the
solar plexus.

Upon completion of the right middle-knuckle fist from a forward bow,
execute a rear-foot-to-front-foot switch (right foot to left and left foot back
into a right neutral bow) and do the opposite side of the technique. Ensure
that your left hand goes in front of your right this time in the transition.

At the end of the technique the right hand should be in a check position, held horizontally across your lower abdomen. Your left hand should
be in the vertical middle-knuckle position (thrusting method of execution)
at solar-plexus height.

Glancing Spear

In the transition to Glancing Spear, a defense for a straight wrist grab, the left hand rotates counter-clockwise to a palm-up position as it is lifted to shoulder height. The right hand is slid up, out, and along the left arm to the wrist. This seemingly insignificant movement is very important. It indicates the function of contouring in finding and securing the following finger and wristlock and elbow break.

If one were to close the eyes and slide a hand along the arm that has been grabbed, it will be easy to find the appropriate position to apply the counter. If one were to essentially grope for it, it would be easy to miss, especially in a dynamic situation versus a static situation. Mr. Parker was emphatic with me about sliding that hand up the arm.

After the hand position is achieved, drop back to 6:00 with the right foot into a left reverse bow stance as the hands are anchored to the right hip, causing the elbow break with the left flapping elbow. Pivot back immediately into a left neutral bow with a left outward elbow to the ribs. The right hand indicates a grab holding the arm in the stretched position down near the right ribs. Continue to pivot into the left forward bow with the right dipping finger thrust to the eyes. The dip ricochets off the back of the left hand, causing one to conclude in the opposite ending position of the left side of Parting Wings. Continue to the second side by duplicating the angling and sliding done to enter the first side.

The dipping finger thrust is an indicator of reversing a principle. In the beginning of the form between sides of Destructive Twins we do an isolation facing the corners that shows frictional pull. The dip in Glancing Spear illustrates frictional push. When the actual technique is done on an opponent, the dip can't really be effective because it does not have travel. You have to push down and bounce up to get the eye-shot. However, if you do have the travel, you can use the contact of the dip to displace the opponent's hand or arm just enough to get an opening. It is a technique I was shown many years ago by Mike Sanders. I have not seen anyone else do it.

The Halfway Isolation

This is sometimes called "the Halfway Horse." Step back with your right foot into a square horse stance facing 12:00 into the isolation marking the halfway point. This is the second horse of the two-horse form mentioned earlier.

Execute a right inward overhead elbow and vertical back-knuckle snap punch, then the left. Follow with a right outward overhead and uppercut/back-knuckle, then the left. Now do twin inward overheads, and then twin outward overheads simultaneously. The sequence can be described as right/left, right/left, both/both.

This may not make a lot of sense or seem to be important to most, but it is. This will help you figure out the test question at the beginning of Form Four, as well as increase your knowledge of motion as applied to the multiple-attacker techniques. Let's take a closer look.

We can start with a common application of the movements in the isolation. Let's say we have an opponent's hand on our right shoulder—say, a side grab. It would be easy to bring our right arm up and over into an inward overhead elbow strike to the arm. This would bring the opponent down and into your follow-up vertical back-knuckle punch to the face or head. It would likely clear the arm off as well.

Alternately, we could come up, under, and around the arm to an uppercut forearm break to the elbow, often called a "wrap." This would bring the opponent onto his toes and into the follow-up back-knuckle into the ribcage. If these techniques were used with the proper footwork they would make good use of torque, back-up mass, gravitational marriage, and borrowed force. But remember, the footwork is left out since this is an isolation. (There are two self-defense techniques taught in the Parker system called Snakes of Wisdom and Marriage of the Rams that use the two "wraps." Knowing these techniques will help because they illustrate applications and how the circles may be continued. More on this in a minute.)

These two directions of movement make even more sense if we consider their effectiveness regarding the position of the grabs on the shoulders. If the grab is more forward of a vertical line dividing your body in equal halves from front to back, the inward overhead works well. If the grab is behind that line, the over-and-under version works. Try trading the movements. You'll see that trying to do the inward overhead against the grab behind the line is difficult, if not impossible. The same is true if you try it the other way, using the under-and-over against a grab in front of the line.

The twin inward overheads work with no changes. The twin outward overheads have a slight difference. In this case, you cross your hands over each other close to your body, then throw the back-knuckles. Why? It is because you need to maximize the use of your pectoral muscles to make this work in application. The straightforward uppercut line reduces the effectiveness of the breaks and the travel on the strikes.

What I think is most important here about this isolation is how it shows relationships of direction and timing. Actually, what is missing is really the key. We see inward and outward (direction). We see one by itself, then both working together (timing). A closer look is merited here.

The two inward overheads, while they are the same in name, actually travel against each other on the clock. A right inward overhead travels counter-clockwise (anti-clockwise for my British friends); a left travels clockwise. And that's never going to change because it is how your body works. The opposite is true for the outward overheads. Stay with me now, I'll show you how this applies to what you're doing in your self-defense.

We have two techniques that illustrate the use of these movements. They are Snakes of Wisdom and Marriage of the Rams. One goes over the arms from the front, the other from the back. So what, you say? Try doing one side of Snakes while you do the other side of Marriage. This shows how you would get both arms going clockwise (right hand does Snakes, left does Marriage) and vice versa for the counter-clockwise. It is workable and is an example of information left out. The isolation points the way, but the student has to do the extrapolation. I have been showing this in seminars for years and it has been an eye-opener. Remembering that isolations may be 1) previews of things to come, 2) additional related information, or 3) things that have been left out will help provide new information. Nobody said those things are mutually exclusive. In this case it fits all three parts of the definition.

Crossing Talon

From the isolation horse, start Crossing Talon. It is a defense for a cross-wrist grab, i.e., a right-to-right or left-to-left. Start by placing the left fist forward and down, indicating the wrist grab. As the right foot moves forward to 12:00 into a right side horse, the left hand indicates the counter-grab by rotating clockwise during the step. Settling into the side horse occurs with the drop of the right forearm onto the opponent's elbow.

Follow the technique pattern but delete the claw rip and knee sandwich, as we did in Short Three.

This version shows the free method of doing the technique, as opposed to the pinned method we saw in Short Three. Both forms do the same technique differently to preserve the information. It may be lost if we do the techniques the same in both forms.

Place the right hand down and out in front as on the other side and execute the opposite side from a left side horse to 12:00. It seems the confusion here centers on the angle of the step into the technique. Should it match the diagonal used in the application? If not, why? It is done to 12:00 instead of the angle for good reason. We have been working the 12:00–6:00 lines heavily in the first half of the form. We have been setting up parallel tracks to work our way back up in the end of the form. We got the diagonal step done in Short Three. If we do it now, it distracts from the pattern of the corner angles we are about to enter with the next technique.

Once done with the sequence, return to the square horse by stepping directly back with your right foot.

Thrusting Wedge

Thrusting Wedge is a defense against a two-hand push, as was Parting Wings. Both can be used against a double lapel grab, too. The major idea here is that both these techniques start from the hand-over-hand central

position, coming up from the energy center. The difference is that they part the opponent's arms using reverse body mechanics. In Parting Wings, the elbows stay anchored and the hands move to deviate the attack. In Thrusting Wedge the hands stay and the elbows move to deflect the energy.

From the point of origin in the square horse, step to 7:30 with the right foot into a forward bow as the hands thrust twin outward claws to the face, elbows out. This gives the technique the wedge it is named for.

Immediately pivot into a right neutral bow or side horse as the hands slide-check out and down the shoulders and arms. The left hand should end at the wrist and pull to the left hip, the hand open and formed to indicate that. The right hand drops down so that the right elbow can continue its travel with full force into an upward elbow to the chin, right hand at the right side of the head to chamber it for the next move.

Now drop the right hammering downward claw to the opponent's bridge of the nose and face with a stance shift and drop. Slide the right foot back the way it came, ending in the square horse.

Slide the left foot around to 4:30 and execute the technique on the opposite side, coming back again to the horse. For consistency, make sure the left hand is in front as the hands come up for the claws. It was in front for the left side of Parting Wings.

Blinding Sacrifice

Another timing change is shown in Blinding Sacrifice. This technique demonstrates how to fill the half-beat in the step between the point of origin and the settling into the neutral bow. The first side is done to 10:30 and the second to 1:30.

Essentially the technique starts with the twin claws from Thrusting Wedge done upside-down. As you move forward to break up the attack by stepping in with the right foot, deliver twin eye flicks, using the forearms to deflect or check the attack. If the attack is a two-handed push, the arms deflect. If the attack is a twin grab to the lapels, or maybe a choke, they are checks. They occur on the half-beat and continue outward, downward, and inward, becoming twin claws to the groin as you settle in between the opponent's feet in a right neutral bow. A hidden front head butt must occur as well, to keep from being head-butted yourself. This is a good place to grab, squeeze, and pull. The opponent will arch up on their toes and help create more travel distance for the next move.

Release the groin grab and reach around behind the back by extending both arms forward and under the arms. Use pull-power back-up mass to deliver twin inverted horizontal back-knuckle strikes to the kidneys while shuffling back with a push-drag into a right 45° cat stance. If you had not done the groin grab to get the opponent arched up, these strikes will do that as well. The hands should pull back toward your body and then move up and outward into twin vertical outward block-type checks. This is another example of a technique that bends the rules of motion. In our system we do not usually let the opponent get their hands above ours. In this technique we purposely run our arms under theirs to get those strikes to the kidneys. There are good reasons for this. One is that it shows us what we can do if we find ourselves in that position, our arms under the opponent's as in a front bear hug. It also matches the initial strike in Striking Serpent's Head but with two hands. We did it one-handed in Short Three and now two-handed in Long Three. Additionally, it is a key to a progression in Form Four.

From the outward blocks, push-drag forward with twin four-finger outward eye slices, settling in a right neutral bow stance. This will cause the opponent to attempt to reach up to cover his eyes. Continuing your action downward, striking the shoulders hard along the way, slide-check both arms, and pull at the wrists. This will cancel the height zone, affect the depth while stabilizing width, and prevent a head butt or kick. The opponent's head should now be below yours.

The pattern of orbital switches and cutting of the circles continues. Both arms now loop up and in to twin inverted vertical roundhouse punches to the temples. We have cut the circles straight down off the eye slices and now do both halves of it coming back up into the roundhouse punches. This is the heart shape used in the delivery of the hammerfists in Grip of Death done in reverse.

Sandwich both forearms inward to strike the jaw hinges while still in the right neutral bow stance. Slide one hand over the other to trap and pull the head down and deliver a right upward knee kick to the face. For continuity one should probably put one hand on top on one side and the other hand on top for the other side in the pull-down and sandwich. The knee strike should be done with limited upward floating of the center of gravity. The returning action of the knee strike is fed into a right stomp onto the opponent's right instep. Therefore, one's weight should be forward to maximize the effect of the stomp. It is never a good idea to lean out of a stomp or stomp kick. Remember that the difference between a stomp and a stomp kick is that a stomp has no supporting leg—that is, you don't stand on one leg and kick then retract; that's a stomp kick.

You could just have easily and effectively thrown a rear-leg knee kick to the face. But in Short Form Three, we have already shown how to do that. Being that the premise of the forms is to introduce new moves and ideas with each form, it follows that a front knee strike should be illustrated. The idea of "what goes up, must come down" introduced in Scraping Hoof with the kicks is reiterated here in this technique. Throwing the rear knee and trying to do a stomp just would not fit the form, but it could be made to work in application.

After the stomp, step back with the right foot (*sans* "extra step") into the square horse, and then go into the opposite side on the 1:30 line. This completes our 45° angles in the star pattern. An observation here is that the angle sequence is opposite of the angle sequence in Short Two, where the back angles are the 4:30, then the 7:30. In Long Three they are done at 7:30, then 4:30. These angle entries are significant in higher forms.

Wings of Silk

This technique, Wings of Silk, is done the same way as in Short Form Three regarding the sequence of strikes. The angles change to 9:00 and 3:00, in that order.

Starting from the horse stance facing 12:00, perform the technique on the line toward 9:00. After executing the forearm break, chamber the hands, momentarily standing in another horse stance.

Reverse the line and direction of the spin used to move out on the line to return to the point of origin. This spin is not used "as is" as a part of Wings of Silk because it won't work. It is used as a rolling body check and could be part of the technique. This is one of the test questions in the form. It seems this section is either ignored or misunderstood. When I first learned it, it was ignored. The next teacher said it was useless and changed that section to make it what he considered to be more applicable. When I finally covered it with Mr. Parker, it was simple. Aren't they all like that?

Having returned to the square horse, now execute the technique and return spin on the 3:00 line, ending once again in the square horse.

Scraping Hoof/Repeated Devastation

An opponent attempts to apply a full nelson, and the counter is a combination of Scraping Hoof and Repeated Devastation.

Already in a horse stance, you have two options for starting this technique. If the horse is somewhat narrow, cheat the left foot out and then in again to begin the body arching necessary to break the hold or trap the arms with the head butt. If the stance is wider, just cheat the left foot in. It would not be necessary to cheat out since the stance is already wide and the needed travel is available. Both versions of this opening move are acceptable. Once again, the rule is "Cheat weak, kick strong."

With the cheat, the arms are thrust downward as in the Short Form Three version of this technique. It is important to remember to lead with the elbows, not with the fists. There are twin inverted vertical punches to the face with the cheat out. Many people have a tendency to raise or flip their elbows up and back to get travel for the downward thrust. It is false travel, really, and it detracts from the effectiveness of the movement. The elbows should drop a lot like Crashing Wings, using the powerful latissimus dorsi muscles to break the grip and trap the arms. Now the fists should be thrown hard with the arching of the body and the head butt. A word of caution here: I do not recommend constantly throwing the head back hard during form practice, as I think it will hurt the neck in the long run. I don't throw everything as hard as possible in the air[13] all the time. The force has to go somewhere, and much of it goes back through the body. Improper timing and alignment may damage joints over time. Hard work is done on the bag or a body because it absorbs the energy. As they say, moderation in all things.

Execute the right back scoop kick, side kick, scrape down, and stomp to the left inner knee, right inner knee, shin, and instep. Duplicate the sequence with the left leg, landing in a horse instead of the "T" position used in the technique.

The second half of the technique is Repeated Devastation, a technique in its own right. These two are together to illustrate the high-line and low-line responses to this attack, and how they can be used in sequence, even though they are taught as stand-alone techniques in the curriculum.

Step toward 1:00 with the left foot into a right reverse bow relative to 6:00. As this is accomplished, pin with the left hand at the right upper arm, using a snaking action to get to the pin position. The snaking is what one would do to ensure the grab of the left hand and the pinning of both arms to trap the opponent's arms. The left-hand grab holds the opponent's right wrist, becoming a pull down and back during the subsequent shift to a right forward bow to 6:00. A right outward elbow is delivered with the stance change, striking the head. The grabbing and pinning checks are maintained throughout. The snaking action to get the grab is as if you were doing Snaking Talon from the back.

Move the left foot back to the feet-together position and immediately step out to 11:00 with the right foot, having now done a front-foot-to-back-foot switch.

Settling in the left reverse bow stance, snaking the right hand, and shifting to deliver a left outward elbow finishes the opposite side of the move.

---

13 "In the air" means you do it as you do in a form, with no physical body in front of you.

There are two discussions here. The first addresses the angles to step toward to get the forward bow stances to 6:00 with the elbows. The second is what you call that switch between the elbows.

I think the angle that gets you to the 6:00 elbow is whatever you need it to be. Step to 12:00 or 1:00, but align yourself to have the bracing angle and proper angle of delivery for the elbow. As to the switch, there are two in the form. One is between the sides of Parting Wings and the other is here. Call them what you want, but they set up the category by being there in this form. Mr. Parker changed the names from time to time in the course of my training. The third major switch is in a subsequent form.

Freeze the arms in position—left elbow and right extended down along the right leg for the pull. Step back into the square horse position facing 12:00. Match the left hand to the right, in fists, while settling. This eliminates unnecessary movement of the hands by leaving the right hand down. The opening position for the final technique is now created.

Desperate Falcons

While executing the cross, step forward with the left foot into a left neutral bow stance. Continue to circle the hands back as in Crossing Talon and using the same timing with the settling. The hands are momentarily chambered at the right hip for travel and control in a "cup and saucer"

configuration. As the opponent bends forward and down, deliver a simultaneous left outward back-knuckle to the head with a right vertical thrust punch to the right ribs or solar plexus. This utilizes borrowed force and is an open-ended triangle to check and control, much like a universal block. Snap both hands back to the right hip into the "cup and saucer" while in the left neutral bow stance. Immediately set both hands in front to indicate the next side of the attack.

Perform the left side of the technique by stepping through to 12:00, circling the hands to the left, and continuing in the mirror image of the right side.

I once asked Mr. Parker about whether or not the technique should be done in a neutral bow or a forward bow. The governing rule is "front hand, neutral—rear hand, forward." The corollary is "both hands, either." I did it with one side in the neutral and the other using the forward. He said it could certainly be done that way to show that idea. I believe he preferred it done with a neutral bow on both sides, leaving the alternative hidden. As we know, the determining factor would be the distance of the opponent, and we select accordingly.

Stepping forward from the right neutral bow stance with the left foot into the salutation horse finishes the form.

You will find yourself a stance width over to the right from where the form was started. This is because of the introduction of parallel tracks in the footwork.

Instructors have "corrected" the form to begin and end in the same spot by changing the footwork, eliminating the parallel track. This is akin to "correcting" the long lines in Long Form Two and Short Form Three for the same reason. These correc- tions delete patterns one finds when mapping out the footwork of the forms from One through Six. Information is therefore lost. In particular the parallel track idea, which is picked up again in Form Five, gets lost to the masses of students. You will find that the two steps back to 6:00 in Glancing Spear and the two steps forward to 12:00 in Desperate Falcons create these parallel tracks. You will also see that they are offset by the aforementioned one-stance distance. All of this is going to lead to some rather interesting ideas involving the star pattern that Ed Parker illustrated for us on the white board. The ideas are developed in the higher forms.

Close the salutation horse with the standard left-foot-in ending to an attention stance. Do the full salutation and bow.

Closing Remarks

Short Form Three was considered to be a demonstration form in the schools I first studied in. Funny, because I saw the head instructor run it at a big Chinese Martial Arts demonstration, and he finished it, but with hesitations. Years later I was able to run it in 19 seconds with the right mechanics. As the demo statement was explained to me, the form was short, had some variety, and looked better compared to the previous four beginner forms. Long Three was said to be just too long. A karate magazine once published a statement about packing a lunch when judging Kenpo forms because they're long. So, I was told that Ed Parker had created Short Form Three as a demo form. Not so, he told me when I got to learning directly from him. In fact, he laughed when I told him some of the things I heard in both the Tracy and Parker schools about things he supposedly did or intended. "They really said that?" he'd say with an incredulous look on his face.

Short Three is a good demonstration form regardless, and a good choice for competition in the intermediate levels. I once taught a dancer with little martial art experience to do it and entered her in the women's white/yellow/orange division at the Nationals and she took first place. Long Three is OK for greens and browns, and lots of people have won with it. I ran it in the black-belt division once and won first place. I chose it because I had a broken toe and couldn't run Four, Five, or Six since I stomped a lot. I can tell you that I took first place in black-belt forms at some time running Three, Four, Five, or Six. My point here is that Short

Form Three is "quick and dirty"—not too short, not too long, hands, feet, knees, elbows, pokes, claws, angles, etc. It just looks good.

A Story About Forms: Ed Parker was approached by a competitor at his tournament, the world-renowned International Karate Championships (IKC). The man asked why it was that he, the Grand Champion winner of black-belt forms, would win $100 while the Grand Champion of the fighting would receive $250. Mr. Parker replied that the fighter took risks and could very well be injured in his quest for the trophy. "Who has ever heard of a world-champion shadow boxer?" he added. The man looked at him, said "I understand," and bowed.

5.

Form Four

Ed Parker intended Form Four to be the last form in the system. It was said that if you understood everything in Four, you understood the system. As time went by, Five and Six were introduced. They are logical extensions of progressions of motion and hold ideas not used or developed in Four.

Four is a long form, longer than any previous. That alone provides a good cardio-vascular workout. As you will see, the length of the form is necessary to get many ideas across and to preserve them for the future. There is a Short Four that is referred to and taught by many teachers. Mr. Parker mentioned it at times, but it was not something required to be learned. It was a nod to the fact that Four is long, and the short version is easier to do. The earlier forms have short versions, and it follows that a short version of Four fits the pattern. It should then follow that there are short versions of Five and Six, and even forms Seven and Eight. I'm not saying there are or should be. I'm saying it is an idea that can be used by individual practitioners to vary or enhance their training. Should you decide to do the short version, you alternate right and left sides of the techniques in their form sequence, e.g. Protecting Fans right side, Darting Leaves left side, Unfurling Crane right side, etc.

How forms are done and varied practice methods were discussed earlier. Ed Parker taught different people different ways of doing the forms, and he did the forms differently at different periods in his life. You will see some people do the forms almost like hard-stylists and others do them with a softer flavor. For the most part the Parker people do them with the same angles, while others have a 90° change in them somewhere. I attribute that to either a deliberate change to say "That's the way WE do it" or someone just plain forgot and taught it the wrong way. Either way, it gets passed down to the students, who can only do what they are taught.

You will also see "signature" moves in the forms. A signature is one move that's done differently from school to school. It was Mr. Parker's way of tracking who learned what from whom. He told me he could tell if someone learned a form from a particular instructor by whether they actually did the signature. Remember, this was back when Kenpo was not a widespread system and there just weren't as many practitioners of the art. It was also easier then to get back to Mr. Parker directly. He had a school you could go to and see him. Later he wasn't around the school that much and it was difficult for just anybody to study with him.

Signature moves are usually subtle. I was taught one in Long Three and one in Four. I didn't know there were signatures until Mr. Huk Planas pointed that out to me. I was then able to go back to Mr. Parker and discuss the idea and placement of the signatures. Over the years of encountering many practitioners around the world and watching their forms, I've seen signatures and had them verified when I inquired about the lineage of the performer. A shuffle here, a big circle there, an opposite hand rotation do actually indicate an instructional signature. The lines are more blurred now since people can learn on video, but you can usually tell they did that because their basics are not normally as strong as with personal instruction. Video is now a lineage of its own.

Overview

A well-executed Four is a nice-looking form and it is good for competition, although a bit lengthy. I suspect that is the real reason for a Short Four: a shorter form is better for competition. I won numerous trophies running Four in both Kenpo and open tournaments. Even Kenpo practitioners will admit that it is tough to watch the Kenpo forms divisions because the forms are so long. How many times can you watch Four without getting a little bored? When I competed at the Internationals there would be upwards of fifty, and often more, men running Four, Five, or Six. It would take hours to complete the division. One black belt even ran those three forms back to back and the following year ran *all* of them from Short One to Six. I salute his athletic ability but it sure did eat up some time. Four is a tough form to do properly, and few make it stand out.

I learned and ran different versions of Four, as well as Five and Six. The first one I learned was pretty poor and it was, in hindsight, no surprise I didn't do too well with it. When I got a more solid version from Mike Sanders, my scores started to rise. I did even better as I got more involved in the Parker system. It took some conditioning of the judges, though. I was competing nationally in the late '70s and early '80s. Being from the Midwest where the Japanese and Okinawan systems had a stronghold, the way I did the original version I learned was not accepted. The judges could see the flaws in alignment and power delivery, even if they didn't know the form. I had a Shorei-Ryu instructor tell me that he had seen Ed Parker demonstrate in the '60s and "He looked like a hard-stylist." What I had originally been taught was too soft, with a lot of meaningless motion. Sanders taught me to harden it up and brought meaning to the movements. That in turn brought more life to the form. So I ran the forms in the Midwest with lower than standard stances, added a *kiai* here and there along with some more power and snap, and got the judges' attention. A heavyweight *gi* helped, too. It popped. That's just presentation—it's superfluous, really.

With all that, the local people could appreciate what was being done since it related more to what they were used to seeing and doing. I got higher scores. But now when I went west and competed in California there was a lot more Kenpo and the standard was different. I wasn't yet doing what was being done out there. Remember, I was in transition between the Tracy-type Kenpo and the Parker system. So there I was doing the lower stances, etc., and it was not "technically correct" for a Parker stylist. After that visit I figured it out. I raised the stances, changed the timing, corrected my form, and won some more trophies. I also ran a few different forms so as to have ammunition in the event of a tie or to play to a mixed panel of judges from a variety of systems. Kenpo has something for everyone, and you can adjust the forms to appeal to most any judge. It's a tough task, trying to be technically correct yet win the gold in open competition. I did it, and made the *Karate Illustrated* magazine National Top Ten in 1980 as well as that of the American Karate Association for several years. If I could do it, you can, too.

Theme: This form is the first of the "live" attack forms—that is, the techniques defend against punches and kicks. Four shows how we handle single and combination punch attacks as well as kick-punch combinations. It's interesting that there are no standard techniques in the form that defend against combination kicks, but the information is in there if you look.

Technique Sequence

Using the names of the techniques as they are taught in the post-1970 Ed Parker system:

Protecting Fans

Darting Leaves

Unfurling Crane

Destructive Kneel

Flashing Wings

Gathering Clouds

Circles of Protection

Dance of Darkness

Thundering Hammer

Unwinding Pendulum

Reversing Circles

Snaking Talon

Circling Fans

Isolation

Defensive Cross

Bowing to Buddha

Prance of the Tiger

Shield and Mace

Five Swords

Twirling Hammers

Closing and Salutation

The opening salutation is the same as that used in the previous forms, Short and Long Three. For a discussion of the usage and execution of the salutation, please see Chapter Two of this book or Ed Parker's *Infinite Insights into Kenpo, Volume 5,* Chapter 3, pages 11–54. For Parker's book I'm the model for the forms and the salutation, a fact mentioned in the book's acknowledgments. They even made a T-shirt with the drawings on it.

Protecting Fans—punch combination

This technique, on its first side, is a defense against a left-right punch combination with the opponent's left foot forward. It illustrates how to handle a combination punch attack by working inside the first punch and outside the second. Later techniques will demonstrate other ways of handling the same combination. Consider it to be like a boxer's attack, a jab-cross combination. It could be used against a straight right step-through punch, a right punch with the left foot forward, or inside a left straight punch. However, most teach it for the combination. If you use it for a boxer's combination, realize that the boxer would likely follow the cross with a hook punch. That's a good reason to do the technique with an extended outward instead of an outward parry. The block would cancel the body better than the parry due to the greater angle of deflection. See a discussion of the block vs. parry idea at the end of this chapter, in "Additional Observations."

Starting from the closed or attention position, execute the standard side of Protecting Fans by stepping forward on the left front 45° angle with your left foot and left inward parry and settle into a left forward bow stance with a right open-hand extended outward block, left hand chambered.

Some chamber the right at the waist, some let it hang.

Pivot to face the right front 45° line with a left horizontal two-finger eye poke and right front snap kick, right hand pulling down into the chamber. Drop into a (square) horse stance facing 12:00 with a right inward elbow, left hand closed and chambered at your left ribs. Note that this angle is not the same as the technique application that drops forward on the right front 45° line. The horse sets up the isolation to come.

Isolation

This isolation may be considered to either have additional information or things that have been left out. In the Parker system there is no form consisting of multiple attacker (two-man) techniques. There is a form called Mass Attack that many Kenpo schools teach, but it is not an Ed Parker system form. Mass Attack contains variations of self-defense techniques from the Parker system. This isolation demonstrates several interesting ideas. The elbow as you sit in the horse stance should really be done while settling forward on the front diagonal, as it would be in the technique. Yet it is done in a horse to start the isolation. If you look at the elbow strike and the chamber hand you will see two short-range weapons—the elbows—with both hands closed.

The next move is done with a right elbow and a left rear finger thrust over the shoulder. Again, the arms are folded but we are getting more reach by using the fingers. To me it looks like Mr. Parker was showing the relationship between the two weapons.

Next is the right straight finger thrust and simultaneous left-rear vertical handsword. Both attack the centerline and both use an extended arm as compared to the previous pair that used the folded arm. The front one is high and horizontal while the rear is low and vertical. Try reversing them; it doesn't work too well. Both are open-handed. The previous pair was both closed, or one open/one closed. This leads us to the next possible combination, which is both closed and using an extended weapon with a folded weapon. Now we execute a left upward elbow (folded weapon) with a right back hammerfist (extended weapon). We are shown the ranges front and back, weapon formations, and horizontal and vertical angles. We will show the methods of execution of thrusting and snapping in the next move, and then two other directions.

The thrusting-snapping combination is like the technique Glancing Salute in that it may be interpreted as a right pin (that looks like an outward block) with the thrust action and a left inward break (that looks like an inward block) with the snap action. There is an argument for a relationship with the two-man technique The Ram and the Eagle. From the completion of the combination you throw twin vertical back-knuckle strikes to the sides to show the side attack lines.

To boil it down, we can say that we now have the elements of working the ranges, angles, and zones for front, side, and rear multiple attacks. If you consider an isolation as a signpost from which to journey down

another path, this one will get you thinking about handling multiple attackers.

The final part of the isolation between the first and second sides of Protecting Fans is what I call the "hunch and crunch."

As you pull your hands in from the twin vertical back-knuckles to uppercuts across your body, drop into a concave stance, all the while keeping your spine straight but tilting forward. Remember that straight

In a concave stance.   OR   In a horse stance.

does not always mean vertical. This is what looks like a hunch, and the punches would be the crunch. Close from this position as if you are closing the form, but do it with the right foot to the left instead. There are arguments about which foot to do this with. I did it both ways and found it makes more sense to do it with the right because it is the only time you close with the right instead of the left, and it's OK because it's not the end of the form. The close at the end restates the "weak to strong" premise of the salutation, which is that we train to make ourselves stronger physically, mentally, emotionally, and spiritually. Closing right to left vs. left to right affects the end position of the form if your footwork is consistent.

After you've done the "hunch and crunch" and close with the claws, step to the right front 45° angle and do the opposite side of Protecting Fans. Hit the left front 45° line with the kick and poke, and drop once again into the horse for the opposite-side isolation, ending at the twin vertical outward back-knuckles. The close is not done after the second side's back-knuckles; you'll go right into the first side of Darting Leaves.

Darting Leaves—straight punch

This technique may be used inside or outside a straight punch. Generally it is taught working against a left on the inside. This enables you to work the centerline in a similar method as the previous technique, Protecting Fans, but inside instead of outside. Long and Short Form One show how to use an inward block as you retreat. Long and Short Form Two show how to use the inward block moving forward. This technique shows how to work in-place. Another relationship here is that while you kick and poke simultaneously as you did in the Protecting Fans technique, you do it with the same side, e.g. right-hand/right-foot, instead of cross-body. The poke is done vertically with two fingers, and it's done horizontally in Protecting Fans. It's simple, really, showing two kinds of two-finger eye pokes, horizontal and vertical. I was originally taught to do a middle-knuckle instead of a poke, with no target or reason.

From your horse stance with the back-knuckles at about shoulder height, pivot to 1:30 into a right 45° cat with a left thrusting inward block. Your right hand will be floating at mid-chest in the vertical two-finger poke formation.

Fire your right front snap kick to the groin simultaneously with your right eye poke. The poke will travel over your left arm, notching itself through your wrist as a form of contouring. Retrieve the kick and poke to their points of origin, but set your kicking leg down and to the right into a horse after retraction. Immediately slide back with the pivot to the left cat and do the opposite side of the technique.

As you retract your left kick, retract your right hand slightly but not chambering, and use it to show the major inward block as you settle in a horse once again by stepping down to the left, timing the settle with the block. This isolates the inward block as the major for the next technique.

Unfurling Crane—punch combination

The odd thing about this technique is that it is demonstrated on the "weak side" first against a right-left punch combination. All the rest of the combination punch attacks are initially shown against the more common left-right punch sequence. That makes this a test question. Now you have to ask yourself why, then go to your instructor and say what you think the reason is.

Step back to 4:30 with your right foot as your right hand continues through from the inward block against an incoming right punch to become an outside downward block. Your left hand will execute a vertical outward block as you settle in the left neutral bow stance facing 10:30, and it becomes a check. Your right hand could be blocking a left kick, making this a defense against a kick/punch-punch combination,

Block, anticipating the kick.   Hammering the groin.

something quite common in Chinese martial arts. We do that very move-ment in Long Form Two.

The typical attack taught for this application is the combination punch, not the kick/punch-punch attack. I mention this attack to explain the downward block position. It seems to me that most people don't even consider that hand position and are surprised when we tell them what it can be. It could even be used against a high-left, low-right body shot that then goes high to your head.

Step-drag forward on the same angle with a left inward/right outward combination block/check inside the left punch. Your left hand becomes a hammerfist forward to the groin.

Immediately deliver a right claw to the face followed by a left rolling back-knuckle to the bridge of the nose. Use "body english" on the strike to avoid disconnected use of the arms. Anchor your elbows.

Slide your left foot directly back to 7:30 to face 1:30 in a right neutral bow stance, and do the standard side of the technique. This is a good example of the principle taught in the first move of Short Form One governing foot maneuvers. The general rule is to step direct when retreating. Instructors are often asked whether the left foot comes in to the right or simply goes to the desired place. If you bring your left foot in to your right in Short One or here in Four, you will be getting closer to the opponent before retreating. If you step direct, you don't. Bringing it in has a pleasing aesthetic to it, making the move look cleaner, but it's a rule-breaker here.

Now you're facing 1:30 and having done the blocks, claw, and back-knuckle, you're ready to go back to the 12:00–6:00 line for the next technique.

Destructive Kneel—straight punch

There are several techniques in this form that share lower-body mechanics with Destructive Kneel. Thundering Hammer, Shield and Mace, and Flashing Wings come to mind. All show how to break down an opponent's stance while striking with the arms. Two others in the group work him while he is still standing, and Shield and Mace works against the leg with your arm. The idea fits nicely—buckle the leg with the leg; buckle the leg with the arm.

This technique illustrates the use of the rear hand to pick off the attack. From the 1:30 line slide your right foot directly back onto the 12:00–6:00

line as your right hand drops down from the previous position, circling clockwise to parry the incoming straight right step-through punch with a horizontal outward parry and grab. Your left hand will follow it almost simultaneously with an inward heel-palm strike to the elbow. You will be doing a step-drag shuffle back to 6:00 in a left reverse wide kneel stance as you do these hand movements. The hands will look like what you do at the beginning of Form Six in the Glancing Lance technique, but in the reverse wide kneel stance. The question I ask is: why do that initial big loop from the back-knuckle to the parry to pick off the punch? Another test question. An answer is a few paragraphs down but should get you looking for a bigger piece of the puzzle.

The wide kneel will check the outside of the right leading leg as your hands catch the punching arm and attempt to break the elbow. The opponent may attempt to pull away or your hands may slip off. Follow him by shuffling to 12:00 into a left close kneel, your right leg breaking his stance down by checking, as your right hand claws his face while your left breaks the right ribs with a back-knuckle and pulling both through to your left side. Your arms create an "open-ended triangle" to keep his arm in check. Your shuffle works like the one in Thundering

Hammer in that you pass by him so he can't hit you with a counter elbow. End with your hands cocked at your left side, left over right at your left ribs.

Reverse direction once more, shuffling to 6:00 into a right wide kneel as your hands deliver a right outward back-knuckle to the right kidney with a left vertical punch to the floating ribs using gravitational marriage. You may hear these configurations referred to as the "cup and saucer" or "stacked" positions. Your wide kneel is driving him down into the ground, and this contributes to the name Destructive Kneel, as this and/or the previous knee checks may sprain or break the leg.

Do the other side by sliding your left foot back to 6:00 with the left hand parry/right elbow break and finish to 6:00 in a left wide kneel, right hand over left.

Another interesting comparison here is that the first technique in the form opened with an inward/outward combination. This one reverses that by going outward/inward. When you read the original *Accumulative Journal* you'll see that Protecting Fans was written with a left horizontal inward parry as the first move. In practice, everyone does an inward parry since it fits the zone of the attack better. Horizontal inwards work better in the mid-zone. Using that knowledge we see that the idea of horizontal inward and horizontal outward would have been displayed in the form and would account for the circle needed to get to the outside of the punch from the Unfurling Crane technique. It certainly would be much faster to block or parry that right punch on the inside from that point of origin.

Flashing Wings—straight punch

One interesting point on the entry to this technique is that it has what looks like two blocks: an upward followed by an inward. The standard technique uses an inward block.

Starting from the wide kneel used in the previous technique, rotate clockwise to face 12:00 in a right front rotating twist stance with a right upward block, left hand chambered. The upward is necessary versus an extended outward block because you are rising in height from the wide kneel, and an extended outward would not give you the same margin for error. Because of your position, the punch needs to be treated almost like an overhand, and you probably wouldn't block an overhand with an outward. This block combined with the off-line movement gained from the rotating twist (about a half-stance to the left) helps avoid the punch. Placing the right foot in the twist correctly allows the left to step forward to 12:00 without obstruction into the left neutral bow with the left inward block that starts the standard technique. A tip: placing your right foot under where your belt hangs usually gets you in the right place, provided you are wearing your belt knot in the center.

Shuffle forward to 12:00 into a left wide kneel with a right inward elbow to the ribs, left hand checking high. This used to be done with a

forward bow, but that has no low-zone check as the wide kneel does. A close kneel works, too.

Rip the elbow through to your left, loading it for an outward elbow to the spine or shoulder blade area (the rhomboids hurt a lot when you hit them) that you throw when you turn back toward the opponent in a horse stance, maintaining the left high check. You people with long arms may be able to reach across with your left as all this happens and rip his face with a horizontal claw in the opposing force line for the elbow. However, if you try this and just can't reach, all it's going to do is diminish the effectiveness of your major moves. The lesson here is that you don't sacrifice your major to get a minor, something Kenpo people seem to do often.

Take the torque from the change to the horse to throw a right outward chop to the back of the neck. Cock your left hand high at the left side of your head only after the right gets there since the right acts as a check. Pivot to a reverse wide kneel to check the leg and drop the left chop on the back of the neck, right hand sliding down the right arm to check. Your left will replace the right sliding check as your right reverses direction along with your stance change back to a left wide kneel.

Strike the throat with a right thrusting chop, delivered almost like a lifting heel-palm. Your right hand will have rebounded off your right knee to get the correct angle and timing on this. Sometimes you'll hear a slap with this as the back of the right hand comes off the leg. If your hand comes from here it will have the proper line of sight for the throat shot. If you take it off and back for the wind-up, you lose that. It may be better to change to Thundering Hammer. That's actually the relationship of the two techniques, anyway. If he stays up you chop his throat; if he drops too much you continue on the circle and do the hammerfist to the back of the neck.

Do a left front rotating twist off the line and facing 12:00 with a left upward block. Step forward to 12:00 with your right foot and right inward block and do the opposite side of the technique. You'll end facing 12:00 in a right wide kneel, left hand high, right hand low.

Gathering Clouds—straight punch

This technique and Leaping Crane illustrate a progression in using the rib rake and strike, with Leaping Crane inserting the kick between the rake and the step-forward/strike. The name Gathering Clouds comes from the action of the arms that looks like you are gathering something together.

From the previous right wide kneel, adjust your left foot to a square

horse position facing 9:00. As you do, execute a left inward parry and right inward horizontal middle-knuckle rib rake. The parry against the right punch moves the attack to your right to open the targets and cancel zones. The small step you did indicates the larger step you would have taken if the point of origin had been a natural stance. I mention this because students get confused as to which foot to move when in this sequence. If you know the technique, you know you step left on the standard side to avoid the attack and get some back-up mass for the rib shot. So step left on the first side, step right on the second.

Immediately deliver a right outward chop to the right kidney and step forward with your right into a right neutral bow with a right inward horizontal elbow to the ribs. Use the ratchet idea in the chop-to-elbow sequence to eliminate wind-up. The elbow is shown as a sandwich in the form for timing and is not applied that way, as it would leave your head open for counter. Your left hand would have to be up.

Now if you imagine you had a square on the floor in front of you when you did the first side, you'll need to get on the other side facing where you were, a kind of mirror-image. Right now you're about two-thirds of the way along the top of the square with your right foot. If you put your left foot behind in a tight rear twist stance, you'll find it is on the corner of the square. Keep your hands where they are for the moment.

Pivot hard out of the twist with a right step to the right into a square horse stance, now mirroring the horse you started in on the opposite side. Taking advantage of the stored energy of the twist stance, use it to fire your right parry/left rib rake with the step. Do the technique on the opposite side, ending toward 3:00 in a left neutral bow, hands in the sandwich position.

Roll your hands in place and palm-up, having your left hand on top, and do a left rear twist stance to 10:30. This can also be done by dropping back into a cat, and then sliding your left foot back in a reverse bow on the proper angle. I think the twist version tends to make you keep your back straighter during the turn. In either case, keep your back straight and shoulders level. Lots of people lead with their hips here, breaking their waist and destroying alignment. By having your left hand on top it will set you in position for the next technique, having your new hand in front as you should. Keep that in mind and you'll have no problem in the next transitions. The rule will guide you.

Circles of Protection—overhead punch

This technique is the first of any in the form to show a new attack line, the overhead (also called overhand) punch. We are on our way to completing the categories of motion in regard to the four basic lines. We've done inside and outside the attack, now we're going under. The last is over, and it is toward the end of the form.

From the previously mentioned rear twist stance, unwind to 10:30 into a left forward bow stance with a right upward parry underneath the right overhand punch. Pivot in place to a left neutral bow with a left upward outward claw to the face, fingers horizontal.

This one-two action not only ensures that you deflect the punch but turns the opponent's head away so he has a hard time throwing the follow-up left punch. The claw hand may also be used to actually block the left punch at or near the shoulder—what is called a shoulder or bicep stop.

Your right hand continues on its circular path back, under, and up into the groin as an underhand claw, as you drop to a wide kneel stance. A forward bow works but not quite as well; the wide kneel lets you hammer upward better. Simultaneous with this your left hand is circling out, down, and in, slamming his right hand against his body and continuing across your own body to check horizontally. Now he is off balance and bending forward. Strike the face with your left outward back-knuckle, shuffling forward here in a left neutral bow if you did not find it necessary to shuffle on the groin grab, which is a pull and rip, by the way. Your right

hand is now either covering at your left ribs or chambered. Don't forget to retract the back-knuckle; lots of people leave it hanging out.

As you retract the back-knuckle you'll start a left front crossover to 4:30, 180° from where you are. Cross your arms again as you did on the transition into this technique but with the right hand on top, palm up. I call this transition "cross your arms—cross your legs." When you complete the crossover with the right step out to 4:30, you do the left upward parry in the forward and finish the left side of the technique.

Dance of Darkness—kick, punch combination

Let's talk about double parries and width zones first. Use of double parries is illustrated in this technique. The kick is deflected by the initial downward parry. The punch is picked up by combination inward-outward parries. It seems to me that the first side of this technique is often executed improperly in that most people like to face square on to the opponent by turning their centerline in the same direction of the attack. The technique is taught starting in a neutral bow, which starts you off as a small target. So, most people are making themselves a big target, then

turning back to the original, side-facing position (as done in the form). It is reverse motion and wasted action. Since you'll already be sideways, just don't rotate so far to get into the technique.

The first parry, an inward with your rear hand, intercepts the incoming follow-up punch below the elbow due to range. The following outward parry with your front hand picks up the punch at the elbow, thus checking the hinges of the punching arm. This following is what creates what looks like a double circle or double parry with the rear hand, a question about the technique that arises frequently. The next turn to 7:30 has both hands moving, with the right being the active one by parrying the kick. The left is coming into position but is still out of range. That positioning is what makes it look like the first circle, and the second, active action is what starts to pick up the punch, then followed by the right.

Now changing from the 4:30 line to the 7:30 line, bring your right foot around three-quarters of a circle behind you to 1:30 into a rear twist stance. This engages pull-power back-up mass to make your right downward parry effective against the incoming right front kick. Having retracted your right outward back-knuckle at the end of Circles of Protection, you won't be working almost straight-armed. Your elbow will be anchored, your ribs better protected, and your arm bent to prevent a sprain or break.

Your left hand will be in the high zone and starting the parry combination I describe in the previous paragraph.

You will rebound out of the twist stance with the inward-outward parries and step toward 7:30 with your right foot into a right neutral bow. Do a left step-through on the 7:30 line as you pull your hands through to the left side of your body, stacking them left over right as in Destructive Kneel. Strike the right kidney and short ribs as you pivot out of the step-through into a horse facing 10:30 and still on the 7:30 line.

Double punch.   Back-knuckle.

Reach up and grab the right shoulder with your left hand and strike the head with a right rolling back-knuckle. You should be pulling down hard to cancel the opponent's height and bring him into the head punch. Consider this to be the claw/back-knuckle section you did in Unfurling Crane, but on the back of the body.

The back-knuckle to the head should cause him to reach toward his head with his right hand. Remember, people tend to hold what hurts. Slap your right hand down hard with your palm up to clear that arm and use his borrowed force to deliver a right inward eye hook to his right eye.

The eye hook will make him move backward, taking the weight off his front leg (the right leg), making it easy to sweep with your left thrusting

Eye hook Poke.

sweep kick. The sweep kick lands a little off-line to keep the form lines clean, so plant your left foot on the 1:30 line in a left front twist stance. The foot sweep makes the upper body move back first before it falls forward, so time the left eye poke as he shifts forward, making him fall into it. That poke is vertical and delivered in a contouring fashion, guide-lining along your right eye hook to make finding the target much easier. The backs of your hands actually rub against each other as you do this. It is the first time they do, making it distinctly different from the two-finger pokes in Long Form Two. I have found that if you do this lancing-type poke in both forms you lose one category of motion.

Pivot out of the twist stance to face 1:30 in a left neutral bow. If you had your hands placed correctly at the end of the first side of the technique, you will find them automatically in the proper position—that is, left hand covering your high zone and right hand covering your middle zone.

Whether you sit for a second in this stance before starting the second side of the technique or just flow through it seems to depend on a few factors. One is that some just like to do it one way versus the other, the flow version being more "Chinese-y" and the other more karate-like (or soft vs. hard, if you prefer). Apparently Mr. Parker did it both ways, and it depends on what era you learned it from him that governs which way you do it. As artists have blue periods or red periods, it seems Ed Parker had hard periods and soft periods. So I can't tell you absolutely which way it goes since I've seen and done it both ways.

After doing the second side you will end in a right front twist stance on the 1:30–7:30 line in that classic twin finger-poke position we like to have our pictures taken in. You have shown the four diagonal lines of the eight directions now, and we're ready to go back to the 3:00–9:00 lines.

Thundering Hammer—straight punch

Thundering Hammer is a big favorite of Kenpo practitioners. It is the first of the hanging-arm techniques to be included in the forms, i.e., the rear arm hangs along the leg instead of being chambered or covering. The other two techniques in the hang family are Dance of Death and Sleeper, and they are found in Form Five. One should know the reason there are the three separate techniques: the opponent may be covering his high, middle, or low horizontal zones of defense, and these techniques attack the corresponding open zones. Beyond this relationship there is the use of the knees to strike and check. Other techniques doing just that in this form are Flashing Wings, Destructive Kneel, and Shield and Mace.

Step out with your left foot from the front twist you finished the last technique in into a left neutral bow stance to 9:00 with a left thrusting inward block, and hang your right arm. You've blocked the outside of his right punch.

Push-drag shuffle forward into a left wide kneel stance to check his right leg as your right arm slams across his lower abdomen as an inward horizontal forearm strike, your left hand chambered high by your left ear.

The shuffle and low-line attack are designed to bring his upper body far forward to preclude the possibility of his hitting you with a right outward elbow. Therefore you can afford to bring your left hand back and up. You sure could do the technique with your left hand covering or checking his right elbow if need be. You could also just whack him in the groin like Dance of Death and not worry about it at all. But we're showing family grouping ideas here and we need this high point of origin.

Change your stance to a reverse wide (or close) kneel stance as your left hand hammers the opponent's left kidney. Leave your right hand down to check his right arm. Yes, I know many people don't do that—they roll their hand up like Flashing Wings. Most I've seen roll it up too far and leave themselves open. Mr. Parker was pretty specific with me about leaving the arm down, but I'd seen him teach seminars doing it the other way. I asked him about that and he said he taught it like that to see if anyone would ask about it or just take his word. Leave the right arm there until the left hand slides over from the kidney shot to control the upper arm, then draw your right out to start the circle over and down into its hammerfist to the base of the skull with the stance change back to the wide kneel.

Angle off with your left foot to the rear 45° angle to the opponent, which is 4:30 and facing 10:30 in a right neutral bow.

Shown with a heel-palm.

When you settle into this stance you will strike the head with a right back-knuckle. Some do an outward back-knuckle; I do a vertical downward hanging back-knuckle.

Some roll the hands into the back-knuckle and others rebound the hand across and off the body. Still others "let it all hang out" using opposing force. Everyone has a reason for his or her way, and I'd seen Mr. Parker do it those ways as well. That said, hit the head and shuffle forward on that line with an underhand claw to the face, left hand checking.

Rotate 180° to your left to face 3:00 to transition to the opposite side. To do this you will need to pick your left foot up and move it to the left about 90° into a left-rotating front twist. Where you put that foot will determine your line of travel for the next move, so make sure it's right.

Work this movement carefully. Poor execution will hurt your knee or ankle in the long run. As you rotate you will deliver a left downward block. This move may be used to block an incoming left kick or as a hammer strike to the previous opponent. Your right hand will be chambered high by your right ear for delivery of the hammering inward block to start the left side of the technique. This blocking order is reversed from the One and Two forms. Those forms do a hammer then a thrust. This one thrusts then hammers. You will actually find that reversal at the end of Short Form Two, but this works the application. Both delete any cocking by reverse motion.

Step forward to 3:00 with your right foot with the right inward block, left hand in place, and do the opposite side of the technique. Your final angle change for the back-knuckle and claw will have you facing 1:30 in a left neutral bow stance. You'll do a rear twist stance with your right foot 180° for the transition to the next technique. Remember that we did one 270° between Circles of Protection and Dance of Darkness. Look for a 90° change down the line. Now you're set for the next section.

Unwinding Pendulum—kick, punch combination

A comparison of this with Dance of Darkness and Reversing Circles is necessary. All are against combination attacks. Dance of Darkness works outside the attack as does Unwinding Pendulum, but does it with parries as compared to blocks. Unwinding Pendulum shows a sequence of inward/outward blocks, while Reversing Circles demonstrates simultaneous use of those same blocks.

As you do the rear twist stance to 1:30 to face 7:30, deliver a right downward block for a right front kick, with your left hand chambered high at your left ear. This should look like the transition between the sides of Thundering Hammer but with the opposite hands.

Pivot in place to a left neutral bow facing 7:30 with your left hammering inward block against the incoming right straight punch, right hand in the

hang position. You are outside the attacks, the best place to be. However, try doing it inside the left kick and punch sometime, or against a left kick/ right punch combination. It will open your eyes, or close one if you blow it.

Throw your right thrusting sweep kick to 7:30, striking the opponent's left inner ankle to spread him out and take his base as your left hand checks high. Plant in a right front twist on the same line and, as you settle, deliver a right underhand crane peck to the groin as your left hand checks.

On the body the check is high near his shoulder or arm to prevent retaliation. In the air the check is done as in Thundering Hammer, contacting your left forearm as the foot stops, for timing.

Keep your spine straight and your shoulders level. Not doing so is a common mistake, and it's done a lot in this and the subsequent forms. I see a lot of leaning and bending. That's bad for alignment and therefore affects balance, power, and breathing. It looks sloppy, too.

Make a 90° angle change behind yourself with your left foot into a right front twist facing 4:30 as your left hand does the downward block and right hand chambers high. Execute the rest of the second side of the technique, ending in a left front twist facing 4:30. Now we'll do that timing change with the blocks I mentioned earlier as we go into the next section.

Reversing Circles—kick, punch combination

This is the technique that's not a technique. Sure you can use it as a technique, but not the way it's been written in the manuals, as most teach it. It breaks too many rules. If you do it for a roundhouse kick it doesn't go up the circle—a principle

we use on all our roundhouse kick defenses. You could step in and jam the attack, though. Maybe you would want to use it for a front kick and overhand punch. That seems to work a little better.

Step directly out of the front twist to 7:30 with your right foot, ending in a right neutral bow. Your right hand does a downward block as your left does an inward block, creating a reverse universal block with the step out.

Pivot in place to a right forward bow stance with right upward parry and a left thrusting outward handsword to the ribs. Pivot back into the neutral bow with a left upward parry/check and right outward chop.

Step-through to 4:30 with your left foot as you deliver the opposite reverse universal block. Make that step-through by bringing your left foot in to your right and then stepping out. This would reverse the idea used when moving into Unfurling Crane in which I referred to the rule of motion stated in the first move of Short Form One. When you step forward you want to close your centerline as you do in the first moves of Short and Long Two. The step, combined with the hand transition, could be applied as an arm break should you decide to utilize the movements as a technique. The first universal block can stop an incoming left kick, and the hand picks up the follow-up punch as you strike the ribs. That strike then slides up the body into a check as your front hand strikes. The top hand would grab at the wrist and the other would become a forearm to the elbow as you step, similar to Crossing Talon.

I describe an application but have stated why I don't think of it as such. I prefer to think of the sequence as showing the timing change of the blocks in Unwinding Pendulum. And the parry/checks done on the upward vertical are a complement to the upcoming Circling Fans technique. That one will do the parries on a downward vertical to show the possible lines, as opposed to how the technique is done in application in the standard curriculum. Hence the name Reversing Circles; it reverses the circles in Circling Fans.

You are now facing 4:30 in a left neutral bow, right hand up and left hand down in the check/chop position and ready for the next technique.

Snaking Talon—punch combination

This technique was originally taught for a two-hand front push. Over the years it started to be taught as a defense against a left-right punch combination. I believe this was to keep the theme of this form intact: it is against live attacks, and working against a push would break that. The technique absolutely works for either, and it's written up both ways in the *Accumulative Journal* and its variations. Either way, it should be done with the hands on the high line, not down by the lower chest or mid-line, as it is frequently done.

Your entire arm should be moving in a figure eight using "Path of Action" (see Glossary) instead of the flippy, ineffective wrist action one sees so often.

Regarding categories, this technique finalizes the progression of handling combinations by working outside the punches. Previous combination punch techniques Protecting Fans and Unfurling Crane correspondingly work inside/outside and strictly inside.

Slide back, step-drag fashion, with your left foot to 1:30 and have your right foot follow, ending in a cat stance facing 7:30. Your hands will be positioned right hand low, left hand high. Your right hand will be bent at the wrist, fingers together, just over your right knee. Your left will be over your right elbow, wrist bent, fingers up, and palm out. Now is a good time to pose and get your picture taken. Keep your back straight, head up, knees bent, and tailbone tucked. This is an example of what Mr. Parker called positional contouring. That's the only hint I'll give you on what this posture means. He thought it was important that we figure this out on our own. It does mean something and it does have uses. One use he described was the way the transition affects the subconscious mind of the viewer. It tends to make them think that the posture "just looks better for some reason" and has more appeal. I believe that was the showman in him. It is like the lines created in ballet that are simply aesthetically pleasing.

Execute a right inward downward diagonal parry outside a left straight punch, followed by a right extended outward handsword block outside a right punch. This action snakes through the arms, giving the technique its name. Your left hand remains in a cover position by your chest.

Your right hand will become a grab and pull-down as your right foot front-kicks the groin.

Shuffle your right foot back to 10:30 and do a step-drag into the left 45° cat stance facing 4:30 and duplicate the technique on the opposite side. From your left kick sit down into a square horse stance facing 6:00 for the next technique.

Upon looking at the footwork in this section, including that in Reversing Circles, you will see what we call "the skating movement." You push forward with your right foot, and then left, then skate backward left, and then right. A zigzag foot pattern is created for the first time in any form. I refer you to Ed Parker's *Secrets of Chinese Karate*, page 78, for insight into his ideas on this foot pattern.

Circling Fans—punch combination

Working outside the punches was demonstrated in Snaking Talon, but using one arm. Circling Fans also works outside but it uses both arms.

I think of Snaking Talon as a "what-if?" of Circling Fans. If you missed the second punch because your left hand was down instead of up (it should have been covering), you pick off the second punch with the same arm. That's another good reason not to practice the previously mentioned "flippy" hand action; it likely just wouldn't work. This version uses a variation of inward downward parries on top of the attacks, which would be uppercuts and gives us the "over the attack" completion of movements.

From a square horse position facing 6:00 with your hands chambered, start a right-hand parry as your right foot begins sliding back to a 90° cat stance (the first one in any form) to 9:00, followed by the left-hand parry.

Fire a right front kick to the groin. With no loss of motion from the right parry, continue your right hand into an uppercut to the bridge of the nose as your right foot replants in the horse, left hand checking near your right elbow.

Pivot in place to face 3:00 to duplicate the technique on the opposite side. Since your left hand cannot start the sequence from the chamber position you will let it move across to the left with your body rotation until it gets to the appropriate position to do the first parry. This prevents such excess motion as dropping the left hand and having to circle it inward.

End the technique with your left uppercut to the bridge of the nose, right arm across your body with the hand checking near your elbow. You are now set for the entry to the isolation facing 6:00.

Isolation

You may be familiar with the "elephant trunk" techniques in the system. If not, here is an introduction. Chinese martial artists often employ an arm configuration that uses the forearm with the wrist bent forward, resembling an elephant's trunk. While we don't use the bent-wrist version as do some systems, we do use the forearms to block and strike and continue to refer to them as "elephant-trunk techniques." Another term for these is "smother blocks," getting this name from the distance at which you would apply them. It is the close range that prevents you from delivering a standard basic block, using the upward block as an example here in the isolation.

Coming directly from the horse stance and hand positions you ended Circling Fans with, deliver a left outward heel-palm to the solar plexus with a right upward smother block. Immediately execute a left upward smother block with a right inward horizontal hammerfist at rib height, followed by another right upward smother block and left inward horizontal hammerfist.

Anchor your right elbow down, creating an anchoring inward block (the first one in a form since the Star Block Set back in yellow belt), left hand chambered at the left ribs.

Deliver a right outward stiff-wrist two-finger slice, followed by loose-wrist inward/outward slices.

Your right hand and arm stop at a point approximately in front of your left shoulder at the corner of the zone of defense. Form the shape of a crane with the right hand and peck across toward the opposite outside corner of the box. As that hand hooks back toward you to the chamber position, maintain the peck configuration and execute a left thrusting inward block and follow with the opposite-side slices and peck. End with both hands chambered in the crane peck position, fingers down.

From the shape of the crane position, still in the isolation horse, deliver twin overhead-type two-finger whips to the eyes at close range.

Extend your arms to mid-range with twin vertical two-finger pokes.

Extend once more to full reach with twin thumb strikes.

Rotate your hands outward away from each other, ending with your little fingers up and thumbs down. Rotate your hands back in the way they came, ending with your palms facing each other, thumbs and little fingers extended and curved.

The mantra for this section is "whip, poke, thumb, little finger, thumb."

Cross your wrists right over left, push-down fashion, as you drop them down to belt level. This is a finishing move to the isolation or the opening to the next technique.

Now let's get to what all this means. As I mentioned, the smother blocks are there because it's really the first time we do them in a form. The application could be for an opponent who is attacking in a windmilling fashion, throwing a series of overhand punches. Execute your first block with the heel-palm striking the solar plexus and the subsequent blocks with the hammers hitting the ribs.

The anchoring inward block could be applied for a right punch with an immediate finger slice to the right eye. Mr. Parker referred to this as "defense-to-offense." You may whip-slice the eyes, then go to the crane hook to move an arm or pick off a punch. He called this part "offense-to-defense." The crane peck may also be used as a strike to the side of the bridge of the nose in this example. Obviously this crane peck may be used to the temple, eye, throat, or even sternum. The demonstration of the stiff-wrist and loose-wrist finger slices is also important. The stiff-wrist version tends to turn the head as a result of its delivery. The loose-wrist version is whip-like in that the timing and method of execution take advantage of the turning of the head by returning the slice more quickly in order to catch the other eye as it turns into your weapon. Ed Parker's finger slices not only took the eye—he was trying to break the bridge of your nose while he did it.

The next section, the "whip, poke, thumb, little finger, thumb" section, shows what you can do if the opponent is moving his head to avoid your eye strikes. The "whip, poke, thumb" section deals with the head moving back away from you. It duplicates the ranges of the Finger Set in reverse, that is, from close to far. You attempt to whip the eyes, and the opponent pulls his head away out of the orbit of the whip. You then extend the hands to poke. He sees that coming, moves his head, and your fingers would hit the cheekbones if you kept going. Your fingers make contact and you rotate the thumbs in. I was shown two ways to do this. One was thumbs up, the other was thumbs down. They both work. One is used when the opponent pulls his head back (the thumbs-up version); the other is used when he puts his head down and your fingers would strike the forehead. One important idea here is being sensitive enough to adjust immediately to these changes to apply the movements. There is a tremendous amount of nerve endings in the fingers, and so there is a lot of information they receive. Your job is to discriminate this information and decide what to do. The thinking in Chinese martial arts is that the fingers are where the energy meridians end, and as weapons, they can do much damage but are also the most easily damaged. This is the main reason for the Finger Set being so important. Weapon formation and delivery along with knowledge of the targets and timing is extremely important. To summarize: your fingertips will tell you when to change from one weapon and angle to another.

When the opponent turns his head in avoidance, your hand rotates and your little finger goes in the eye (keep it curled). When it rotates the other way the thumb goes in. There are other places to use this idea, such as in the Grip of Death technique. When the opponent turns his head away from your attempt to hook his philtrum with your fingers, your thumb can hook under the jaw into the facial nerve. While doing this part of the isolation, keep your elbows bent and execute as a tearing type of action.

Finally, drop your hands heavily into the cross-wrist position. This can strike the collarbones or the pectoral attachments, rake the body, or trap a kick. Drop the hands down to the belt line before stepping back into the next technique.

Defensive Cross—front kick

The influence of the crane system shows in this technique. This really looks like a long-hand technique, especially with the hanging rear hand 180° off the front hand claw, followed by the lifting back-knuckle strike. This and Prance of the Tiger are the most crane-like moves in the form.

From the right-over-left crossed-wrist position at your waist, you will slide your right foot back to 12:00 to create a left forward bow stance to 6:00. With this your hands will trap and hook the incoming right front kick by forming a left shape of the crane to hook the article as your right hand traps on top of the foot and ankle, then pulling to and past your left hip from your center. This action causes the opponent to lose balance by making him start to do an airborne front split.

He will want to throw a follow-up punch, probably a right, and the unbalancing (along with the next move) helps prevent or minimize that. Your hands are in a hang position on your left side, so throw a right hanging outward and downward back-knuckle strike to the head. If a punch is on the way, use it to block the punch.

Your left hand will be in the hang, about 180° off your right hand. As the right hand pulls through and down, throw a left overhead claw to the face. As it strikes, your right hand should be in the hang position, again about 180° off the left hand. I like to have my right hand palm-forward in the hang to get some torque for the next move, but I've seen many who like it palm-back.

With your left hand in contact with the head, right front snap-kick to the groin to bend the opponent forward.

His head will move down and away from the face claw, allowing you to hold his head down for the follow-up lifting back-knuckle.

This is an example of moving the head off the hand instead of your hand off the head. This idea is popular in Chinese martial arts. Your hands don't move relative to your body but they do change position. I relate it to the two ways you keep from getting hit, which are 1) move yourself (the target), and 2) move him (the weapon).

Since your groin shot brought him down and forward and crowded you, you'll have to step back down to your point of origin in the forward bow. As you do, you throw the right upward stiff-arm lifting back-knuckle to his face or head. It will sandwich him since you are still holding his head with your left hand. You will see this kick/back-knuckle combination again in Form Six but with a step forward instead of back to show the range differences.

You will show the sandwich in the form by hitting your hands together, right knuckles into left palm, timed as your right foot lands. There is a rule in the Kenpo system that you don't back up as you strike. Some people think you are backing up here, but you're actually striking *up* as you settle *down.* Look at the techniques taught in the system that use the front-kick/stiff-arm combination. This is obviously an example of what to do when your opponent doesn't react the "right" way (bending forward instead of moving back). This is a real "Ed Parker-looking" technique, very fast and strong with the back-knuckle/claw combination.

Drop your hands down to your waist again, this time with your left hand on top. Step back with your left foot to 12:00 and do the opposite side of the technique, ending with right-over-left sandwich in a right forward bow stance facing 6:00. The next section with Bowing to Buddha is quite interesting for several reasons. One is that it will flip the back-knuckle sandwich over. Another is that it is done from a kneeling position and shows the switch that was left out of Long Form Three, but on your knees instead of your feet.

Bowing to Buddha—front kick

I look at this technique as an introduction to a transitional position—in particular, that position between being down on the ground and standing. It is one of the most sensible ways to position yourself while moving up or down. The opposites are represented in that this form shows you how to drop down to the kneeling position, how to stand up from that position, and how to switch from knee to knee.

I question the application as it is taught by some. I do not believe this move should be used against a roundhouse kick from the front because it breaks some Kenpo rules of motion. One rule we use in all other defenses against a roundhouse kick is that we angle off, away from the apex of the kick. We don't angle in this technique. Many instructors teach the technique using a "windmill" block—that is, an inward/outward open-hand combination. Normally we use open hands for parries and closed hands for blocks. That's another broken rule. Now picture a Muay Thai fighter lining a roundhouse at your head while you're down on one knee. Still want to do that windmill block? You have no bracing angle and you can't angle off on that knee easily. These, among other arguments, are why I teach the technique for the straight front kick, as I originally learned it.

Drop in place on your left knee and form a kneeling stance as your right arm blocks the incoming right front kick with a horizontal downward forearm block that converts to an inward block position. Your left hand is chambered at the ribs. This blocking action of the right arm is like that done in the technique Raining Claw. It has to be done like this unless you want your forearm broken. The change to the inward position deflects the kick and keeps your arm from having to take all the force. A strong kick to your head on such a low line has a tremendous amount of force, and I don't recommend taking it all with your forearm—I've met guys who got theirs broken like that. The angle change also helps line up the next shot, which is a right upward elbow to the groin.

This elbow is part of the two-in-one timing done in many techniques, notably Raining Claw. You will step-drag shuffle forward on your knees as you strike the groin with the elbow on the step, and your left hand shovels up to the groin right after as an underhand heel-palm claw with the drag. Like the claw/ punch timing in a properly done Raining Claw, the elbow hits on the half-count, the heel-palm claw on the full count. The heel-palm "serves up" the testicles, bringing them up and forward as the right arm cocks at your right ear. Immediately smash down on your left palm with your right downward hammering back-knuckle sandwich.

Transition to the elbow

OK, you're wincing, so you got the idea. Jump-switch on the ground into the opposite kneel stance with your left downward forearm block. Since it is a switch, you didn't gain or lose ground and are in the same spot you ended the first side. This technique is the reason you see so many Kenpo people with worn-out knees on the *gi* pants and why some

wear *judogi* pants instead—they have reinforced knee sections. Hawaiian Kenpo systems like to work on the knees, and this is just a small signpost of that. There used to be a few techniques in our curriculum that started on the knees and some that ended or transitioned through the kneeling position. In today's curriculum, this is the only one remaining.

Knowing that the groin shot will bring him down and forward will prepare you for the grafting of this technique with the next, Prance of the Tiger, in your practice sessions on the body. Otherwise there is a good chance he'll fall on you. Regardless, we've seen the relationship of the upward and downward smother blocks, the upward and downward back-knuckle sandwiches, and the kneel and jump switch, so we're ready to move on to another crane-like technique.

Prance of the Tiger—flank uppercut punch

This follows Bowing to Buddha, in which power was used on the down-line, to now show how power is used going upward. We call the down-line power either gravitational marriage or marriage of gravity. The up-line power fits the definition of back-up mass but some like to call it reverse gravitational marriage.

The attack is a right uppercut to your head from the 45° angle at 7:30. From the back-knuckle sandwich stand up and back, sliding your left

foot back into a left 45° cat stance facing 6:00. It is important to sit back into the cat instead of drawing the right foot forward all or part of the way. Dropping back gets you away from the upward line of the uppercut. Standing straight up and/ or coming forward keeps you in the path of the uppercut. It may help to consider the function of an uppercut, which is to strike the stomach and if that misses, the chin. The uppercut attack will be blocked by your left push-down block along with a right stiff-arm lifting back-knuckle to the chin as you rise.

The right hand may be used to block a follow-up left, with the chin strike as an insert, or to clear the uppercut away when you continue the circle with it as if doing an inside downward palm-up block. The bottom portion of the circle may be used to rip the ribs as well. Your left hand will cover high as the right hand circles down. The timing is to stand up with the push-down and circle the right hand, completing the circle as you sit in the cat.

Immediately throw a left thrusting sweep kick to the opponent's right shin, followed by a right side kick to his left inner knee with a simultaneous right outward back-knuckle to the face or head.

This is a side chicken-kick to 7:30. Keep the angle in mind since we are going to throw knife-edge kicks to the four corners when you consider this technique in Shield and Mace. This technique will do the 4:30 and 7:30 angles, and

the next technique will show the 10:30 and 1:30 angles. This kick combination is the closest we get to a flying kick in the system. Our high forms show the side chicken-kick, front chicken-kick, and chicken scoop-kick.

From the right side kick, retract your right foot and plant down in a right 45° cat stance facing 6:00 with a right push-down block. Chamber your left hand at your left ribs on this side of the technique, forcing yourself to do a full circle into the inside downward block versus the half-circle you did on the first side. Continue into the left side of the technique. Retract your left side kick from the 4:30 angle and plant it to 7:30 in a left forward bow stance with your hands stacked palms facing each other, right over left. This is the opening position for the next technique.

Shield and Mace—straight punch

One element that makes this interesting is the "move yourself" idea. There are really three ways to avoid an attack. They are 1) move the attack, 2) move yourself, and 3) move both. The standard method in this technique is shown in the form, which is to stack your hands and move off on the angle, then throw the check and block simultaneously. Lots of people get punched due to bad timing or position, so many of us teach the technique in application with an inward parry with the step and settle with the check and punch.

If you look at the outward block you'll see it's not really a block. It can't be—it doesn't have the right angle of incidence to be a block because of the rotation of your body. So, it's a check. Besides, we don't use the vertical outward to block; we use it to check as in Unfurling Crane. There it's block, check, block, check. Major/minor–major/minor.

Regardless, this technique uses the rear hand to do much of the blocking/checking/parrying work, as do Destructive Kneel, Circles of Protection, and Prance of the Tiger. Destructive Kneel works rear hand outside. Circles of Protection works rear hand under. Prance of the Tiger works rear hand over. Maybe you would say Unfurling Crane uses the rear hand inside to complete the category.

Pivoting from the forward bow stance, you will deliver a simultaneous right vertical outward "block" outside the right straight punch and left straight thrust punch to the ribs in a horse stance. An observation here is that in the previous technique you faced the 90° line and the attack came from the 45° angle. Now you face the 45° angle and the attack comes from the 90° line. Drop your stance down into a left wide kneel (a close kneel works too), checking the right leg, with a right downward hammerfist to the right kidney or right hip area, left hand pressing his arm to check.

Striking in the hip area hits a branch of the lateral cutaneous nerve. Striking to either area will cancel the height zone. The action of blocking outward and then hammering downward is an example of useful reverse motion. Your right arm simply reverses its path from the check to the hammer.

Change back to the horse stance, using the torque to help you pull the opponent down by his right arm with your left hand as your right continues to circle counter-clockwise. A reverse wide kneel may be used here in place of the horse. Transition through this stance into another left wide kneel stance with the right hand horizontally clawing the face and eyes, your left

hand maintaining the check on the right arm. The hands make a horizontal figure eight with these movements. A finger hook is sometimes used instead of the claw, specifically targeting the right eye.

Your right hand will continue on the circle, your left-hand check "jumping" off and on the opponent's arm to let the right arm through to its intended target of the back of the right knee. Your right strikes the knee as a chop, complementing the angle of the thigh, and buckling the leg out as you drop your weight down into a wide kneel. It works the same way as a looping downward roundhouse kick does in the technique Reversing Mace.

This also demonstrates how the hand can be used to buckle as the leg usually does. This movement opens a line to the opposite knee by moving the leg so you can fire a right-side knife-edge kick to the support leg at 10:30. In Form Five's Circling the Horizon you'll strike the back of the

knee with your hand as well, but it's with the other foot forward so you know both ways. Keep your left hand high by your right shoulder to check. Retract the kick directly back, planting it to 4:30 in a right forward bow stance, hands stacked left over right. Pivot out and do the technique on the opposite side for an attacker coming from 3:00.

Retract your left-side knife-edge kick and plant it down toward 9:00 so that you now face 12:00 in a square horse. Stack your hands at your right hip, left over right, ready for the next technique.

Five Swords—roundhouse punch

This is where you'll find the inside line to defend against a single punch. The rest of your single straight-punch techniques in this form are outside the attacks, making this the lone example of working inside. The message here is that it is better to be outside the arms than inside. In addition, we are using the same downward and inward block combination we used in Unwinding Pendulum, but on the inside instead of the outside.

From the square horse stance facing 12:00, start stepping forward to a right neutral bow stance while delivering a left outside downward block and settling with a right thrusting inward block. The downward block deflects the incoming right front kick, and the inward block handles the right punch. Your left will chamber at your left hip after the block.

Immediately throw your right slicing outward chop to the neck as you start your turn to the forward bow stance, and complete the turn with your left straight-finger thrust to the eyes. Pivot in place back to your right neutral bow stance with a right vertical finger thrust to the solar plexus, left hand covering. You should have used the same timing as the standard technique and the opening moves of Long Form Two.

Slide your left foot back to 4:30, creating a right forward bow stance to 10:30 as your left hand outward-chops the left side of the neck. Your right hand will be chambering at your right ear as you settle in the forward bow. There are many versions of this transition—some do it in a twist

  stance, some people claw instead of chop, others exaggerate the hand position or the timing—this is the way I do it.

Drop into your right neutral bow on the 10:30 line as you deliver a right hammering inward downward chop to the back of the neck, left hand covering. Remember here that the rule we established in Short Form Two

will come into play to make our next transition easier: When we are in a neutral bow to the corner, our feet will point at the wall. I mention it here because there is a tendency to over-rotate with the final chop and get the feet misaligned. That causes us to have to rotate and step further than needed, making the transition clumsy.

Your right chop will now become an outward and downward hooking action as you step through to 12:00 with your left foot to a left neutral bow stance to start the other side of the technique. That hook may be used to clear the head out of the way or pick up a left kick. The right hand then chambers at your right side. Execute the opposite side of the technique, ending on the 1:30–7:30 line in a left neutral bow stance with a left downward chop and right-hand cover. We are ready for the final technique in the form, with the opponent firing a left straight punch from 12:00.

Twirling Hammers—straight punch

The "push" power used in Five Swords is juxtaposed with "pull" power here. The lower-body mechanics are the same in both techniques, that is, neutral bow to forward bow to neutral bow. Five Swords pushes the strikes out away from you, while Twirling Hammers pulls the strikes in toward you. Like many forms, similar techniques are placed sequentially to point out their relationships. Ed Parker didn't just put them there without good reason.

With the left punch on its way you will pivot into a left front rotating twist stance with a left extended outward or extended upward block, right hand chambered. Step through with your right foot to 1:00 into a right neutral bow stance as you deliver a right looping overhead punch to the back of the opponent's head, chambering your left hand at your ribs.

Pivot into a right forward bow stance as you strike the left ribcage with a left inward elbow while cocking your right hand at your ear as if you were going to do a hammering inward block. In the application you simply drop your right elbow to check the left arm as you elbow the ribs, but in the form we are looking for full range of motion.

Pivot back into the right neutral bow with a right inward horizontal hammerfist to the left kidney as your left hand checks the elbow, outward-hooking style as if carrying a pizza. Your elbow should have driven the body back a bit and turned him so that the left kidney is presented in such a way as to have proper angle of incidence on the hammerfist. Often the partner does not react to the elbow and is turned at an angle that would have the hammerfist skimming the target, the kidney and hammerfist being almost parallel to each other.

Crossover with your right foot and right extended outward block, then step out toward 11:00 and do the left side of the technique. The final position will have you on the diagonal line in a stance with your centerline facing 1:30.

Another interesting point here lies in the footwork used to get into the technique. It is the mirror image of that used in the transition from Destructive Kneel to Flashing Wings and its second side. There it is a right rotating twist, then a left, while here it is a left rotating twist and then a right. Both are done with the upward and outward action of the blocks.

Closing

The close of the form is called "the triangle close" for good reason because that is the pattern you make.

Coming from the right-hooking check/left hammerfist position, you sweep your left foot toward 4:30 as in a crossover sweep. As you complete the sweep your left hand will cover your right in the salutation at the right shoulder. Yes, this may be used as a foot sweep at the end of the technique.

Plant your left foot at 4:30, making the top point of the triangle, and leap off on that same line with your right ending in a one-leg (crane) stance, hands still at the shoulder. The point at which you land is the right bottom corner of the triangle. Reasons for this line include angling off an incoming attack and practicing balance. As you sit in the crane your left foot should be wrapped behind your right knee, a classic position. In the process of all this, be sure not to move your centerline excessively to the right. In fact, it should move as little as possible. That contributes to stability and ability to counter-attack, the root of reasons I mentioned earlier.

Now plant your left foot directly to 9:00 so that you sit in a square horse stance to 12:00 as your hands come from right to left to present the

salutation. Your stance should settle at the same time your hands come out. You have completed the bottom side of the triangle by settling at the left bottom corner. I describe the footwork as "point-corner-corner." You have the three points of the triangle but not the three sides. You'll pick up the travel along the "missing" side at the end of Form Five.

The triangle is a reference to a Chinese training device called the "plum flower stumps" or *muy far chong*. See page 54 of Ed Parker's *Secrets of Chinese Karate* for a diagram of the basic configuration. It is popular in many Chinese systems, and he and I spoke of it a few times. The curious part of it lies in the name. I've been told the name comes from what you can't see, not what is in the layout.

Close with your left to the right as you normally would. Do the salutation and bow. Remember to close first, then bow.

Additional Observations

- The use of an outward parry in the first technique, Protecting Fans, is significant enough to be a subject of discussion. For most it seems arbitrary, no big deal, do it either way. It works fine both ways. However, you will find that this first technique and the first technique in Form Five are related, and that should dictate which way to do it. Destructive Fans has been called Protecting Fans turned sideways. If your opponent were to step-through forward with his right foot instead of keeping it back, you would find yourself in position to change to Destructive Fans. Then changing from the extended outward into the parry would pull him in more so you could pull off the hammer and sweep. The basic idea in the standard Destructive Fans is that the opponent managed to gain your centerline and you are in danger of getting scooped or buckled, so you hammerfist him and kick his foot out to close the line.

- The first isolation may be done in a horse instead of the concave stance. I argue for the concave, and I previously stated one reason why in the description. Another reason is that there were no concave stances in any form prior to this, and this was to be the last form in the system. Thinking in that way, you'd have to include this stance. Form Five came later and took care of that, so maybe that accounts for the variation. Think about this, too: We have isolations to the front in Long One, Long Two, Long Three, Four, and Six. We have them on the front diagonals in Long Three. We have one facing the rear in Four. But there are not any to-the-rear diagonals.

- Why are there no roundhouse kicks in the forms? There are if you think about it. Take a look in Form Five.

- The third switch shows up in this form. It is the jump switch, done in between the sides of Bowing to Buddha. It's disguised since you're on your knees. The other two were shown in Long Form Three. What is the foot position in the kneeling stance here in Bowing to Buddha? Try working the technique with your foot with either the instep on the ground or your ball of the foot making contact. See which one works better for you, and keep in mind how many movements you have to do with your foot to stand up in either version.

The categories of blocks and parries contained in this form are interesting. There are:

Single blocks   Double parries

Single parries   Block then parry

Double blocks   Parry then block

Then consider that they work inside, outside, over, and under. Some work with a strike, some strike after they do their job. This is important information.

- Extension Four! I did a version of Four that is the evil brother of Short Four. I did every technique in the form in its full version or with its extension if there was one. And you thought Four was long anyway....

- When were the later forms created? I have a copy of an exam-grading sheet from 1964 (reproduced on the facing page). It lists the forms up through Six. The form was made out for Kenneth Lee Metzler. I also have his first-degree black-belt certificate, and it is dated September 19, 1965. The grade sheet here is for his brown-belt test. Given the fact that you spent eighteen months as a brown belt by IKKA standards before testing for black, he likely took that brown-belt exam in early 1964. Based on this evidence, the high forms after Four existed prior to 1964, something I've heard argued enough times to merit including it here.

- In Defensive Cross the proper footwork to make the technique work is hidden. The first side of the technique is incomplete, while the second side holds the actual footwork. It really takes two steps to draw the opponent into the splits position I mentioned. You should step back with the left as you start the hook and trap and immediately go into the second step. Since you start the second side with the right foot already back and then do the step left, you actually have the correct footwork shown in the form. You can also think of this technique as being Five Swords with the other foot forward. The following technique, Bowing to Buddha, is like Five Swords too, only upside-down. They all have similar timing.

Advanced

FORMS: Long III
Form IV
Form V
Form VI

International Kenpo Karate Assn.
PROMOTION RECORD

STUDENT: METZLER KENNETH LEE
LAST / FIRST / MIDDLE

Basics	COMMENTS	Poss. 5 SCORE
STANCES: Basic—		
Riding Horse		5
N. Bow and Arrow		3.5
F. Bow and Arrow		4.0
R. Bow and Arrow		4.0
Cat		4.0
	Sub Total	
KICK:		
Front		
Snap		4.8
Power		5
Lateral		4.8
Wheel		3.5
BLOCKS: Basic—		
Inward		
Outward		5
Rising		4.5
Downward OUT		4
Downward IN	too wide	3
Push		4.5
SPECIAL:		
	Sub Total	
FORMS:		
Long I		
Long II		4.2
Short III		4.4
Black Belt Set		4.5
	Sub Total	

Present Rank U / R WHITE / BROWN / BLACK ☒

Advanced	COMMENTS	Poss. 5 SCORE
FORMS: Long III		4.5
Form IV		
Form V		
Form VI		
TECHNIQUES: 1		4.15
2		
3		
4		
5		
Unit Score for Tech. in addition to Required (5 Point Poss.)		
	Sub Total	

Free fight ☐   Challenge + −
Teaching: Sup.   Sat.   U.Sat.   NA

WRITTEN THESIS: Approved ☐   Disapproved ☐
THESIS SET: Approved ☐   Disapproved ☐

Promotion approved by:

Total Possible ____
Total Attained ____
Score Differential ____

Disapproved if Not Signed.

Recommend Promotion to:
WHITE   BROWN   BLACK

6.

Form Five

It is obvious that the name is from the place the form takes in the numerical sequence. Form Five is also referred to as "fulcrum form," "takedown form," "surprise form," and "go from where you're at form." They're all accurate since they all describe what is going on. The form consists of techniques that take the opponent down (you generally need a fulcrum for a takedown, hence the term "fulcrum form"). Many movements come from points of origin other than those normally practiced, and that's why it's called the "surprise" or "go from where you're at" form. This is the reason the salutation does not close after the prayer hands position: you're surprised with an attack from the side and your hands are already up, so GO.

Overview

Form Five is an often-misunderstood form. It does not flow in the same manner as Four or Six and is shorter than they are. It's not particularly well-suited to tournament competition although many have done well with it, but not like the other high forms. However, it is a very interesting form when you analyze what is contained herein and understand its place in the system.

Along with the aforementioned takedown and point-of-origin ideas, the form fleshes out some concepts Mr. Parker had, hinted at, or did not include in Four. Themes include the coordination of opposing hands and feet in crossovers, counter-balancing movements, sophisticated foot maneuvers, and the comparison of takedowns and strike-downs, all of which are shown in Form Five. Also, consider that if an isolation is not moving the lower body in order to direct attention to the upper, might we also keep the upper still as we work the lower in isolation? See the footwork in this form and make your own decision. I think you'll have a better appreciation for the form when you understand these components.

Technique Sequence

Destructive Fans	Sleeper
Dance of Death	Brushing the Storm
Leap of Death	Falling Falcon
"Three on a Line"	Circling the Horizon
The Back Breaker	Leaping Crane
Three on a Line Redux	Closing and Salutation
Hopping Crane	

Opening Salutation

As I mentioned earlier, you do the standard salutation but do not close. When showing the prayer position, you'll stay there in the horse. This is what indicates being taken by surprise.

Destructive Fans—straight punch from side (flank)

The parry sequence that opens Form Four is reversed here in Destructive Fans of Form Five. This technique uses the rear hand outward first, then the front hand inward. Four starts with the rear hand inward, then the front hand outward. Interesting, but maybe it's not very important. This correlation depends on how you do Four. Some do it with a parry and an extended outward block (as I do), and others do inward/outward parries. An old version of the *Accumulative Journal* reads with a horizontal inward parry to start Protecting Fans. I've never seen anyone actually do that, but it's interesting.

From the prayer position you will look to your left to see the incoming straight right punch. Step slightly back off the line with your left to

a modified horse stance so that your feet still face 12:00 but you have a toe-heel line to 9:00. With your step your right hand does an outward parry and your left circles clockwise into an inward parry. Continue the circle of the right hand into a hammerfist to the solar plexus, timing it with the settling into the modified horse. This is the previously mentioned Protecting Fans "turned sideways."

Execute a left front crossover sweep to the back of the right leg like you did in Dance of Darkness in Four and stack your hands, right over left, at your left hip as you settle in the front twist stance. The hands hide the actual application of the pull-down on the attacking arm and overhead claw to the face. The sweep is the first part of what we call a "double drag-out" and stretches the opponent out to set them up for the following spin-sweep. This crossover with the stacking hands is the first indication of a series of this type of movement in the form. You'll see the hands stacked in this manner in several techniques. They are demonstrations of timing and position. You'll see them stacked on the same side and opposite sides. They're done for balance, for a standard oppose, or to enhance gravitational marriage.

From the sweep you will spin 360° clockwise, taking out the leg you just swept with a right reverse roundhouse sweep and striking the right kidney with a right outward back-knuckle in the process. Keep your left

hand high and covering. The sweep drops the opponent down on his left knee and causes him to start to turn his back to you.

In the standard version he comes down on his knee more facing you, and you'll do the prescribed vertical punch / front stomp. How he is positioned is determined by whether you swept him or caught him instead with a spinning buckle. For what we are doing here it is the version in which his back is to you, so you check across his shoulders with your left hand and straight-punch to the head with your right. Therefore, your right hand must be above your left when you do this. You will be on the 3:00–9:00 line facing 9:00 in a left forward bow stance at this point. This angle is about 30–45° further around than the standard and is done this way for the sake of the form. It keeps the lines set.

From the forward bow, cheat your right foot back to the 3:00 toe-heel line, like an inverted cover. Your hands are now crossed palms-up, right over left. As you turn to face the 3:00 angle your hands will start the outward / inward parry sequence and finish with the left hammerfist as you settle in the horse to do the left side of the technique.

Do the opposite side and end it facing 3:00 in a right forward bow stance, left punch over right check.

Dance of Death—straight punch

Dance of Death is actually a fairly common term for movements in karate. *Kata* are often referred to as a "dance of death." The name here comes from how one "dances" on the back of the body in the second half of the technique. What's interesting is that you step back on this version as opposed to forward in the standard. This and the other two techniques in this group, which include Thundering Hammer and Sleeper, were intended to show what you can do when your back is to a wall, and therefore they are taught stepping forward. Beyond showing the hang position as a workable point of origin, the obstacle behind you is the reason for the hang position of the arm. There is a possibility that if you cock your hand to chamber, you'll hit your elbow on that obstacle. Of course, you can step back if there is no obstacle and your hand is hanging, so that's the message here.

The straight right step-through punch is coming at you from your left side. The difference now is that you have your right foot forward, while in the first technique you were side-on to the opponent. It is as if you were caught in mid-stride as the punch comes from the side and you had to respond from that position.

You will be coming out of the right forward bow facing 3:00 by stepping back to 6:00 with your right foot. As you step back your right hand

will do a downward parry (some do a downward block), your left will follow with an inward parry, and you'll settle in a left neutral bow stance facing 12:00 with your right arm hanging naturally. The other two horizontal zones of defense we hinted at in Form Four with the introduction of Thundering Hammer are picked up in this form with this technique and Sleeper.

Pivot to a forward bow with the right ridge-hand (upward vertical reverse handsword) to the groin, left hand checking against the arm.

Right step-through forward to 12:00 to a neutral bow stance as your left hand slide-checks down his body and right leg into a leg pick as your right inward elbow strikes him at the hip or low ribs. Some people step a little more to 11:00 to an inverted stance in the form; I just don't do it that way. The leg pick pulls hard to assist the takedown and ends up at the ankle with the leg trapped against your body to check it. The opponent is now on his back, probably suffering from a concussion and/ or cracked skull.

Now that you are standing between his legs and he knows something bad is about to happen, he'll try to close the legs like a clamshell. This is why it is important to hit the left inner knee with your right outward hanging back-knuckle strike—it keeps the legs open. You should be transitioning into a wide kneel stance by now as well, since the opponent will not only clamshell, he will try to roll away. If you are in a close kneel you don't have the lateral stability that the wide kneel lends, and you may go over with him when he rolls. Continue the circle of your right hand and drop into the wide kneel with your right finger slice to the groin, maintaining the left-hand trap on the leg.

Slide your right hand toward you along his leg to keep the knee in check since it will tend to flex when you do the groin strike. Pivot from the wide kneel into a right forward bow stance facing 12:00 as your right hand makes the shape of the crane vertically and turned left, with your left hand positioned fingers-up near your right forearm. This is a stylization of the grab and twist on the foot at the toes and ankle that we do to turn him over on his stomach.

Continue the travel of your hands across your body to the right hip in the stacked position, left over right, as your left foot stomps the opponent's lower spine. The stomp is done either as a crossover or a forward bow, though the crossover is preferred. Time the stack with the stomp on the 1:30 line. Keep in mind that a stomp is different than a stomp kick. A stomp has no supporting leg while a stomp kick does. Your foot should be aligned with the spine to best fit the weapon to the target.

Leap off the body to 4:30 onto your right leg in a one-leg stance facing 10:30. You should be facing the opponent. Many people like to turn their back to him at this point and throw in an additional kick to the ribs or kidney. That angle does not allow you to see what he may be doing with his lower body, while facing 10:30 does. He may be rolling, kicking, grabbing, or trying to get up. You can see all of this if you don't turn your back on him. Besides, you'll get that shot to the short ribs/kidney in anyway when you drop down onto it with your left foot in the next move.

Drop from the crane into a left close kneel stance to 10:30. Use this for gravitational marriage on your left kidney stomp and the accompanying right downward chop to the back of the neck. The stomp is not really a stomp; it acts more like a pinch or "vice-like move." It is your ball of the foot that makes contact rather than the heel. Using the heel to stomp would make the drop awkward due to the angle of your foot. Your left hand should be covering or checking his body by being positioned near or under your right arm. The stomp hits the right short ribs and will cause the back to arch, bringing it up into the chop, so the left-hand check may be used to control that if necessary. You may actually get the kidney if the factors are right or you break the short ribs and lacerate the organ.

Draw your right leg up high, as you did in the first front crossover stomp with your left, and stomp his upper spine between the shoulder blades, right foot matching the spine angle, moving toward 10:30. Stack your hands on your left hip, right over left, as you do for the marriage of gravity.

Leap off the body to 10:30 onto your left leg into a one-leg stance. Your right leg will be cocked high, as will your hands. Your left hand will be almost fully extended upward along the line of your right leg, and your right hand will be cocked diagonally across your body near your left shoulder. This loads everything for the next move, which is the right back stomp kick to the head to 4:30. Throw your hands down along with the stomp kick to engage marriage of gravity and use directional harmony. Remember to bend your left knee and breathe out as well to enhance the power. Some will argue that the extension of the arm(s) is unnecessary and/or extra motion. Mr. Parker used some large movements in certain positions because the opponent was so incapable of response due to injury or position that it made the big movement possible. He used to say the opponent was "fully braced to accept the shot."

Retract the right kick toward 10:30 as if you were going to cover out in a twist stance. Place your hands on your right hip in the stack position, left over right, as you settle into the twist stance. This is the point of origin for the opposite side of the technique. However, this is a good time to talk about the "plus X" principle. The "plus X" principle is used again and again in Kenpo. It's also called "lines and angles" with the plus being the lines and the X being the angles. Simply put, it means that when your opponent is on the plus lines you go to the X angles. If he's on the X you go to the plus. This ensures good angles of delivery, entry, and incidence. In this technique you cross his body on the X for the stomps to keep him pinned and carry out the leaps to the angles to stay aligned for the strikes without having to worry about glancing off. It's the same reason you move up the circle to 4:30 in techniques like Five Swords. It helps keep you from having your strike buffered by the shoulder as you would if you step too far up the circle.

For the second side of the technique you will pivot counter-clockwise to face 6:00 with a left downward block as you step back to 12:00. Deliver a right thrusting inward block as you settle in the right neutral bow stance. The blocks are here to illustrate the "push-power" of the blocks as opposed to the "pull-power" of the parries used on the first side.

Do the left side and end by leaping off to 7:30, do the left back stomp kick, and drop into a left front twist stance as if covering out. Position your left foot so that you can turn out into a horse stance facing 9:00. Your hands will be down to show an exaggerated natural position, and you'll immediately step-drag shuffle back with your right foot to 3:00 into a left reverse bow stance to 9:00.

You will be doing a right open-handed extended outward block and grab at the right wrist with a simultaneous left inward heel-palm strike to the opponent's right elbow to start the next technique. A common variation is to use an outward horizontal parry as in Destructive Kneel in Form Four, those two being paired techniques.

Leap of Death—straight punch

As I've mentioned before, techniques are sometimes placed in a sequence to illustrate relationships. Dance of Death demonstrates stomping with one leg at a time, while this technique, Leap of Death, does it with both legs at the same time. The cocking action of the arms and legs is the same as Dance of Death, both being drawn up close to the body before delivery. Differences in foot maneuvers are also shown: the leap and the hop. This has a leap, and Hopping Crane (a few techniques later) has a hop.

From the shuffle with the parry and elbow break facing 9:00, immediately shift back into a left neutral bow stance with a left outward horizontal back-knuckle to the opponent's right ribcage while your right hand maintains the grab at the wrist. Continue the flow of the left hand up along the right side of his back to his shoulder and grab. Keep your right forearm in contact with his body to control and check. As you do this, pivot hard into a left reverse bow and pull your right hand down to your right side. This will force your opponent face-down to the ground, head toward 3:00. Try to get him to land so that your right foot is next to his waist (use his belt as a marker). This will prevent him from rolling away or being thrown too far to finish the leap. It is another example of the elongated circle that Mr. Parker said was a hallmark of Kenpo.

From the reverse bow (a forward bow relative to the opponent's position), leap up into the air, cocking your hands and feet as you do. Draw your legs up under you as your draw your hands up to your chest, cocking all four weapons at once. This is going to use total gravitational marriage for the landing. Your feet will stomp both kidneys and slide off to the sides of the body. The kidney stomps will arrive just before the hands, causing him to arch his back and provide borrowed force for the double heel-palms that fit his skull. The thrust of the palms will drive the head back down into the ground, compounding the concussive effect of the strikes. By landing and then dropping into the low diamond stance you will maximize the effect of the palms and ensure your reach and stability. This is a good example of directional harmony, too.

The palms are done with fingers out so that they not only fit the target but then are able to slip easily around to the front of the head for the next move. Cup his chin with both hands and jerk upward as you convert your stance into a concave stance. This tears the attaching front neck muscles (the sternocleidomastoids) and damages the atlas/axis area that the skull sits on at the top of the spinal cord. Your knees act as the fulcrum to make this work. Too often we see people drop into the concave with the heel-palms. That's too early. It puts the brakes on the heel-palm strike and adversely affects the timing of the pull up.

Slide your left hand back toward you, contouring the head. Use it to brace the head and/or grab the hair. Spin the head toward you, pushing with your left hand and pulling with your right to break the neck. The 45° angle you normally need to break a neck is not as necessary due to the previous neck pull that changes the angle of the head. That 45° angle is shown in the next technique, as well as in Leaping Crane. You pull your right arm up through the break so that it chambers up by your right ear for full travel on this and the next move. Take care not to change stance while you do this break. Many students pivot into a close kneel and back to the concave while doing the neck break and following chop. Closer examination of that shift will show that you would unconsciously push the target down away from you with your left knee as you try to gain power for the chop. A little "body english" is OK; just don't pivot too far. Having maintained control of the head with your left hand, deliver your right inward downward chop to the bridge of the nose, effectively sandwiching the head.

Now you pivot to your right and drop into a right close kneel stance. Deliver a left outward downward heel-palm, contouring the back of the head to sandwich it again into the ground. Mr. Parker really liked the idea of that, so much that he called it the "concrete facial" and included it in his *Encyclopedia of Kenpo.* Your right hand covers at your chest or chambers at your ribs. The knee drop drives him into and pins him to the ground as well.

Mentally mark the spot your right foot is in. In your next move you will replace that foot with your left in that spot. Using your late opponent's body as a springboard, take the rebound from the knee drop and feed that energy into a right looping downward roundhouse kick to the head. Spring up out of the knee drop with a counter-clockwise turn and throw the kick with no loss of rotation. Bend your support leg as the kick drops to enhance the marriage of gravity. Try to stay at about the same height you started at when you begin the turn, then drop. Trying to gain too much height is often detrimental and leads to loss of balance. Your hands will stack at your right side with the kick, left over right. In the actual technique, your hands are up and covering. If you can't remember what side the hands go on, it is the side you kick with. This form gets confusing as to which side they go on since there are so many examples of how to do that using direct- and counter-rotation and opposition movements.

That final foot replacement and kick have you working on the 3:00–9:00 line. You are currently working toward 3:00 and going to start what looks like a crossover toward 9:00 for the second side of the technique. From the looping downward roundhouse kick, plant your right foot in the twist toward 9:00 as your hands begin the parry and elbow break. Step out to 9:00 with your left foot as you pull and commence with the back-knuckle to the ribs and do the left side of the technique.

"Three on a Line"

This gets its name from the three foot maneuvers in the transition: 1) the crossover into the twist, 2) the loop to the close kneel, and 3) the spin to neutral.

You have finished with the left looping downward roundhouse kick, and your hands are stacked on your left hip, right over left. Plant your left foot into the crossover to 3:00. That's maneuver #1. See the photos below.

From that left front twist stance, loop your right foot around and down into a left close kneel toward 9:00. That's maneuver #2. Spin counter-clockwise to 3:00 with your left foot, ending in a left neutral bow stance and looking to 3:00, hands stacked on your left throughout. That's maneuver #3.

A word about head position: You've probably been looking down to where the opponent would be. If you know how to apply this section and want to show it, keep looking down. If you aren't sure, keep your head up (as above) and spine vertical. I'd recommend the head-up version for tournament competition when there are judges unfamiliar with Kenpo forms. If a judge knows how to read the form, looking down shows that you know where the body is. Otherwise most hard-stylists like the straight-spine, head-up postures. Know that the head being down, even slightly, often contributes to loss of balance in the spin step.

You're now facing 3:00 in the left neutral bow, and a straight right punch is coming in from 4:30. Your hands are on the "wrong" side of your body, that is, they're on the left while the punch is on your right. For tournament competition you may want to put a head snap in for emphasis, making a soft move look hard. Don't do these a lot; they're not good for your neck. Now you are set for the next technique.

The Back Breaker—straight punch from the side (flank)

One comparison with The Back Breaker and Leap of Death is that the former pulls the opponent down from the back while the latter pulls down from the front. The Back Breaker also matches up with Destructive Fans in that the parries are changed up. This one is rear hand inward/front hand outward while Destructive Fans is rear hand outward/front hand inward. They are both used for flank attacks.

As the right straight step-through punch comes in, you step to 4:30 with your right and parry the attack with a left inward/right outward combination, settling in a right inverted neutral bow stance.

Continue to step toward 4:30 with your left, followed by your right so that you end in a left neutral facing 10:30. As you step, your right hand will roll to a palm-out position to check and then grab the opponent's

right shoulder/trapezius area. Your left will
duplicate the grab on his opposite side as
you step with your left foot. The rolling of
the right arm and hand acts to contour his
body and control width-zone changes; the
subsequent left grab then controls height
and depth as well. The act of grabbing
with both helps control all the zones, and
it assists in breaking the waist backward
to reduce or nullify his leverage. Keeping

your forearms in contact with his back as you grab will provide protection should you lose your grip, as they look like the first move of Parting
Wings. It occurred to me that while we normally grab the *gi* and pull to
break the balance, Mr. Parker probably did not have this luxury when
he was street fighting as a young man in Hawaii. I presume many of his
opponents in that warm, sunny climate were not wearing shirts, or light
shirts if they did. Would the shirt move too much or tear away? After
a little experimentation I found that the grabs should be at the clavicle
and squeezing the trapezius muscles, which causes a lot of pain. I offer
my apologies now to my students who volunteered their bodies to this
excruciating research. That area is called the supraclavicular space, and
you can pinch some assorted veins and arteries (including the jugular
vein, carotid artery, phrenic, and maybe even the vagus nerves). Knowing
that Mr. Parker had large, strong hands and that he liked to grab and tear
makes this a perfectly logical insight into the technique. Remember that
occupying the opponent's mind with pain makes him less likely to hit you.

In addition I was reminded that there are some inserts to be done
along the way to the grabs, both with the feet and hands. These, too,
make sense when one considers the fact that just parrying and attempting to get behind the opponent without doing any damage until you get
to the knee strikes reduces the probability of the technique being successful. If you count the moves, there are four before any real damage

gets done: 1) Step with parry. 2) Step behind and grab. 3) Step again and grab. 4) Pull and knee. Inserts may be done on the first and/or second moves to occupy his mind, which is, as they say "mo betta."

We're behind him now and have essentially disappeared from his line of sight. (I'll have more on disappearing in the "Additional Observations" section at the end of this chapter.) Pull hard down and back just below your shoulders as you throw a right knee to the lower spine, striking at the junction of the lumbar and thoracic vertebrae. This happens to coincide with what the traditional Chinese arts consider to be a major energy point. Continue to pull down so that your hands end at your waist and drop his upper spine between his shoulder blades on your left knee, which is another major energy point. Your stance needs to be a very solid left neutral bow or high wide kneel to support the weight of the dropping body. This pull and drop occurs as you use the back-up mass of your right knee retraction, timed so that everything happens at once in the settle.

With the opponent balanced and braced on your left knee, release your grabs, brace the left side of his head with your left hand, and shoot your right hand heel-palm through his right jaw hinge to break it. Immediately cup his chin with the right hand as your left hand braces his head and/or grabs his hair like in Leap of Death. Push hard with your left hand and jerk back high to your right ear with your right hand to snap the neck. The finish position of this has him looking at you. Ugh.

Maintain the brace with the left hand and chop the bridge of the nose with your right hammering inward chop. Convert both hands into claws and drag them in toward your body.

Follow the same path and bring both arms up to cock them for the twin looping downward back-knuckle strikes that follow. Deliver those strikes as if doing the rolling back-knuckle you do in Unfurling Crane and others. These strikes are taught as striking the collarbones. They work better if you strike the front of the shoulders at the muscle insertions, or even the biceps. After all, you did claw him in the face, and he will probably be trying to cover it. Your back-knuckles to the biceps will clear the arms out of the way for the next move. When asked if all this motion was necessary since the circles are somewhat large, Mr. Parker said the opponent was injured and "fully braced to accept the strikes."

Continue the circles out, around, and down into twin claws to the face. Time the claws with a left step-through reverse into a right wide kneel. The movement of the leg will remove the brace, causing the body to drop. Moving it too soon makes the body fall away from the claws and you won't get the impact or the control you want to direct him to the ground.

The claws put him where you want him and help sandwich him into the ground. The hands will stay in the claw formation in between your knees to keep him down and cover your groin.

Many do this last move in a reverse wide or close kneel and have good reasons for doing so. However, the form will require a wide kneel— that is so you don't have excess motion for the next move, the transition back to Three on a Line. Try not to cheat your rear foot up to help support him in the transition to the claw-down. In the application, which has more moves, you'll find that if you do so your feet are in the wrong place, making you unable to hit the jaw target with the side-of-heel kick. Most times that little extra step is why you can't.

➤ *Three on a Line Redux*

From the wide kneel/claw position at the end of the first side of The Back Breaker, rotate clockwise into a right front rotating twist stance. Pick your right foot up as you rotate and use your weight to drop into the twist. Stack your hands on your right hip, left over right, throwing them with the stance for the back-up mass. This faces you toward 10:30. The next moves will not truly be on the 3:00–9:00 line as they were earlier on the first side. It's like you'll bend the line by moving up on the angle and *then* changing to the 3:00–9:00 line.

From the front twist you will loop your left leg up along the diagonal and down into the right close kneel stance, then spin clockwise to come out on the 9:00 line. You will end facing 9:00 in a right neutral bow stance with your hands stacked again, right over left, on your left hip. Keep your center and your head vertical during the spins on both sides, not letting yourself bob up and down. That's a general rule anyway.

Do the opposite side of The Back Breaker to 7:30, ending in a left wide kneel stance toward 1:30. Now you're ready to do Hopping Crane, a rather strange but useful technique.

Hopping Crane—downed attacker

The application typically used for Hopping Crane is on an opponent who is down on his stomach with his head turned away from you. Think as if you had done the first part of Leap of Death but threw the attacker too far. In addition, you hadn't hurt him, so he starts to get up. He's out of range for the leap, so another foot maneuver is necessary—in this case, the hop. It was explained to me as being like the opponent's arms are their legs. In the rest of the form we take their legs out in a variety of ways, so here we treat them like they walk on their hands.

From the left wide kneel used to finish The Back Breaker you will execute a left front rotating twist stance, picking your left foot up off the ground during the rotation and stacking your hands at your left side,

right over left. The stack moves in the same direction as the twist and is completed as your foot plants. This will have you facing 12:00.

Step-through forward with your right foot to 12:00, transfer your weight to it in a one-leg stance, and hop forward. The hop, like any other foot maneuver, is designed to cover distance. In this case you use it to adjust your range so you can step down with your left slightly to your left and sweep his arm out with your right foot as it comes into the opposite one-leg stance. The slight side-step to the left helps to get your back-up mass moving to aid the sweep and creates a set of parallel lines. These 12:00–6:00 lines cross the 3:00–9:00 parallels created in the earlier Three on a Line sequences.

As your right leg sweeps the arm, your arms will swing horizontally to the opposite side.

This action acts as a brake to help you keep from over-running the opponent as you hop forward due to the counter-force the arms gener-ate. In the event you are using the technique to take down a standing man, your arms will strike across his chest as your right knee hits the back of his left leg, like the knee and kick in the tech-nique Courting the Tiger.

Finish the technique with a right-side stomp kick to the head or ribs. Your arms will still be out to the right. To do the other application, utilize a side kick to his right inner knee. The mechanics of this are the opposite of the stomp kick in Dance of Death, where the arms go with the stomp kick, while here they are opposed to the stomp kick.

Retract the stomp kick into a front crossover to 9:00–10:00 as your hands stack on your right side, left over right. You'll step and hop up the left parallel line you established a minute ago.

The left sweep out and kick will get you back on the original 12:00–6:00 line. Retract your left kick and place it to 1:30 as if covering out, hands stacked on your left side, right over left.

Pivot clockwise to face 6:00 in a right 45° cat stance. Your hands will form the same positional contouring configuration used in Form Four going into Snaking Talon.

Your right hand will be down and your left hand up. Keeping your hands where they are, stomp your right heel down hard into the ground and launch off it with a left step-through forward to 6:00. As you finish the step forward, execute a left thrusting inward block, leaving your right arm in the hang position as you settle in the left neutral bow stance. You're in the initial position for Sleeper.

Sleeper—straight punch

The hanging-arm category is completed here with Sleeper. Dance of Death earlier showed the low-zone counter-attack, and Thundering Hammer in Form Four showed the mid-zone counter-attack; Sleeper completes the category by counter-attacking the high zone.

What is really interesting about this technique is the heel stomp used to launch into it from the transition. That stomp symbolizes the heavy drop used to keep the opponent off balance when you step-through behind him in the third move of the technique. You don't show the drop where it belongs; you do it early. So sometimes you'll hear of the technique being done "backwards."

Shift hard into a left forward bow stance and throw the right inward diagonal inner-wrist strike to the left side of the neck. This looks like and

acts much like what is commonly called a "ridge-hand." It *does not* strike with the same surface area as a ridge-hand, which we call the reverse handsword. It strikes with the bony inner wrist to the soft target of the side of the neck. You'll get the carotid artery, jugular vein, and some nerves with the strike and squeeze. The impact causes internal bruising and swelling, while the squeezing that follows cuts off the blood supply to and from the brain. This move knocks an opponent unconscious very quickly, hence the name Sleeper.

It's important to know that you won't throw the strike like a ridge-hand in that it should not circle in but thrust up instead. Throw it as if you are going to hit his right armpit with an upward finger thrust and then change it to the inner-wrist strike. Here is why. When you block the punch you impart energy to it that moves it to your right. If you circle from your right with the inner-wrist he may be skilled enough or lucky enough to block it because you gave him the momentum and maybe even the position to block much like an inward block would. Besides, you haven't done any damage yet, and he may just plain see it coming and stop it. If you sneak it up under his arm it is hard to see and very strong. Typically you'll see people do this with the left hand opening from the block and the right arm striking that hand, primarily for the timing. In application that wouldn't happen because the left hand would be pressing against the offending arm and the right would be slipping under with no opportunity to make contact in such a way.

Now step-through forward with your right toward 6:00 into a neutral bow stance. As you settle, clamp your left hand onto your right arm and anchor your elbows. This is the actual sleeper hold. It is also where you would have dropped your weight to start the takedown, but you did that in the stomp down and launch in the transition.

In the real world the sleeper hold presses on both sides of the neck simultaneously. The version we teach in the regular curriculum is the "safe" version, pressing on one side only. (More on this under "Additional Observations" at the chapter's end.) The form version we show here is the one that strikes the right jaw hinge with your left outward heel-palm and then scissors both sides of the neck. Your right inner-wrist presses on the left neck; the left outer forearm presses on the right side. The slap and clamp you did just a moment before hides the jaw hinge strike and the scissor.

Slide your left foot behind you to 6:00 into a rear twist stance. This line is done, like some other lines, for the sake of the form. It is not the line you really want to use, but this move keeps you on the 12:00–6:00 line we are working through this technique and the next.

As you pivot in place out of the twist stance, your left hand will claw outward. Continue to pivot into a right neutral bow stance facing back the way you came toward 12:00, finishing with a right downward back-knuckle strike as you settle in the neutral bow. Pivot into a right forward bow stance with a left push-down, right hand chambered at the right ribs. The claw rips across the face, the back-knuckle strikes the man down at his face or chest, and the push-down either hits him again where necessary or acts as a cover. This is another example of the back-knuckle/claw sequence we have been working on since the third section of Long Form Two. We see it in Long Form Three and lots more in Form Four. Take a look at Unfurling Crane, Destructive Kneel, Dance of Darkness, Thundering Hammer, Defensive Cross, and Bowing to Buddha. The series is picked up again with different timings in this form. You see it in Destructive Fans, The Back Breaker, Circling the Horizon, and Leaping Crane. Notice the relationships of back-knuckle, then claw; claw, then back-knuckle; back-knuckle with claw; and see them done same hand, alternating hands, both hands together. Applications show them done inside, outside, and over, front of the body, back of the body, etc. There is lots of information there.

Anyway, the claw would pull him down over your right leg, possibly breaking his back as you back-knuckle him. The push-down might then be used to push his body off your leg as you slide your right foot back to 6:00 to form the left 45° cat stance facing 12:00. Your hands will form the positional contouring configuration, left down, right up, as you did to start the first side of this technique. Do the left stomp down and step up with your right foot to start the second side facing 12:00.

You'll end the second side facing 6:00 in a left forward bow stance with a right push-down and left hand chambered. Now you're primed for the only weapon defense technique in the form.

Brushing the Storm—overhead club from side (flank)

One of the interesting facets of Brushing the Storm is that it uses essentially the same entry footwork as The Back Breaker to get you in position behind the attacker, but the hands "split." You can use your hands inside,

outside, over, or under an attack. In The Back Breaker your hands work outside the attack. In this technique, one hand works outside and the other works inside. By looking at other standard techniques to see similar methods and timing while using differing angles of delivery, you may find additional relationships.

From the left forward bow stance, step slightly to your left as your left hand executes an inward parry outside the right overhead club attack, right hand chambered.

Follow with your right foot sliding into your left and arcing back onto the 6:00 line as your right hand delivers a lifting upward heel-palm to

the chin, with your left hand covering your ribs. The step ends in line behind the attacker's right leg so that your feet have described a scallop type of foot pattern, which can be seen in the Universal Pattern. The heel-palm stretches the opponent up and back, ready to accept the next strike.

In the technique application you will step behind the opponent with your left foot into a left close kneel stance and strike the solar plexus/ sternum area with a right inward ver-

tical forearm strike. Some delete this forearm strike from the form, and it appears later in Falling Falcon (however, that uses a thrusting forearm, which is different). The reasoning here is to make one take a hard look at the strike and note its applications as a mid-range weapon. A forearm is seen in Long Form Two with the front arm, and Long Form Three in sandwich form using both arms and as it is here with the rear arm. In application the forearm shot uses borrowed force from the chin strike and sets the opponent up for the next move. Some use a twist stance with the strike, but looking at the close kneel you'll see that you need less rotation to accomplish the job, so it's faster. Some people will use some form of elbow instead of the forearm, but I think the forearm fits the logic of the form better. If you show the forearm there's no harm done. I've seen it both ways.

Pivot in place into a horse stance, much as you did in Dance of Darkness in Form Four, and using the same alignment. Drop your right hand down and in toward you to deliver an inward underhand heel-palm to the groin. The action of the right arm in this technique is very much a ratchet action—it strikes the chin, then ratchets down to the chest, then ratchets again to the groin—using economy of motion. Your left hand will remain high to cover your face and check him at the shoulder and upper arm.

Slide your right hand down along his right leg, contouring it to capture the right leg at the knee. Pull the leg out from under him in a leg pick that is the same as the one used for the takedown in Dance of Death, only on the back of the body. Simultaneously you slide your left hand down his flank to push him down, to his right, and cancel his height. Your right leg will be circling back behind you to 6:00 to use the back-up mass of your body to help the leg pick. In the technique this angle is to 1:30 relative to the opponent, but in the form we stay on the 12:00–6:00 line (again for the sake of the form). Your step and pull are completed as you settle in a left neutral bow stance to 12:00 with your right hand cupping at your hip, palm-up, and your left hand in the push-down position.

Continue by sliding your left foot back to a left 45° cat stance and deliver a left front snap kick to the groin. Retract the kick and set it behind you to 6:00, ending in a right neutral bow stance to 12:00, hands still in the push-down and cupped position.

Step-through to 12:00 with your right foot and right inward parry to start the second side of the technique, traveling up along the line to end facing 6:00. Fire the right front snap kick to the groin and retract it to 3:00 into a rear twist stance on the 3:00–9:00 line. Pivot in place to a left side horse stance facing 9:00 with your guard up. You're in position to start the next technique. This is the only time you start a technique from a side horse stance.

Falling Falcon—front lapel grab

Essentially the same takedown as the Sleeper, Falling Falcon does it from
the inside of the arm instead of the outside. This where we may see the
reappearance of the vertical forearm we deleted from the previous technique, depending on how you were taught.

The opponent grabbed your left lapel with his right hand. Starting
from the aforementioned side horse stance, you pin his hand with your
left and step-through with your right foot as you strike with the right
vertical forearm. The strike hits near the head of the humerus, just below
the shoulder joint itself. The combination of the strike with the step, which
ends behind the opponent's right leg, takes him down. The reaction to the
strike is quite different depending on whether it is placed at the humerus
or at the shoulder. If you hit at the shoulder or above, it tends to move
him backward more and makes the rotation into the takedown more difficult. When you strike the inside upper humerus, the upper arm wants
to separate from the joint and the body goes with it as a defense against
the separation or dislocation. The force is more in line with the rotation
needed for the takedown, making the move more effective. In the real
world you prefix or insert this first move to keep him from punching your
lights out with his left. But that's all omitted here to emphasize the use of
the vertical forearm strike. With this rewrite I have to point out that omit-

ting the forearm is not critical, and that the two forearms are distinctly different. This point is an example of a signature version given me by Huk Planas, and whether you do the form with or without the forearm in Brushing the Storm is inconsequential.

You will pivot to your left after the step-through and in to a right reverse bow stance facing 3:00. The opponent will hit the ground more on his left side as you maintain your grip with your left hand and immediately wrap your right hand, palm-out, around his wrist. As you secure the grip you can release your left hand. Twist your right toward you to rotate his elbow joint upward as you start to rotate to a left reverse bow stance. As you complete the stance change and rotation, your now-freed left hand strikes the elbow joint with an inward heel-palm to break it. Imagine how this person is feeling at this point since you have probably dislocated his right shoulder, slammed his body down, and bounced his head off the ground, then twisted the dislocated arm and broken or sprained that same arm. No telling if he damaged his left arm in the fall, too.

Slide your left hand up his arm to meet your right. Pull up toward you with both arms as you deliver a left knife-edge side stomp kick to his head/neck. Mr. Parker used to like to say, "Help him up!"

Snake your left hand around his wrist much as you did your right immediately after the takedown. This traps the arm to prevent the chance of him freeing it during your transition. It is important to remember in these sorts of contact manipulation techniques that you're both going to be slick from sweat or blood, and that fine finger control is reduced due to stress. Escapes from wrist grabs are done by going out by the thumb, a principle we learned as beginners. By doing this snaking action and grabbing, we are minimizing his escape opportunities. Now pull the arm over toward your left hip to stretch it.

As with the other hand snake, you wait until your grab is positive, twist the arm, and release your right hand. I strike the inner elbow with the right inward heel-palm at this point, but most people skip this and go on to the next move, which is to snake the right hand around the wrist again, accomplishing the two-hand trap again, but with the thumbs down, inverted from the first one. Consider that the strikes to the elbow will tend to make the body arch, which, in this case, will open the next targets.

Kick the right elbow joint as you trap. Use the right side of your right shin to make the contact—don't hit with your shin directly. You can, but it hurts you more, unless you train for that like a Thai boxer or Kyokushin stylist. This is the third elbow break. You wouldn't likely do all this but now you have tools, timing, and targets to do any one of them. The body is arched, so retract your shin kick into a right back scoop kick to the

kidney. Retract that into a right front crossover stomp on the 3:00 line. This last section of kicks is done like you're wiping your feet off. It feels like three wipes. You'll be in a right front twist stance with your hands in the last trap position. The looping kick we do in the technique is normally not shown.

Pivot in place to face 3:00 in a right side horse stance. Step-through with your left foot and do the opposite side of the technique.

At the conclusion, when you do the left kicks, you'll land in a very tight left front twist, having set your left foot down more toward 7:30, as if stepping on your own toes. This will set the proportions of your stance so that you can turn out into a cat stance for the next section with no adjustments.

Circling the Horizon—straight punch

This is Leaping Crane "upside-down." The zones struck are reversed in Circling the Horizon in that we hit the head, torso, then leg; Leaping Crane hits the leg, torso, and then head. The name of this move comes from the horizontal line made by the attacker's punch that you circle around for the initial vertical back-knuckle and following elbow.

Pivot out of the front twist stance into a right 45° cat stance with a right rolling back-knuckle. Your right hand was on top on the last manipulation, so this should be no problem. The back-knuckle acts as a cover as you turn toward the obscure zone, and it may be used as a block for the incoming straight right punch. It would ideally strike at the nerve center just above the elbow joint as you drop into the cat and follow immediately with a left overhead claw (there's that back-knuckle/claw sequence again) to either strike the face or check the arm.

Step forward with your right foot into a right neutral bow stance with your right thrusting vertical back-knuckle to the face or temple, left hand checking down just below your right elbow. The temple strike is bad, and can kill him in short order. The bone plate of the skull is thin here, and an artery routes through the area. A subdural hematoma that puts pressure on the brain may result from the impact. The variation I like is to punch the nerve under the cheekbone (zygoma). The knuckles fit just right, and the reaction to the strike is dramatic. In either case their hands usually come up to their head, opening the next line of attack. In the case of the facial nerve strike, their legs usually quit working and they go down immediately. I thought that was a fable until I hit a guy in a street fight and tagged him right there. It worked as advertised.

Shuffle forward in the right neutral bow stance with a right inward elbow to the right ribcage. In the form you do it with a sandwich, for the timing. In the application you need to keep your left hand up to check his elbow. Remember the saying, "Gaps in your checks leave gaps in your teeth."

Drop down onto your left knee, leaving your left hand up to check, and execute a right chopping hammerfist to the back of the right knee.

We saw something like this in Four, but with the other foot forward. Dropping on a knee is a typical Hawaiian Kenpo technique. It tends to get you out of his immediate line of sight and is quite surprising. The gravitational marriage and complementary angle work like the looping downward roundhouse kick in Reversing Mace, and the strategy is similar to what you did in Leap of Death. The hammerfist travels down and back to the hang position much like Sleeper.

Shoot your right leg back hard as your right hand strikes his chest with a straight heel-palm, left hand checking. This is the same standard-oppose takedown you did in Long Form Three in Dominating Circles, but on your knee.

Here is something to think about. The general rule for heel-palms is that you don't strike the chest with a straight heel-palm because you can hurt your fingers. Usually you do the torso strikes fingers-in or fingers-out. You could use the fingers-out version here but not the fingers-in. Fingers-in would misalign your arm and possibly damage your shoulder. You get away with fingers-up to the chest here because you backed him up with the rib shot, and your body drop changes the angle of delivery enough to save your fingers. Of course there are other variations; however, I find this version to be safe and effective.

The opponent has fallen on his left side with his back to you and head toward 9:00. Pull your hands to your right hip in the left-over-right stacked position as you kick straight forward with a right front snap kick while still on one knee. The kick drives forward and plants, acting as a ratchet point from which to step-drag shuffle your body forward as you did in Form Four's Bowing to Buddha. The kick is not exactly a snap kick, but it's not a thrust kick either since you can't roll your hips as you should in a thrust kick. It hits the right kidney with the ball of the foot, travels over the body, and then the heel hammers down on his solar plexus or mid-section. These are the reverse mechanics of the final kicks in the standard application of the previous technique, Falling Falcon. This one is ball/ heel, that one was heel/ball; the ball kick would drop on his solar plexus.

Cheat your left foot in and over to your right as you start to stand up and turn to face 6:00. The foot should adjust enough to position you in a left 45° cat stance as you unwind to 6:00. The thing to remember on these cat stances is that you don't want to be backing up as you do the rolling back-knuckle. Adjusting the foot will take care of that so all you have to do is rotate and sink. Follow with the right claw and do the rest of the technique. You'll end facing 6:00 on your right knee with your hands on your left hip. I think it's easier to remember to put your hands on the same side as the kick in this section because it sure can get confusing in this form.

As you stand, move your right foot behind you on the 3:00 line into a rear twist stance, keeping your hands on your right. Pivot to your right to face 12:00, taking that energy into the next technique like you did in the transition between the sides of Gathering Clouds in Form Four. Now you're into the final technique in this form.

Leaping Crane—straight punch

Leaping Crane is a "strike-down" technique instead of a takedown technique. That means that we take the man down by striking him instead of by tripping, sweeping, pulling, etc. The idea is the same as just plain knocking him down with a punch in the face. It would be different if you stepped on his foot while you punched him since that would create a levering action.

Having taken the energy from the unwinding action of the twist stance, your hands will drop to your sides as they did in Form Four in the Gathering Clouds transition. You leap to your left onto your left leg to avoid the straight right step-through punch. As you leap the left hand will do an inward parry outside the arm, and your right will rake across the right ribs with a horizontal inward middle-knuckle strike. The leap moves you off the line and provides back-up mass for the rake. You will find yourself in the crane stance with your arms crossed over your chest, left over right. The position allows you to get full travel and effect on the parry and the rake, as well as load the following kick.

Immediately shoot a right snapping knife-edge kick to 1:30, striking the right outer knee. This will break and/or buckle the leg inward toward the opponent's centerline to close it. Do the kick with no lean away, as this will cause you to travel back through the point of no return and you'll have to fight your way forward through that point to get moving forward into your next shot. Be sure not to rotate away into a thrust kick either since you'll just have to rotate forward again, back the way you came, which is reverse motion and unnecessary. This is a nasty strike to the knee that at least results in cartilage damage, if not a broken leg. It drops him down onto that knee, possibly smashing the kneecap (patella), and closes the centerline to keep him from punching with the left. It will cause him

to start to rotate his back to you as if he were trying to spin. And please retract the kick; don't let it hang. More on this in "Additional Observations" at the end of this chapter.

As your right foot plants to 1:30 between his legs, you simultaneously deliver a right outward back-knuckle to his left kidney. This causes him to arch back toward you and also stops his rotation. There is a lot of borrowed force in this since you set him in motion with the kick. Keep your left hand up in the cover position to check his shoulders if needed. He may spin fast enough to hit you with his left arm if your check is down. Even worse, it could be an elbow to your groin.

Using the borrowed force of the arching caused by the kidney strike, you ratchet your right inward elbow to strike the head. Your left hand will sandwich his head with an inward heel-palm. This movement uses a "reverse whip" to accelerate it, pulling your right hand back as you move into the elbow. It also travels on a diagonal unlike any other sandwich we have done. That is due to the kidney being lower than the head, and most of our ratcheting-type sandwiches are done on the same plane. Some like to change the timing in the application a little to hit with the heel-palm first to turn the head into the elbow. It works—it just has offset timing. The targets should be the jaw hinges, or possibly the temple. I've seen a lot of people do it short, maybe hitting the mastoids, and that causes the head to "squirt" forward out of the vice created by a sandwich.

Reach around with your right arm, under your left, and cup his chin. This can be a bit awkward. It is akin to the heel-palm and claw rip in Crossing Talon when done in application. That is a vertical move; this is the same done on the horizontal. The rip was left out of Short Form Three and reappears here. Rip your right hand back and up to your right ear in the hammering position as your left hand pushes, palm out and fingers in (outward heel-palm style), and you pivot to a right forward bow stance.

This is intended to break the neck by holding the body stationary to act as the fulcrum. In other neck breaks in the form you use both hands on the head to pull and twist. This is another way to get the break. This is going to turn him to his left and toward you again, so your left hand had better be checking him at the shoulders to stop that. Your right foot needs to be inside his legs in the event he falls forward and tries to kick, intentionally or not. If you set it outside his front leg, as I have seen many do, he can pitch forward and back kick with no obstruction. Your leg position helps control him on the vertical, much like your arm does on the horizontal.

Another way to do the break is to contour over his head, slide down his face, and cup the chin. Yank up and to your right and break the neck with no danger of the rotation feeding back on your centerline. It's even easier to get the chin because your left arm doesn't get in the way. I do the form one way on one side and the other way on the opposite side just to remember the variations. However, it is supposed to be done with the hand going under and around.

Pivot back to the right neutral bow stance and hammer down hard with your right inward downward handsword to the side of the neck. As in The Back Breaker and Leap of Death, which share the chop, you should watch how you deliver it. A common mistake is to draw the hand back by your chest or ribs and then thrust with the chop. This makes the angle flatter and creates more of a sliding action than a hammering action. That, of course, takes what should have been a major angle of incidence strike and gives it angle of deflection. It is also an example of what going too fast can result in.

If you did the neck break the second way, the chop goes to the bridge of the nose, since the opponent turns his face toward you. The philtrum or throat would be possibilities also. If you break the nose you might even slip in an eye hook on the way out.

Front scoop-kick the groin with your right foot and then kick his upper spine with your left front kick, a combination called a chicken scoop-kick. Your hands will pull back and stack on your left, right on top. Time the stack with the second kick for opposite force. Plant your left foot down as a crossover into a front twist stance to 3:00. This may be used to stomp his right ankle. Something to watch is that you don't anticipate the stomp and have your body dropping down into the twist as your left kick is still in flight (a common mistake). This detracts from the effect of the snap kick, so bring the kick back under you and then plant. The loss of power is a result of falling off toward the right as you kick instead of keeping your mass moving forward, then planting to the side after impact.

Leap out of the twist stance to 3:00 into the crane stance and do the opposite side of the technique. With the final kick your hands will end at your right side, stacked with the left hand on top. Drop into the front twist stance on the 9:00 line. This will act as the top point of the triangle we use in the close, as in Form Four.

Closing and Salutation

You will make the triangle, but by closing the opposite side from the one in Form Four. Leap to 7:30 onto your left leg in a one-leg stance as your hands come up to your right shoulder in the salutation. Plant your right foot down to 3:00 into the salutation horse stance. Just because the triangle is left-handed does not mean the salute should come from the left side. In a Shaolin-based system, as we are, the salute always comes from the right. Close left to right and do the full salutation.

Additional Observations

- What if you started the form and did it with the standard technique angles? You'd be 30–45° off immediately with the first side of Destructive Fans. I found that if you did that you would wind up facing 12:00 anyway at the end of the form.

- Pull the kick back in Leaping Crane. By leaving the leg out to drive the opponent down, you are forced to abandon your margin-for-error position created by retracting the side kick. You certainly can force him down, but you are committed to that and it is very difficult to change lines if need be. Being in the crane allows you to choose among the following: follow up with the back-knuckle, cross out, change lines of entry, fire another kick, etc. Leaving the kicking leg out also allows him to trap it in the crease of his knee and take *you* down, intentionally or not. It could break your ankle in the process. I've just found it to be safer to retract the kick. You'll see this position again in Glancing Lance in Form Six.

- The concave stance is also known as the "double close kneel." Just as your front foot is turned in on the 45° angle in a neutral bow stance, so is the close kneel, whose root stance is the forward bow. Bending the

The kick left hanging. Opponent leans back and traps the leg.

back knee differentiates it. By having both knees turned in and both knees bent, you'll see why it gets the name.

- The neck breaks in the form are done by:

  1) twisting the head with both hands,
  2) twisting the head while the body acts as the fulcrum,
  3) by striking instead of twisting.

The Back Breaker illustrates the two-hand method, Leaping Crane shows the one-hand method, and Dance of Death has the striking method. The twisting methods have to be done on a 45° upward angle. The striking method uses brute force on a delicate area. One of my black belts, Frank Triolo, did a thesis technique using a twisting neck break and named it "Panorama." It got his point across.

- Form Five is the killing technique form. If you could morally justify doing the full sequence of some of the techniques in this form your attacker would die. He *might* die in some of the techniques in previous forms, or just wish he was dead. Look at Dance of Death, The Back Breaker, Leap of Death, and Sleeper. These are killing techniques. Broken spines, necks, arms, legs, crushed tracheas, cracked skulls, bruised kidneys, lacerated internal organs, fractured or broken ribs, and punctured lungs abound. Smashed testicles, too.

- That shuffle you did to get into the first side of Leap of Death is the only shuffle to a reverse bow in any form. You'll win the trivia contest.

- *Standing on the body:* Some of the common questions are "Won't I slide off his body?" and "How do I keep my balance while I'm standing on him?" The thinkers are considering how contouring affects your base in these types of moves, as well as how the opponent may be moving from the impact or trying to escape. You will almost certainly lose your balance if you are working too high—that is, not breathing out and sinking your center while doing the stomps or stomp kicks.

  The Russian system has a drill to condition you to keep the body in balance. One partner lies face down, and the other does squats while perched on their back. The top person must work on balance while the bottom person relaxes and breathes. It is mutually beneficial.

- *There are three ways to take a body down:* 1) Take out the top while the bottom is stationary. 2) Take out the bottom while the top is stationary. 3) Take out the top and bottom simultaneously. All three are shown in the form. Go find them.

- All too often I see Kenpo practitioners just beating on their partner. They have either forgotten or are unaware of the old judo maxim from Jigoro Kano, which is: "Mutual welfare and benefit" or also translated as "Together we both shine." Good words. Better if they are lived.

- *"Disappearing" in The Back Breaker:* There are martial arts stories about practitioners who could disappear in combat. It's not magic; it's technique. If you do your footwork correctly, that is, in timing and pattern, you can disappear too. The footwork in The Back Breaker and Dance of Darkness will get you into your opponent's obscure zone faster than any other methods. Combine that with keeping him busy with impact and he'll be looking around to see where you went and will swear you disappeared. Mike Sanders did this to me back in 1976. We were sparring and he got behind me and took me down so that I was in a sitting position. I looked over my right shoulder and didn't see him. I looked over the left and didn't see him. I looked at my brown belt who was watching and said, "Where'd he go?!" He stated the obvious, that being "He's right behind you!" "I know! I can feel it!" I said because Mike was still hitting me. It was weird. And, of course, he laughed at me. But it was a good lesson.

- Sleeper holds are techniques that create pressure on the jugular vein(s) and/or carotid artery(ies) and may cause unconsciousness, stroke, brain damage, or death. They were popular with police forces for many years until a few suspects died from their use and police officers became restricted by the law and couldn't use them anymore in most states. Yes, it was improper use (crushing the throat) and probably some excessive force (too long and/or too hard) that caused the deaths. Some states have allowed use again of these techniques. There are states in which NOBODY is allowed to use them by law. When I was in bodyguard school in the early 1980s, we were shown a variant that completely avoided the throat and got the job done without the sharp-edge version we use in Sleeper. If law enforcement personnel use something like a sleeper hold, it's like that. The version we teach to students at the lower level is a *relatively* safe version that works. It doesn't get both sides at once and reduces the chances of accidentally killing someone with it. The form version is a different story, and is the way a sleeper hold should really be done. Be careful with these things. Whenever you work on someone with pressure or strikes to the neck, you have to be careful. In today's world there are more instances of people dying from clots released into the bloodstream by this sort of pressure. It's attributed to our diet, and the substances breaking loose from the blood vessel walls get into your system and clot somewhere important, which can be a Very Bad Thing. Here is the story.

What we are creating is called blunt trauma. This can possibly cause death in four ways: 1) a clot, 2) a tear in the artery, 3) released plaque, or 4) a leaking blood vessel. A clot can float around until it finds a place to settle, usually in a smaller vessel, where it chokes off blood flow and can cause an embolism. This can result in blindness or stroke. A tear in the artery is called a dissection, and it essentially swells where the tear is and blocks the blood flow. Released plaque can do what the clot does, and most plaque build-up is found at the junction of the braches of the carotid artery, which is where we happen to strike. Damaging the blood vessel can cause it to leak, which is called an aneurysm. The result of a strike may take days, weeks, or even months to appear. Maybe this is another foundation of the *dim mak,* "delayed death touch," we hear so much about.

Studies show that sudden head turns, hyper-extension, and trauma from strikes can cause any of the above. Young people (twenty-five and younger) are more resilient and can take being choked out with a sleeper hold without too much concern. Cranking the Sleeper on an older student may not be such a good idea, as you can "crack" the artery and cause a problem. Arteries become brittle with age, thus the concern. However, in the fast-food generation, even in the young group I mentioned they are finding more arterial plaque than before. That can put them at risk just as if they were older. This is not a medical text, so suffice to say: be careful with what you do in practice with the sleeper holds and neck crank techniques. Stretching the neck from a twist or impact can result in the damage to blood vessels that I mentioned, as well as hearing loss, blindness, unconsciousness, stroke, or death. Those "head snaps" you practice in the form can do it, too. Please read the paragraphs below by Dr. Marc Rowe for a medical look at the sleeper hold. He and I published a lengthier article on this subject in the *Journal of Asian Martial Arts* (2009, volume 18, number 3).

Note that with a sleeper hold, the pressure is on the neck, not the trachea.

A heel-palm breaks the right jaw hinge and then the hand continues and clamps on for the "double" sleeper hold.

Implications of Sleeper Holds
by Marc Rowe, MD

To understand how the sleeper hold causes unconsciousness and can, on rare occasions, result in a stroke or death, we need to review a few anatomic and physiologic facts and learn a little bit about atherosclerosis (hardening of the arteries). The brain needs oxygen to function. If a portion of the brain receives no oxygen, it dies and the victim suffers a stroke. If a large portion of the brain or the whole brain is deprived of oxygen for several minutes, the brain and the victim die. Each side of the brain gets oxygen-rich blood from a pair of arteries, the right carotid and vertebral arteries and the left carotid and vertebral arteries. The vertebrals lie deep in the right and left sides of the neck and are protected by a bony canal. This makes them difficult to compress or injure. The carotids are more superficial and exposed and are therefore easily compressed and vulnerable to injury. Compression of the carotid artery on one side stops blood flow in this vessel, suddenly reducing the amount of oxygen the brain receives. The brain still receives blood from both vertebral vessels and the carotid artery on the opposite side. A momentary period of unconsciousness or weakness and loss of coordination and balance occurs. The victim collapses but suffers no permanent injury. This is what happens if a sleeper hold is done properly and the victim has normal blood vessels.

Injuries and deaths that have occurred during application of a sleeper hold are usually the result of improper technique, positional asphyxiation, or vigorous struggling by the victim during application of the hold. However, serious complications and even death can occur, albeit rarely, even when the hold is applied properly and the victim does not struggle: here is where atherosclerosis of the carotid artery comes in. Due to genetics, improper diet, smoking, lack of exercise, age, and diseases such as diabetes, the inner lining of the arteries becomes prone to retaining deposits of fat, cholesterol, calcium, and cellular debris. This build-up results in plaque formation. The plaques narrow the vessels' diameter, reducing blood flow to important organs.

Now let's think of a carotid artery with plaques being vigorously compressed by a sleeper hold. The vessel is weakened and more susceptible to injury. It can rupture or develop a weak spot, an aneurysm that may later rupture. Compression can dislodge portions of the plaques, and pieces are then carried along in the blood stream toward the brain as an embolus. Downstream they lodge in an artery deep in the brain and cause a stroke. Although atherosclerosis is commonly associated with older individuals, the present overfed, under-exercised generation is developing diseased blood vessels earlier in life.

7.

Form Six

Overview

Form Six is one of the best-looking forms in our system. It is also called the Flowering Hands form. Every technique is a defense against a weapon. It's sophisticated, flowing, dynamic, and has a ton of information in it. The key idea here is that once you start moving, you don't stop. This is the closest to the Taiji principle that we get.

Theme: Figure eights are continuously used to tie the techniques together and facilitate that flow we look for in this form, the aforementioned "flowering hands."

The Kenpo knife techniques illustrate numerous ideas and methods. The two most likely grips are blade-out and blade-back. Both are shown by inference—that is, techniques selected for this form include defense against both types of grip. Ed Parker's principles of "divert, seize, control, disarm" must be utilized in each technique, but not all of them in every technique. An analysis of the techniques reveals a variety of attack lines with high, middle, and low lines shown from the front and sides, even from the rear.

Technique Sequence

Glancing Lance   Raining Lance
Unfurling Lance   Capturing the Storm
Clipping the Lance   Circling the Storm
Thrusting Lance   Escape from the Storm

Entwined Lance   Defying the Rod

Capturing the Rod   Twisted Rod

Broken Rod   Isolation, Close, and Salutation

Salutation

The salute starts the same as in the other forms from Short Three and up. The difference in this salutation is that you come off your legs, brushing with the hands up, to the "I have no weapons" position.

After the prayer position you brush down off the legs again and circle your hands in and down to the twin push-down position.

Your fingers will point at each other as they reach the final position. You will actually rise a bit by straightening but not stiffening your legs as you do this, the opposite of what is done in most internal systems' movements of the same type. The salutation is done this way because the hands are circling the opposite direction of the normal close. It is another example of opposites and reverses.

Glancing Lance—mid-line knife

A big variant here is found in the way many people teach the first step back. A "new" version of Form Six is taught with a step back to the corners, while the "old" version is done with the step directly back to 6:00. I believe the new version is a correction for a non-existent problem. The problem seems to be that people couldn't get the technique to work so they changed the attack. The original attack had a right step-through, and it has been changed by some to a left step forward. This change makes the attacker's centerline easier to hit, although it makes the second part of the technique harder to do. I believe the underlying problem lies

in how the original attack was being done. The attackers over-rotated their bodies on the thrust, and that made the centerline almost impossible to hit using the intended lines and weapons. The front kick would have to be a roundhouse to strike the groin, and the eye hook would be harder to get. Rather than teach the partner attacker to thrust and position himself more realistically so one could potentially use the rear hand to strike, check, or disarm, some practitioners changed the attack. All too often the same problem exists in the instruction and practice of other techniques, particularly the punch defenses.

The attacker thrusts with a right straight step-through mid-line knife, blade forward. If the attack is on the low line you can't do this without getting cut. You're probably going to get cut anyway, but why increase the likelihood by trying to snake that hand under and out? In addition, I think the attacker is going to thrust and then try to pull the blade back, likely rotating it for another cut on the way out. I think that too many

people practice the techniques as if the attacker is just going to stab and then stand there. My experience in weapon systems tells me that he's going to feel your contact and change lines. The Parker techniques take that into account. Mr. Parker would have changed lines on you; I know because he demonstrated some of his knife techniques on me.

Slide back to 6:00 with your right foot into a left neutral bow stance as your right hand strikes the outer wrist with an extended outward-type chop, and your left hand strikes the elbow with an inward heel-palm to check and possibly break the arm. Keep your elbows anchored to protect your torso and enable you to do an open-ended triangle if he changes his attack line when you go for the block/strike.

Immediately start to deliver a right inward two-finger hook to the right eye (either one or possibly both). You'll be throwing a right front snap kick to the groin between the block and the eye hook. However, by thinking of continuous motion from the block to the eye strike you'll have a better chance of getting the timing right. Too many people break the moves up and can't keep themselves covered in the event that the opponent draws the knife back for a second cut. By sticking with him when you make initial contact with the extended outward you can get the counter-attack in more easily and effectively. The front kick becomes more of an insert. Your left hand is continuing to check his arm while you kick and hook, and your right knee will check his when you settle from the kick to 12:00 in a right neutral bow stance. The settling and the eye hook will be together.

Leap onto your left leg to 9:00 as if doing Leaping Crane as your right hand loops counter-clockwise down and out to clear his arm, and your left hand covers high by your right shoulder. This creates a universal block-like open-ended triangle. You will find yourself in the crane and ready to kick.

Shoot a right-side snap kick to his right outer knee to break and buckle. Your right hand will be continuing from the clearing action you did, changing orbits from the vertical to the horizontal. Your left hand continues to cover, and you retract the kick like you did in Leaping Crane. As your kick plants between his legs to 1:30, your right hand will strike the right jaw hinge with an inward-hooking heel-palm strike. The flow and drop here is what Mr. Parker called "body fusion." He used it by hitting with an almost stiff-arm strike with the drop and rotation.

Your right hand will now cup the chin and anchor against his back, over his right shoulder. This locks the neck and possibly allows you to strike diagonally down into the right kidney, if you do the slip-off version.

Strike the left mastoid process with your left inward-hooking middle-knuckle strike, using the borrowed force of the inward heel-palm to pull him into it. If you cupped his chin you can hold him in position with the neck lock while you strike.

Slip your left hand across the shoulders to check them as your right hand continues on its horizontal figure-eight path to become an inward elbow to the head. There is a continuous flow from the inward heel-palm to the inward elbow that is referred to as a "condensed" figure eight. I like to think of this motion as speed-bagging his head.

In application this technique is done by throwing the side kick to 3:00 or even 4:30, depending on how hard he lunges. I had a conversation about this technique with Mr. Parker that resulted in a demonstration. I remember it vividly because it hurt. He told me the technique is actually two techniques in one. The first part is to be done when you have a hands-down point of origin. The second part is done when the hands are up. There is a little tendency to get caught in the transition between the first and second halves since you actually have to leap over or around the opponent's right leg to hit the one-leg stance. Again, if you do the "corrected" version, the lines change and the technique has to change with it.

Slide your left foot up and into your right foot into an attention stance as your hands close inward to the twin push-down position. You are at the top of a line you created.

Step back with your left foot and do the left side of the technique, ending facing 10:30 in a left neutral bow stance.

Unfurling Lance—high-line knife

The name comes from Unfurling Crane. It is used because the last half of this technique is done like the last half of Unfurling Crane. Mr. Parker said the timing is "1–2–3, 1–2–3, 1–2–3."

Take the energy from the ending inward elbow of Glancing Lance and let it take you to your right into a 45° cat stance to 3:00 as your right foot slides back into the cat and your right hand delivers an inward-hooking middle-knuckle strike to the medial nerve of the opponent's attacking right arm. Your left hand will follow the right to either check or strike the same arm. The check may

be done as an outward parry, the strike as an extended outward chop. I prefer the chop as a back-up for the middle-knuckle, since they both strike the nerve and contribute to the attacker dropping the weapon.

Fire a right front snap kick to the groin immediately after the left-hand move and keep your hands circling horizontally to repeat the middle-knuckle and check sequence. The middle-knuckle will strike higher on the arm, still attacking the medial nerve but in between the bicep and tricep muscles inside the arm.

If he bends forward a lot from the kick, your middle-knuckle might go to the temple.

As your foot plants in a right neutral bow stance to 3:00, your left hand will become an outward-hooking check against the inside of his arm, and your right changes from a circular path to a straight line with an outward elbow to the solar plexus. You would probably make that check into a grab, especially if he had not dropped the knife. If you did grab, however, you could not continue to the designated technique and you would have to break the sequence at this elbow strike. Some people do this elbow as an elbow sandwich. I don't since it doesn't really put you in position to do the check or the following back-knuckle.

This is where the crane part of the technique begins; it picks up where Unfurling Crane left off in Form Four. Strike the bridge of the nose with a left hammering claw and then a right rolling vertical back-knuckle that immediately reverses course and becomes an underhand hammerfist to the groin. The back-knuckle is done while in the right neutral bow stance. The hammerfist occurs as you slide your left foot to your right while starting to turn into the opponent, keeping your knees bent. The turn will enable you to do the following front scoop kick with good alignment; the bent knees keep your center of gravity from rising, and they contribute to power. Drive your right obscure vertical elbow up under his chin as he bends from the groin shot. A ripping claw that travels up as if you were going to put your hand on the ceiling follows the elbow. This is an either/or movement. If you caught him with the elbow, the claw probably won't get him. If the elbow missed or had less than intended effect, the claw would get him. As the right hand arrives at the apex, your left will strike his solar plexus with an outward heel-palm and your right foot scoops the groin. This is the "Unfurling Crane." (Living in Florida, I had the opportunity to see first-hand how the crane spreads its wings to dry them and saw how the name came to be.)

Drop your right arm, leading with the elbow and not the hand, into a hammering inward chop to the left side of the neck as your right foot turns in to a side kick to the right inner knee. Be certain to rotate your body back toward the left for the torque, and keep your left hand covering in the mid-zone.

Retract the kick, plant it to 3:00, and face 9:00 as you go into the left 45° cat stance to start the second side of the technique.

Plant your final left side kick to 9:00. Keep your left elbow anchored with the chop out, and drop back with your right foot to 7:30 to a twist stance facing 1:30 as you drop your right elbow along your right ribs to block the next attack.

Clipping the Lance—low-line knife

The use of an elbow block in any form shows up here for the first time in Clipping the Lance. Elbows as strikes are shown in the low forms, and this is the first time we intentionally demonstrate an elbow block in the transition to an open-ended triangle leading to the technique. This is a variation on the standard technique, Clipping the Storm, which is for a low-line club thrust.

The attacker is approaching from what is essentially your right side or rear flank, aiming for your exposed ribs with the knife in his right hand. As you pivot out of the twist stance to a left side horse stance to 1:30, your right elbow drops and the hand extends into a downward parry. The elbow starts the deflection and the parry then forms the bottom of the open-ended triangle.

The completion of the rotation to the horse stance is done with your left hand chopping down with a thrusting handsword to the radial nerve. Your right will end cocked at your right ear. The strike to the radial nerve should cause him to drop the knife. The photo below shows the variation in which we strike with a heel-palm to the elbow instead.

Hammer down with your right downward-thrusting chop as your left hand cocks across your body at your right shoulder, pivoting slightly to a left neutral bow stance. I aim this chop to the radial nerve again but higher on the arm. One reason is that it increases my

chance that he will drop the knife. Second is that it will force the arm back into his body so I can check it against him much like in Raining Lance. Be careful not to chop in toward your left—it may re-orbit the attack, and I have noticed that many people have a strong tendency to do this. The term "re-orbit" refers to when a force exerted on an attack or body causes the attack or body to continue on an arc or circle and return to the originally intended target.

Throw your left thrusting handsword out to his throat as your right hand chambers at your right ribs and you pivot back to the side horse. Notice that the sequence you have done so far is simply the mechanics of Parting Wings, but turned on its side.

The throat strike causes the opponent to reach up to his throat. Check his arm(s) down with your left hand as it retracts palm-down. As this happens, poke him in the eye with a right vertical two-finger poke with a shift back into the neutral bow. This will cause him to reach up again, opening his ribs.

As he opens the target you start a right step-through forward into a right 45° cat stance, striking the brachial plexus at his armpit with your left hand. This strike is an inverted outward middle-knuckle. The target area is where the major nerves of the arm come together and also where a concentration of lymph nodes is located. It is very sensitive, and a hit here will cause him to drop his right arm to cover it. Alternate targets would be the low ribs or sternum, depending on how he is positioned. Your right hand will have drawn back to your right ribs, chambered.

Complete the right step-through forward along the 1:30 line into a right neutral bow stance with a right straight heel-palm thrust to the chin or side of the head. Your left hand will have checked down and now covers your right ribcage.

Be aware that as a general rule a cat stance means kick. In this case the cat stance indicates that you can catch him with a knee strike, most likely in the thigh.

Slide your left foot back behind you to the front twist stance to face

10:30, dropping your left elbow, and do the left side of the technique. You'll end the technique in a left neutral bow stance to 10:30 with a left straight heel-palm.

Retract your left hand into a thrusting inward block as you draw back into a left 45° cat stance to 12:00, right hand chambered at the right ribs for the transition to the next technique.

Thrusting Lance—low-line knife

We are showing the opposite side of the cat stance/inward block section done in the beginning of Long Form One. In that form we do a right cat with a right inward block followed by a left inward block. In this form we do a left cat, left inward block, followed by a right inward block. Since the left hand was high for the preceding heel-palm, the delivery of

the block is more like that at the end of Short Form Two, when you go from the heel-palm to 7:30 and face 1:30. Just don't let there be any holes between the blocks.

Continue the left step-through reverse back to 6:00 as your left hand drops to cover the low line and your right delivers a right hammering strike to the forearm of the incoming right knife attack. There is some camouflage here. The right inward block isn't really a right inward block, and it hammers even though it's in the thrusting point of origin. Your left arm will hang along your left leg, lined up for its follow-up shot.

Thrusting Lance is taught as a standard self-defense technique starting from a right neutral bow stance, hands up. There you angle off to 4:30 with your left foot as your right arm smashes down on the opponent's radial nerve. What is typically left out is the low-line downward parry with the left hand to create the necessary open-ended triangle. I believe it was left out of the technique but kept in the form to see who was thinking. I learned the technique without the downward parry, and the manual didn't have it in there either. When I realized the form had the line in it, I put the parry into the technique. So, for my lineage, there is no difference in the technique and the form.

You will find yourself in a right neutral bow stance to 12:00 with your left arm hanging and your right arm approximately horizontal. If you know the technique you'll realize why horizontal is necessary. Your right hand will grab at the wrist as you push-drag shuffle forward in the neutral bow with a left underhand claw to the groin.

Think of your right hand as being a fixed point that you shuffle up to. You would in application since you grabbed his arm and want to control it. If he pulls back, you go with him. End with your right hand over your left forearm, the grab disappearing in favor of a timing slap on your forearm like in

Thundering Hammer. In fact, that's the same shuffle claw, but with the rear hand instead of the front.

Slide your left hand back under your right and rotate both hands to the right into the "I have no weapons" position you used in the salutation,

A head butt is a good insert.

only now you hold it down by your waist. This configuration indicates a wristlock. The actual hand position is 180° off this, so it's more camouflage. Your elbows should be in and should actually slide along your body as a guideline until they are centered. You will do a right step-through reverse back to 6:00 as you do this, transitioning through a left neutral bow stance into a left 45° cat to 12:00. You should hit the cat and the wristlock position together. Remember not to raise your center of gravity as you slide back.

Execute a front-foot-back-foot chicken kick as you pull your hands back toward your right hip. Your left foot hits the right ribs and your right hits the chest. Pulling keeps the opponent off balance and uses borrowed force.

Slide your left hand to his right elbow as your right hand draws back to the hang position during the settle forward into the right neutral bow stance, still toward 12:00. In the application you do this on the 10:30 line. Here we're working a 12–6 line for the form pattern.

As you settle, strike upward to the face or head with your right stiff-arm lifting back-knuckle. Pull it up and through, rising up a little with it for the back-up mass. Rotate your hand downward and drop your weight with a vertical downward back-knuckle strike to the head. Mastoid, base of the skull, or temple are the likely targets, depending on head position. Continue the path of the right hand down and through the target, maintaining the left-hand check near your right hip.

Continue to flow with the right hand by circling it counter-clockwise, then in and down to strike the upper spine just below the neck with a diagonal inward downward hammerfist. Use your right elbow as an imaginary fixed point and throw a right diagonal downward outward hammerfist to the base of the skull. The path you have described here with your hands is the same as the figure eight you did in Hooking Wings. In that technique you did the eight, then the vertical elbow/claw strokes. This one reverses it by doing the vertical strokes, then the figure eight. You should once again use "body english" on the diagonal strikes to engage your back-up mass. I just hate to see someone waving their arms around, totally disengaged from the body.

That right downward outward diagonal will travel down and through the target and become the downward parry line for the second side of the technique. Simply step back to 6:00 with it and you'll be in the left neutral bow stance to 6:00 and ready for the other side.

Take the travel of the final left-hand downward outward diagonal strike that you complete this side with and feed it into the next technique.

Raining Lance—overhead knife

Raining Lance is the only technique in which we deal with the blade-back "ice pick" grip attack. Overhead attacks and their differing ranges and weapons are shown here and in Capturing the Storm, Circling the Storm, and Brushing the Storm. In this case the opponent is stabbing down with his right on the first side of the technique.

Your left hand circles clockwise from the hang position it was in at the end of the previous technique, now its point of origin. In doing so it changes orbits and picks up the outside of the attack, which is coming from the left side. It does so as a type of inward downward parry, riding along with the downward force. You will be turning toward 9:00 into a left 45° cat stance as you do this parry, and simply point your right fingers at his thigh with minimal movement (from horizontal to vertical) from the hand's previous position. It is unnecessary to re-cock your right hand to

do this. We call that "pumping." Your hand was already down in position to allow you to make the bottom part of the open-ended triangle. Pumping the hand opens the line, and there is a possibility he'll take that line to cut you. Most knife-fighters would, switching from vertical to horizontal slices. I have seen Mr. Parker teach this using the rear hand first for the high-line parry, followed by the left hand on the same line. It opens that bottom line, and it's dangerous. He taught me, and many others, with the left-hand high-line and right-hand low-line open-ended triangle. I believe he did that other way just to see who was thinking and would ask him about it. I did, and that's another story for another time. In any case, this is designed to close his centerline.

With the triangle created and your left hand following his downward energy, slide your left foot forward to 9:00 to a left neutral bow stance to engage your back-up mass and let him stab himself in his right thigh.

Your hands will be crossed at your wrists in a smaller triangle. As with any other step of this type, your left foot will not pass his right heel. This is a position check and prevents him from attacking on your low line. His weight should be on his right leg, which would stop him from kicking anyway, but he might try to turn out and away, which presents the possibility of a back scoop to your groin. Your leg would automatically check it off by its position. The muscle of the leg may spasm when stabbed, and you want to cover your low line for the same reason.

Shuffle forward into a left wide kneel stance as your right arm ratchets into an inward elbow to the chest. Your left hand maintains the pressing

check on the weapon hand, which is still stuck in his leg. Chances are he won't feel the stab immediately if the knife is sharp. But by the time you get to shuffling forward the message is getting to the brain and the hand is trying to pull the knife out, possibly with the right hand assisting or trying to hit you or push you off. The leg will try to pull away. You probably would, if you were stabbed in the leg. That will be made difficult by your pressing check with the hands and the pressing check of your right leg in the wide kneel stance. You'll need a wide kneel here for its lateral stability and therefore its resistance to pressure from this angle. In addition, since you closed his centerline on the first move, you'll need to re-open it for the elbow. Pull hard to your left to open him for the elbow and you'll also get good angle of incidence and width-zone cancellation for the next two shots.

Pivot in place to a reverse wide kneel to maintain the leg check. Replace your left-hand check on the weapon hand with your right by sliding it down along his arm from the inward elbow position. Your left hand will "jump" up and behind your right to strike the throat in an inverted web strike. The jump is much like that done in Shield and Mace in Form Four. The left hand is making a half-circle on its way up to the throat. This will be complemented in a moment by the following web strike. The web strikes are also known as "tiger mouth" or "crab pinch." They are shown in this technique as two halves of a whole, the throat strike being the bottom half of the circle and the next strike shows the top.

Pivot back to the left wide kneel stance as your right hand continues the circle it started on the way down to the check (moving clockwise) and strikes the head. It slams into his philtrum as a chop and rolls up into a double eye strike, your thumb in his right eye and your index and middle fingers in his left. You could just leave the fingers there as a poke or you could flex your hand and pinch his eyeballs, which is what Mr. Parker liked to do. It is like striking the bridge of the nose but from the inside.

Continue your right hand down counter-clockwise, making a full 360° circle with it as you turn yourself to 3:00 into a right 45° cat stance. That circle allows you to pick up the outside of the left-hand attack with your parry, and you can drop into the neutral bow with the last 180° of the circle. Your left hand was already down and checking while the right was traveling, so it has the low zone covered and doesn't need to pump into position. Remember that on both sides, the bottom hand of the triangle turns the back of your hand toward the blade so the arm acts as a guideline to the leg. (The triangle configuration, as mentioned, has two sides with the third side open. That side is where the weapon hand is and your arms make the other two, as a guard.) It is common in knife systems to do this to minimize the effects of cuts received while defending. They almost all agree that you would rather take the cut on the back of the hand than the palm. Less blood, less chance of getting muscles, nerves, ligaments, and tendons cut. You'll have better ability to grab; it's tough when your palms are cut, bleeding, and were sweating to start. Hence the pronounced knife-hand position, pointed at his leg.

Also watch how you get into the initial neutral bow stance. Lots of people put an unnecessary shuffle in at the neutral bow and shuffle again at the elbow. Shuffles go where they are needed, and that is usually at the short weapon, the elbow in this case.

Do the technique on the opposite side to 3:00, ending with a left strike to the eyes and the right pinning check in a right wide kneel stance.

Step up to 12:00 with your left foot into a left neutral bow stance as you execute an upward cross block, right over left (right hand closest to you), to start the next technique.

Capturing the Storm—overhead club

The series of open-ended triangle cross blocks started in Form Four is finished here in Capturing the Storm. The universal blocks in Reversing Circles and the downward crossed blocking parry in Defensive Cross cover the sides and bottom of the imaginary box used in the basic Zone of Defense. The upward cross block opening this technique completes the box.

From the step forward (in the application you step a little more toward the left front corner) and the cross block, redirect the energy of the right step-through overhead attack back and down into a strike with the opponent's own club to his right shin as you pivot to a left forward bow stance. Notice that the previous technique did the same thing, redirecting the weapon into the body, with a shorter weapon but started on a complementary plane. This one blocks instead of parries and opposes the attack on the same plane.

Your hands should be closed as you block to prevent hurting your fingers, and then open on the redirect into the flowering-hands position. The flowering movement is done by rolling your wrists together clockwise

to prevent his slipping through (with the possibility of a butt strike, as in butt of the weapon, removing your teeth); you then go to a twin palm-out "butterfly" position. The butterfly traps the hand and club while directing the shin strike. Like the "I have no weapons" flowering move in Thrusting Lance, the butterfly is not what you actually do in application. In application you would grip the hand and weapon in a death-grip.

The redirect and flowering may be done in a neutral bow or by shifting to a reverse bow and back into a forward bow. I like this reverse-to-forward version. It adds power and tends to keep the opponent a little bit more off balance. The club should strike him just below his knee at the top of the shinbone. This is the patellar tendon trigger point, and the strike there causes the leg to straighten. That's a good thing since it gives you some room to work on the next move. Drive the club and hands upward like a golf swing, stretching his right arm up and out. This will expose his ribs for alternate strikes, keep him off balance, and open a path for you to walk through on your next move. It doesn't help his shoulder joint, either.

Maintain your grip on his arm with your left hand. (What kind of grip? Death-grip.) Slide your right hand up to grab the club near his hand. Do a right step-through forward to 12:00 (10:30 in application) as you start to peel the club out of his hand at the thumb. Do a left step-through reverse to 12:00, spinning under his extended right arm, and pull his arm down hard to your left hip. Your right hand will have extracted the club when it was over your head, allowing you to hammer it from a

12:00 position down to 6:00 to break his elbow as you sit in a side horse on the 12:00–6:00 line, your centerline to 3:00. This position puts you in Crossing Talon on the front side of the arm. This is important to know for a few reasons, but mainly that if you lose the club, which you probably will, you need to be able to control or break his arm with your hand or arm. If you don't pull his arm across to your left hip as you strike down, you will be too far off your center to do that effectively.

The arm break will cause him to arch his back, lifting his head. Assuming you still have the club for the rest of the technique, strike the back of his head with it in an outward horizontal stroke and pull it back and down toward you to strike the shin again. After pulling the shin strike through, retrace the line and strike the back of the knee, hitting the popliteal nerve to bend the leg. Round off the corner of the triangle and strike diagonally up and back to his head as your left foot sweeps his right and your left hand maintains a check on the weapon arm. The head strike should go to the bridge of the nose, and is done with a flick action. The Filipino stylists call it a *florete,* a "flower." You'll end in a left front twist stance to 6:00, right hand high and left hand low with the palms out.

Right step-through forward to 6:00 and do the left side of the technique. End in a right front twist stance to 12:00, right hand low and left hand high.

Circling the Storm—overhead club

I don't do Circling the Storm for the straight thrust as it's written in some manuals. I use it for an overhead butt strike attack. The range works better than trying to pick off a long-range thrust with an inward block. It keeps his elbow checked since he's going to fold it to hit you with (if he knows what he's doing), and you can reach him with an inward elbow. If he's trying to crack your skull with the club equivalent of Raining Lance, this move works just fine, with no range or checking problems. This technique is the short-range equivalent of Flashing Mace. If you look at some of the techniques in the system you'll see that they demonstrate the four

possible range combinations of kicks and punches, knees and elbows—
that is, long/long, long/short, short/short, and short/long.

Step-through forward with your left foot to 12:00 and execute a left
inward block to the outside of the right strike, right hand chambered.
Deliver a right inward elbow strike to the ribs as you did in Flashing
Wings with your right step-through forward to 11:00, slightly off the line.
Your left hand will check against the arm as you step.

Turn back the way you came to face 6:00 in a left forward bow stance
with a left outward elbow to the right ribs or solar plexus, the target
depending on how far he turns from the first elbow.

Your right hand will precede the elbow to make sure you don't get
hit with his arm (likely elbow) as you spin. The elbow combination is the
same as Flashing Wings, and the footwork is the same as Flashing Mace,
in which the handwork is an example of long/long, using your fists.
Flashing Wings is short/short. If you caught your opponent with the first

elbow and he moved away, you could spin and use the outward back-knuckle to the ribs, making it a short/long combination. You could start like Flashing Mace with the head shot and change to an elbow for the rib shot, making it long/short. There are other places in the high forms that indicate this concept as well.

You're in the left forward bow stance to 6:00 with the left outward elbow and high right check. Leap back on the line onto your left foot in a one-leg stance as your left hand chambers and your right travels horizontally on the high line to cover. That hand is actually a claw to the face but it's hidden in the form. The leap uses the back-up mass it generates to power the claw. Shoot a right snapping side kick to either leg, striking the back of the knee.

Continue the flow of the right hand by making it into a counterclockwise circle moving inside your left hand and striking down and out to the kidney as you plant down from the side kick. This is Leaping Crane behind the opponent instead of in front. Use the same rules. Consider that he is showing the high-line rake compared to the mid-line, think about how to position yourself to kick either leg due to the angle change, and then determine how either kidney could possibly be struck depending on which leg the kick went to.

This is where I stop the technique in application, as the lines would be a little different, and cover out. I believe that if you successfully did the side kick and heel-palm, the man would be out of position to do the rest of the technique as described in a manual. This technique was not even written down in a manual back when I learned it. It didn't find its way to paper until 1981, and Ed Parker did not write it. I was taught it as a combination of concepts, as I will describe momentarily. I agree that parts of it will work. I don't agree that they will work in this sequence in its entirety.

Slide your right arm vertically, contouring his body. Your left hand moves little or none. Change the orbit of your right arm from vertical to horizontal to check across his shoulders. Your right hand will, depending on interpretation, either rake back and forth as it did in the Finger Set, or orbit from back to front and return. Your left hand will take its place as a check. When the right hand returns to the horizontal, your left hand will make a large circle counter-clockwise from front to back toward 6:00. It will end forward again in an underhand crane peck with your right hand at your left forearm as in Thrusting Lance, as your left foot crosses over forward, settling in a left front twist stance. This is largely an examination of how you move to strike and check, changing from vertical to horizontal, and how your hands must move to check the vacated positions when you do so.

Here is where the argument of what is happening starts. The technique, as written in the 1981 and later manuals, continues from the side kick and kidney shot by sliding the right arm up the opponent's back, checking the back of the shoulders with the horizontal check, sliding over his head to cup the chin for a neck break, returning to check, and then sweeping the back of his right knee and striking the groin with the peck. Fine. This tells me that your side kick was not very effective and did not drop him to his knee(s). That, in turn, tells me that the rest of the technique is based on that premise. If so, then yes, maybe the rest will work as advertised.

I like to think I kicked him hard enough to drop him. In that case he will not be in position for me to get the rest of the sequence in, especially the last groin peck. I think you would agree that it would be difficult, if not impossible, to get low enough with the proper body posture to hit the groin. OK, let's say he's going to fall slowly enough that you can get the groin shot in. You've kicked his legs twice and cranked his neck—chances are he's not going to stand there since neck cranks take the legs out. However, if you do the second part as a second technique, all this is different and those problems go away.

I was taught that the second half is done on a man who is facing you instead. The principles don't change, just the body position. That kidney shot could have been a strike to the groin, causing him to bend. The vertical elbow strike is now an obscure vertical elbow to the chin. Check horizontally with your right across the front of the shoulders and rake the eyes with claws as your left hand checks. Replace the shoulder check to control the width zone in what we call a "bar check," sweep-kick the front of the leg at the shin or knee, and get the groin peck. It seems to work easier, better, and you get the last shot in with the intended borrowed force.

Right step-through forward to 6:00 into a right neutral bow stance with the right inward block and do the left side of the technique. End facing 12:00 in a right front twist stance.

Escape from the Storm—overhead club from side (flank)

Escape from the Storm is Brushing the Storm (see the previous chapter for the application photos) with an alternate ending. In this one your weight is on your front leg with the leg pick; in the other it's on the rear leg. The

underhand crane peck pattern is the reverse of the overhand figure eight in Thrusting Lance. It shows how to apply the front crossover and crane peck you did in Circling the Storm on a horizontal body vs. a vertical body.

From the right front twist stance and looking to your right, lace your left leg behind your right knee through a one-leg stance as you do a left inward parry outside the right overhead attack. Step down as you execute the parry and right step-through forward to 3:00 into a right neutral bow stance with a right lifting heel-palm under the chin, coming up from his obscure zone.

Left step-through forward to 3:00 (1:30 in the application) into a left close kneel stance with a right inside vertical forearm strike to the sternum and solar plexus, left hand checking outside his arm. You may have left this out in Form Five, but it's back in context in Form Six. Unwind into a horse with a right underhand claw to the groin, left hand now checking the upper arm or shoulder.

Continue by sliding your right hand down his leg for the reverse leg pick, capturing his leg at the knee. It is a common mistake to do the pick below the knee. That's bad because it usually triggers the folding action of the leg, which may result in his scoop kick to your groin or even your face if you are bending down too much.

Yank the leg out from under him as your left hand assists by pushing down on his flank and sliding with pressure to his right hip. Slide clockwise to the rear with your right leg to 3:00, ending facing 9:00 in a left forward bow. Your right hand will cup near your hip to show the ankle grab; your left will be in the push-down position in front of your right hip. The push-pull of your hands and the elongation of your step into the forward bow stance accent the drawing of the leg. Your attacker should be pitching forward to catch himself with his hands. He will still be on his left leg, creating a triangle to support himself. If you yank him hard and don't control him, he will fall down and make the rest of the technique unnecessary. Ed Parker was a large, strong man with a lot of upper-body strength. This sort of technique suited him. It's harder for smaller people.

Do a right front crossover step into a front twist stance as you anchor your elbows and drop your weight. This drop will put his right knee over your right knee, with intent to break it. The anchor is shown by doing the shape of the crane with both hands, timed with the drop. It is inherently a soft move and looks like it doesn't have much power. Gravitational marriage is what makes it work. Be sure to have your right lower leg vertical to support the impact. If it is not lined up correctly, you risk hurting your knee. If you know the ending of Raining Lance, you see the same alignment in the back break, but from a different stance.

Make a counter-clockwise 360° circle with your left open hand and strike the right leg at the inner thigh to move it away and open the groin. Legs are larger, longer, and heavier than arms, and you will need the travel of the circle to move it. Speed demons like to shorten the circle, but you will see that they usually use reverse motion and don't move the leg much. Keep in mind that you have done a lot of damage already, and a little wind-up like we use in The Back Breaker is OK.

Immediately pivot out of your twist stance with a right underhand crane peck to the groin as your left hand covers. You'll momentarily be in a right neutral bow as the right hand strikes. Pivot to a right reverse close kneel and deliver another underhand crane peck with your right hand, backhand fashion. These two groin strikes tend to make him raise his hips and keep him off balance as well as open him for the next strike.

Slide your right hand onto his hips to check them and keep them in position as you hammer your right heel up into his groin. The hip check will make this act as a sandwich. If you turned enough to the reverse close kneel, your foot will fit the target appropriately. If you did what most people do for the sake of speed, your foot will not fit the inverted V made by his legs up to the crotch. The foot will tend to be somewhat diagonal, and your heel will hit his right inner thigh. When you do the application ask your partner to tell you where you're hitting (you should be doing this anyway), and if you're catching the thigh then practice turning to the stance more.

Keep your right hand on his hips, cross back toward him with your left foot into a front twist stance to 9:00, and circle the left hand counter-clockwise like you did in Circling the Storm to strike the groin. Use another underhand crane peck or an underhand claw, usually a peck. You will end facing 3:00 in a left front twist stance with the underhand groin shot.

Lace (thread) the right foot through as you did on the first side and do the technique to 9:00. This is another example of the first move of a technique being the last move of the previous one in the transition. Your right knee would be striking his tailbone after the groin shot. So, this looks like the same opening crane from the first side, but it's actually the last move of that sequence.

Entwined Lance—high-line knife

Entwined Lance is considered to be Calming the Storm with a foot sweep, and it uses the rear hand to deflect the attack. There are relationships to Scraping Hoof and Triggered Salute as well. Scraping Hoof fits here in that the inner knee kicks we did behind us are now done in front. Triggered Salute pins and hits, but works on the outside with the pin. Calming the Storm also has a simultaneous block/strike combination but works on the inside. This technique works the simultaneous actions but with a parry. So you have a category that includes a block, parry, and a pin, working outside and inside, with a simultaneous counter-strike.

I taught a seminar at the 1993 Internationals. At the conclusion I had a brown belt approach me in the hallway. "*My* instructor taught me Triggered Salute with an outward parry," he said. I answered that he could

certainly do that but then the opening move would basically be Calming the Storm. I got no answer. I think people forget that there are lots of ways to do the techniques, but that the standards give you the ideas to discover the variations, both workable and not.

This technique is a stand-out because it breaks an established pattern in the form. You did knife and then club techniques, and you're about to go into the gun techniques when you suddenly have one lonely knife technique in the sequence. This is a message that you can interchange the techniques. Many techniques taught for guns can be used for a knife, and some knife techniques can be used for guns or clubs. It is a lesson I have not heard many instructors pass along. Nobody told me about this—I figured it out. All I needed to do was ask. But I had to think first because to learn you must know the right questions to ask. And to know what to ask, you must know the base information correctly. If you don't you probably won't get on track. Those who don't know or understand the applications and angles, etc., won't get the most out of the forms. The forms become mere exercise.

Turn hard into a left front rotating twist stance to face 12:00, picking your left foot up and adjusting it to your left for proper alignment. Your left hand will parry the inside of the incoming right high knife thrust with an outward hooking parry similar to that hooking check in Unfurling Lance, and your right will be positioned horizontally, palm-down, under your left elbow for the next move's line of sight.

Take advantage of the torque generated by the twist stance and use it to move forward to 12:00 with your right foot into a neutral bow stance. Strike the throat, not the side of the neck, with your right thrusting outward chop as you plant.

The next part of the technique incorporates three movements simultaneously. Retract the chop toward your left side, raking the arm as in Lone Kimono as you go. The rake rips the radial nerve and should cause the attacker to drop the knife. It is really to keep him from reaching back to cover his throat; the initial chop should have gotten him to drop the knife. The rake will act as a check as your left hand goes along for the ride, using his energy to launch a straight finger thrust to the eyes. As in Unfurling Lance in the early part of the form, you would probably grab the weapon arm as soon as possible. (What kind of grip? Death grip, sir!) Therefore, you could delete the eye poke and work the rest the same. You could grab with the chop, rake with the right, and then grab with it to get the left eye poke in. Re-grab with your left and continue. Possible, but a bit tricky with sweaty hands, maybe some blood, and loss of fine finger control. I don't recommend it. The base technique shows you how to work with the sliding and striking checks to maximize effect in minimal time. Keep in mind that you might work it like that against an empty-hand attack instead. As your right hand is raking and your left is poking, your right leg will be at work. It will pull back toward you into the chambered position, sweeping the inside of his right (lead) leg at the ankle to pull him off balance and into the eye poke. Your leg will be cocked, and your foot will probably be to the left of your left leg for full travel on both the sweep and the next kick. Mr. Parker once lamented that he couldn't use all his weapons because he had to stand on one leg. This technique is a good example of his thinking along those lines.

Kick the inside of the opponent's left knee with your right side kick. Retract it as you normally would and plant down into a right neutral bow stance, still to 12:00, as you strike the right ribs with your right horizontal outward back-knuckle. Your left hand will show the grab on his wrist, but keep your elbows in for the transition to the opposite side.

Rotate in place to the right front rotating twist stance, hooking with your right arm, left hand horizontal, and step forward with your left to 12:00 to start the second side.

You will end that side in a left neutral bow stance to 12:00 with the left back-knuckle and right check.

Capturing the Rod—front gun

The term "rod" comes from what is now old slang for a gun. Back in the 1950s you were "packing a rod"; today you may be "carrying a piece." The first side of Capturing the Rod is a defense against a right gun pointed at your chest or your head.

Step to 3:00 with your right foot as your left hand deflects the gun with an outward parry-like check inside the wrist. Your right hand will be grabbing the hand and gun, so your hands will be close together at this point. The parry, grab, and step will happen simultaneously. In the application your right hand will slice across the eyes, most likely hitting the attacker's left eye.

This uses the rule of taking something with you as you cross your body. It will make the next moves easier as well since he will want to pull his hands back. Try to grab the hand and gun as much as possible to restrict his ability to turn the barrel on you. When I was in bodyguard school I was taught that if someone tried to take your weapon away, you were to try to get the end of the barrel on him somewhere and fire. It might not have been major, but you shot him and got his attention. I have seen many a practitioner do this technique without really checking the gun, leaving the gunman able to turn the gun on the defender. There's a place called Gunpoint—don't go there.

Use a left straight finger thrust to the eyes, riding his pull back and putting a wristlock on him with your left forearm as the major tool. His wrist should be bent back toward him with his palm toward you.

Bring your finger thrust back and manipulate the hand and wrist into a spiraling wristlock by turning the hand and gun (if it's still there) clockwise and remembering to keep the barrel turned away. Do a right step-through reverse to 9:00 into a left neutral bow stance as you do the twist and lock with the same triangle configuration you utilized in Thrusting Lance, since it is the same lock. Again, keep your elbows in, sliding them along your torso for power and control. The twist will turn his centerline away from you, canceling his options with his left hand. The

Consider that the opponent may use a two-hand grip on the gun.

pull-down cancels the height, negating his legs. He will turn and bend toward 6:00 (3:00 relative to the way you are facing), presenting his right ribcage and head. The twist may simply be a wristlock, but with a little extra force it will break the wrist and possibly cause a fracture in the arm. That alone should disarm him.

Pull your hands to your right side as you deliver a right step-through front snap kick to the ribs or chest. Your left hand will check his elbow as your right hand pulls the gun back and away to strip it from his hand. This action will provide opposite force for both moves. Pulling to your right is essential. It continues the checking of height, width, and depth. I've seen many people do techniques that use this lock and pull to their left hip. I think it feels awkward but that is not the point. Pulling to the left re-opens his width zone and enables him to come around with his left to grab you, probably at the leg(s). It also repositions your right hand to where it can't work the strip and strike.

As your right foot plants to 3:00, your right hand will stiff-arm strike him in the face or head. You should have the gun in that hand, making this a pistol-whip movement. Your left hand will check the elbow, and your right knee will check his leg at the knee. Typically you will see this done with the right hand looking like an underhand reverse hammerfist, since that's how you would be holding the gun, striking with the butt. This hand position will easily lend itself to a stiff-arm lifting back-knuckle if you lose the gun by just turning your hand one-quarter of a turn to have your knuckles up. The stiff-arm lift is often used here in the form. It complements the front kick/stiff-arm strike you did in Form Four at Defensive Cross. That technique shows you what to do with your long weapon in the event the opponent falls toward you; Capturing the Rod shows that you have to step toward him. (The chicken-kick in Thrusting Lance shows us how to fill a half-beat between the lock and the kick/strike.) Another general rule is used here. You don't normally step back when you strike, yet you appear to in Defensive Cross. You get away with it because the opponent is closing on you as a result of the groin kick. A kick in the ribs often moves him away, as it does in the gun technique. You could switch to other weapons, but then we lose some of these ideas.

To start the opposite side you will cheat your left foot behind you and slightly to your left. I've heard this called an "incorrect cover." That would be incorrect, but it does convey the idea of how to move your foot. It shares some characteristics with a cover in that you stay in the same spot, face the opposite direction, and change lead sides. A technically correct cover would be done with the right foot and would get you to the same position, facing 9:00 in the left neutral bow stance to start the second side of the technique. The reason for stepping with the "wrong" foot is simple. The application of the left side of the technique starts with the left foot stepping forward, and this simply indicates that. Another reason is that it keeps the same line we were just working on. The correct cover would have us moving laterally off it, which is the function of a cover step.

Do the opposite side of the technique and end facing 9:00 in a left neutral bow stance with the left stiff-arm strike. You're going to head off to the 45° angles now.

Broken Rod—rear gun

"Broken Rod" refers to the elbow break you do in the course of the technique. In the previous technique we went inside the attack; now we're on the outside.

The footwork is reversed. In the application you step forward; in the form you go back. There are a couple of reasons for this. The main one is that the form lines show you how to get to the same diagonals in the same order as Long Form

Two. We have to fit the puzzle pieces together, and it starts all the way back in Short Form One. The first steps with a downward block in each of the first four forms are different. When you know all four of the first forms you have all four possibilities. They are:

1. step away left and block right,
2. step forward right and block right,
3. step forward left and block left,
4. step away right and block left.

What this has to do with Form Six is that we are going to the 4:30 angle first like we did in Short Form Two but we do it by spinning into it, going the opposite direction as the step in the low form.[14] It is related to the spin back to position in Long Form Three between the sides of Wings of Silk. That spin is in the wrong place for the application but works when "corrected." The spin here in Form Six is done with the opposite foot for the sake of the form. If you did it with the correct foot you would have the same maneuver as in Short Form One, i.e., step away and block down.

---

14 Here "low form" refers to the aforementioned Short Two. Martial artists often refer to the beginner and intermediate forms as low forms.

Another consideration is how you get your back parallel to the gun so if he manages to shoot you it probably wouldn't hit your spine. The twist stances don't do that as well as a forward bow stance does, plus they get your feet going in the wrong direction and may actually move you into the attack more than you want.

Forgetting all that for the sake of the form, you step back with your right foot to 4:30 in a front twist stance. As you pivot out toward the corner, you deflect the right-hand gun pressed into your lower back with a right back elbow block. Your left hand will start to chamber at your left ribs as you do this. Continue to pivot toward 4:30 in a right neutral bow stance as your right arm continues its path and your right hand seizes the wrist and gun like you did in the previous technique. (What kind of grip . . . ?) Pull to your right hip to pass the weapon hand to your right, away from you. This will also anchor it for the next move.

Left step-through forward to 4:30 with an uppercut forearm break to his right elbow. Ideally you will pull his arm close to you so that your body checks his arm and the gun is past you. Too many people get lazy when they do this. They tend to orbit around the gun hand, but let it float back toward him. It usually results in the gun hand being on their centerline. It is as if they don't think the man will be fighting back. In that position the attacker may shoot you in the groin or leg. If you pull past you, that possibility is eliminated; the man is off balance and the arm is easier to break or sprain.

Note that the transition would end with the gun just past your right hip to prevent his turning the barrel toward you. Also note the foot pin.

The break will get him up on his toes with his back arched, as we have examined in past techniques. Drop your left hand down from 12:00 to 6:00 into the groin as a hammerfist while maintaining the right-hand grabbing check.

Continue the path of the left hand up along the other side of the circle from 6:00 to 12:00. Contour his body as a sliding check as you do, stopping at his right shoulder. You could crack him in the head with your heel-palm on the way if you're feeling mean.

Step-through with your right to 4:30 in a right forward bow stance as your left hand pushes hard to help your right hand strip the gun down and back and keep him turned away from you. Your arms will end on a 45° angle, matching the line of your rear leg. It looks very much like a classical kung-fu posture called the "willow leaf palm." Some people use a twist stance here instead of the forward bow. I don't because I find that it forces me to re-rotate a little too much to get into position to strike from my strip. If something went wrong I don't think I'd have as many options to respond with.

Pivot counter-clockwise into a right side horse stance, the same side horse you would have ended that line with in Long Form Two. While pivoting you will strike him under the chin or in the face with the butt of the gun to stand him up, letting your arm travel upward over your head to 12:00. In the second half of the pivot you bring the gun down in a clockwise half-circle and hit him in the solar plexus with it as you sit. Show this strike as a horizontal inward hammerfist. Your left hand will cover at your ribs, checking his right arm in application. This half-and-half pivot and strike is the same as seen in many techniques where we do two-in-one timing. It's a lot like the end of Twirling Hammers in Form Four. It is also another example of pistol-whipping as in Capturing the Rod.

Bring your left foot around behind you to 7:30, making a 90° angle change. Plant in a twist stance, pivot to your left, and do the technique on the opposite side along the 7:30 line. End in a left side horse stance with the left hammerfist.

You are going to move up the same 1:30 diagonal you would in the Two forms. In keeping with the spin we did to open this technique, we will spin to these next two directions as well.

Defying the Rod—front gun

Defying the Rod gets its name from the similarity it has with a technique called Defying the Storm. That similarity shows when you lever his arm, resulting in the same position in both techniques.

Slide your left foot back behind you to 1:30 into a rear twist stance as you stack your hands on your right hip, left over right. Pivot counter-clockwise as you simultaneously deliver a left open-hand extended outward block, right front kick, and a right straight finger thrust. It's not really a block since it doesn't fit the definition of going force against force. It's a force against a "neutral force," as Ed Parker liked to say. The left hand strikes the right arm just above the wrist to deflect the right hand that is holding the gun. Your right foot hits the groin as your right hand pokes the eyes. Float your weight just as you do in Conquering Shield in Short Form Three.

As your weight drops, your left hand is now grabbing the weapon arm and your right arm is sliding down along that arm using frictional pull, your hand stopping just above the inside elbow. As the opponent  bends forward from your drop, catch him with your right flapping elbow under his chin, using your right hand as a fixed pivot point. The flapping elbow is first shown here; it doesn't appear anywhere else in the forms. The strike will probably cause whiplash, injuring the neck, along with the possibility of broken teeth, a split lip, or maybe he'll even bite his tongue.

Slide your right hand up his arm to his shoulder, hooking your hand at the crease between the arm, shoulder, and the back. This will give you the longest possible lever for the next move. All along, your left hand has maintained the death grip on the weapon hand, which may or may not still hold the weapon.

A common variation of this technique has you reach all the way across your body with your right to grab the weapon hand as well. You would then lock down on the elbow joint by anchoring your arm to your body, allowing you go for the next levering move. I wouldn't do that for the reason that you are reaching across your own centerline and allowing what is called a "pass line." It would be easy for the opponent to check your right elbow at that point and tie up both your arms. Sure, you kicked him and poked him and elbowed him first—that should slow him down and allow you to pull it off. But it's a bad position, one that can be avoided by using the lever with the hand instead of the shorter elbow tool.

OK, so let's call it "category completion" and say we are showing that type of lock with the hand-and-elbow manipulation. Sorry, we have that position in Spiraling Twig on the initial turnout for the elbow break, and it's done from a better point of origin. One of my black belts, Charlie Cockrill, does a theme class called "Don't cross the centerline unless it's safe to pass." The idea is based on the principle in our system that you always take something with you when you cross your body. For example, if your right hand is on your left side, it strikes as it comes back to the right. Five Swords is a good example. The right hand starts on the right, moves to the left to block, and then does a slicing chop on the way back to the chamber on the right side. Charlie's class emphasizes how to effectively use your inserts and keep from getting checked off.

From the lever position you will step back to 7:30 with your right foot and end in a left forward bow stance facing 1:30. In the application the angle is 4:30 to the opponent. Here in the form we are holding the diagonal line. As you step back your right elbow anchors and travels back with your right hip as your left hand pushes upward. The arm ends in a vertical position as you sit in the forward bow. It looks a lot like you are turning a big wheel when you do this. Do it with a lot of force to not only get that arm up but to cancel his height, width, and depth zones. His free arm should involuntarily reach for the ground since he will be heading face-first for it. It is a survival reaction, like blinking your eyes to keep sand out.

Press down on his wrist with your left hand. This is a wrist compression and will make the coming strip easier since it acts like a wristlock and makes the hand want to open. Maintain control with your left hand and strip the gun away by pulling it out straight up. Don't let your own hand go past vertical as you do this—that's just wasted motion.

Maintain that left-hand grip. Drop your right hand down on his head or neck, striking with the butt of the gun. Continue to bring the hand around, counter-clockwise, passing through the head. When your right arm gets to the high front 45° angle it will trigger your right step-through knee strike to the chest using the same timing as Locked Wing did in Short Form Three. This will result in a sandwich, with the gun hand striking the spine, left hand covering. Plant forward with your right foot to 1:30 in a right neutral bow stance. The sandwich is normally shown with a right heel-palm with the knee strike. You could do this if you lost the gun in the process of defending yourself, in which case you eliminate the strip line and go right to the sandwich or use the last moves of Defying the Storm.

Now slide your right foot back behind your present position, chamber your hands on your left in the stack, and pivot clockwise to 10:30 to start the opposite side. End facing 10:30 in a left neutral bow stance.

Twisted Rod—side gun

The wristlock you do in Twisted Rod is the same as one you learn to defend against as a lower rank in the technique called Twisted Twig, hence the name. I think when I learned it the name was Green Gun. Apparently that was because the technique was taught to green belts.

In this version the attack is a right gun held at the right side of your head. In the application of the standard technique the attack comes directly from the front. The message here is clear. Do the techniques from the front, back, and sides. Change the zones from high to low as well.

From the left neutral bow stance to 10:30 do a left rear crossover toward 3:00. As you make the twist stance your hands come up, your right hand making contact with the outside of his right arm. Your right hand should be executed as an extended outward block, hand open. Your left hand should be up as well, near your left shoulder as if matching the posi-

tion of the right. The function of the rear crossover will actually take you toward 4:30 but you are looking for a 3:00–9:00 line for the two sides of this technique. What is happening here is that the opponent senses your reaction and starts to retreat. You have to

stick to him to prevent loss of control of the weapon, which dictates the crossover maneuver. Finish the maneuver with the right step-out to 3:00 into a right front twist stance.

Left step-through forward to 3:00 as your left hand grabs his wrist in front of your right hand, ending in a left neutral bow stance. Your arms don't move since they are twisting the wrist by a combination of applying pressure to the back of the hand with your right forearm and bending the wrist with your left hand. Step-through forward with your right as your right elbow stays anchored and you pivot to your left into a right reverse bow stance. The turn puts pressure on the wrist and makes the takedown, tripping him over your right leg so that his head ends up toward 9:00. The weapon, in this case a gun, may be pointed at him as you twist his wrist.

This is one of the few takedown techniques that have the man land on his back. Most have him land on his side to eliminate the use of the other natural weapons. Shovel-kick his right ribcage with your right foot and immediately stomp his left collarbone with the same foot and plant to 10:30. If he were on his side, you couldn't do the stomp kick to the collarbone; it would be turned away and parallel to the angle of delivery. The shovel kick breaks the right ribs, which would have him curl in

and toward you. The stomp stops him from curling in too far, possibly closing targets and even trapping your leg. Breaking the clavicle is bad. It can affect lots of nerves, arteries, and veins. Breaking it on one side also takes out the opposite side because the survival reaction of the good side is to come to the assistance of the damaged side. When you strike a standing man on the collarbone and fracture it, the weight of the arm pulls it downward, creating a lot of pain. The other hand will automatically sling the arm to take the pressure off, which takes that arm out of commission as well. On the other hand, if the opponent is insane or drugged, all bets are off. On the supine man, striking the collarbone causes the back to arch noticeably before all that other stuff happens. This is a reason why you need to plant your right stomping foot above the right shoulder for the next move. It will check off the right arm. Planting below the right arm may not.

After the plant you pivot to the left and drop into a left close kneel stance facing 4:30. The drop into the close kneel serves to crush the throat with the right knee, close the entry line to your groin, and check off the right arm. Your right hand will simultaneously poke downward with a straight finger thrust to the eyes. Maintain the wristlock on the weapon hand with your left hand.

Step behind yourself with your right foot into a rear twist and do the crossover and step out on the 9:00 line to do the opposite side. You'll end the technique facing 7:30 in a right close kneel stance, having finished a triangle pattern with the two sides of the technique.

Cross behind yourself with your left foot in a tight rear twist stance. Step out to 3:00 with your right foot as both hands chamber at your sides in a square horse stance to 12:00. Time the chambering with the settle in the horse.

Isolation, Close, and Salutation

Standing in the horse stance facing 12:00, do the first hand movement of Glancing Lance, that is, the right-hand outward chop to the wrist with the left-hand inward heel-palm to the elbow. Use the same timing, but without the footwork.

Hands are in transition.

Loop your right hand counter-clockwise, over and down as in the second part of the same technique as your left hand pumps horizontally into the same inward heel-palm position. The right hand is hooking as it does so and may be used as a shape of the crane. This shows the over-and-under methods of picking off the knife attack while remaining on the same orbit. Repeat the process on the opposite side, left under and left over.

Your right hand will now make a 360° circle from its point of origin, picking up the gun attack as in the opening move of Twisted Rod. Your left hand will reach across to show the grab after the right hand ends in the vertical position, having now traveled one and one-quarter circles and accomplishing the deflection and counter-grab. The counter-grab is shown as an inward elbow sandwich even though that's not what you would actually do.

This is essentially the same line as used in the opening of Glancing Lance. You have rotated your right arm into an inward elbow position to indicate the wristlock as done in Twisted Rod. Duplicate that outward circle with your left hand followed by the right, doing the opposite side of the sequence and ending with an elbow sandwich.

Slip your right hand back toward you along your left forearm into the first step of the salutation, crossing into the right front twist stance with hands left over right. It feels a bit strange to do this in this manner since we are used to doing the elbow sandwich with the heel-palm continuing out away from the elbow instead of in. Finish the salutation as you did at the beginning of Form Six.

What you will hear most about the isolation is that it is the first and last techniques of the form, which it is. Yes, it's a knife defense and a gun defense. Yes, it goes over and under. But what does that really mean? It does show that you can handle an attack by going over it or under it, and that it is interchangeable for use against a knife or a gun. The main point, however, is that the first movements work on the same plane, which is vertical. The second set of movements start on the vertical and change to the horizontal. That shows the orbital switch idea. OK, fine. Why do we need that? We need it because the idea of changing orbits lends itself to stripping the weapon. The logical progression is that we can take the weapon and use it—and we do that earlier in the form. If you are a proponent of the Form Seven and Eight school, you see the logic perpetuated in their demonstration of Kenpo concepts regarding the use of the club and knife. It would make sense that if you take the weapon you should know how to use the weapon. It is a sub-theme of this form anyway, as shown by the techniques comprising the form. But consider also that if that idea is true, shouldn't we have a gun form? I'm being facetious, but the logic would dictate that one get familiar with the workings and use of a firearm. It can and does make a difference at times.

Additional Observations

- The Crane family techniques in Form Six appear in Circling the Storm and Glancing Lance. The second half of each is where you'll see them. Circling the Storm uses a high-line rake versus the mid-line rip of Leaping Crane. The hand in Glancing Lance actually goes vertical instead and then changes to an inward line. Contrast that with the outward line in Circling the Storm and Leaping Crane. In those you leap with the rip, and then strike outward after the kick. In this one you strike inward after the leap and kick. Then there is the Unfurling Lance association in which you get to the one-leg stance and strike with both simultaneously instead of sequentially.

- There are a lot of middle-knuckle strikes in Form Six. What they show is completion of some lines that started back in Short Form Two. Short Two has the vertical line down line, Short Three has the upward line, Long Three has the vertical thrust line straight ahead, Form Five has the horizontal rake line; Six adds the inverted hand position on the outward line. That's all four—in, out, up, and down. It's done as a rake, snap (whip), hook, hammer, and thrust. It's primarily used as a nerve strike, normally hitting a specified nerve or plexus, which is a gathering of nerves. What is not included is interesting as well. There is no straight middle-knuckle thrust in any technique or form in Parker Kenpo. I believe it is because of the nature of its alignment when thrown in that manner. Years ago I was sitting as a judge on an all-style black belt review board. I was a third-degree black back then. A candidate for fourth black was running his forms. Out of curiosity I asked him about a straight middle-knuckle punch he did and what else he knew about that particular hand formation. He said, "Well, we do that many different ways." I leaned forward, anticipating new knowledge. He excitedly said, "We do it this way, AND we do it this way," and he demonstrated the horizontal and vertical fist positions. That was it. I was disappointed. Mike Sanders had shown me several ways to throw the strike, and I later picked up some more from Ed Parker. There is a key relationship between the form sequence and the techniques as they used to be taught that shows the usable lines. Knowing those lines prevents damage to your hands and maximizes effect. It also gives you the keys to figure out why Parker did some of the moves the way he did in the forms.

- It seemed to me that the underhand claw to the groin in Thrusting Lance was awkward. Not so if he's pulling back as you shuffle in. Then I looked at Capturing the Rod. It's the same thing except you go over your counter-grab instead of under. Your right hand is in the same position in both techniques, and you simply go over or under it. It's a common principle in many other systems.

- A comparison of blocking and parrying an overhead attack shows up in the side-by-side placement of Raining Lance and Capturing the Storm. The knife is handled by two hands, as is the club. What is different, and significant, are the orbits of those actions. Both use the weapon against the opponent wielding it. However, you can't use the club technique for a knife; you'll likely get trapped and cut. In fact, there's a problem inherent in the upward cross-block anyway. It's easy to check it off with the free hand. In my mind it's workable, but there are better alternatives shown in the system. The upward cross-block position is better used as a transition on a carry-over type of technique when you need both hands to get from inside an attack to outside. It's just a frozen example of what you might do with an open-ended triangle on the vertical.

- Other Chinese systems have an application for their salutation. The salute is composed of self-defense techniques. Our salutation is applied in Twisted Rod. Take a look at the footwork and hand positions and you'll see what I mean.

Closing Comments
No Excuse for Poor Execution

There is a little bit of the soapbox in this section along with technical observations. Keep your fingers together. I've seen numerous versions of this form done, many with poorly executed hand formations. We're a hand system, and this is a high-level form. There really is no excuse for this. There are reasons, but no excuses. A black belt in Kenpo is supposed to be an expert in the use of the hands. Demonstrating poorly formed natural weapons does not indicate an expert in my book. You're telling me, or the judges, that you can't even keep your fingers together or that you can't curl them into a claw? Maybe you're an all-about-me person and could care less about what we think. What about you? Want to hurt your hands when you hit something? Go ahead and use that crummy open-hand formation. These shapes you make with your hands and arms are different for every weapon, and they affect muscle and bone alignments for each one. Sure, you can get away with your little finger being out of position when you actually hit something. But having space between each finger when you do a heel-palm does not make it the compact unit you want. You won't deliver the power and have the effect you really wanted, and you take a chance on damaging your hands. Besides, this is form. You want it to look your best. I once was approached by a fourth-degree black belt, a competitor, at the end of his form division at a tournament. He ran Six and wanted to know why I gave him "the lowest score in the division." For one, I had not. It was low, but not the lowest. I proceeded to describe the flaws that included neutral bows that looked like diamond stances, kicks too low and some on bad angles, and the splayed fingers. Needless to say, he was not happy. You know, he turned around and went to the musical/creative division and did one of the better performances I've seen. Maybe he turned his anger into fuel, an "I'll show him" sort of thing.

Being a fourth degree, he's been around a while. He should be able to take some critiquing. At that level I'd want to know how to make my form better. After all, the next step is fifth black, a professor level. I'd probably not dump all that stuff on a lower-level student. So I told him what I thought. I was the first Parker Kenpo stylist to make the National Top Ten way back in 1980. I took a lot of criticism, both from within and without. I worked at perfecting my technique. I wanted every little detail as perfect as possible. It was reflected in my scores and resulted in a national ranking. You don't get the gold with your fingers sticking out. Make it clean, precise, fast, and powerful. It's not easy. It takes sweat, self-discipline, and hours of work. It feels good when someone watches your form and compliments it. It is personal satisfaction when you can see the video or just run the form and know it was a job well done. Then go out and take that same drive and apply it to your job, relationships, hobbies, etc. You don't have to win—you just have to try.

Aim the kicks where they are supposed to go. If the technique calls for a groin kick, aim it where groin height would be, not down to the shins. Normally on a standing man the kick would be at your own groin height. That is because you index the techniques to your body size when you shadow-box. One of the reasons for doing form is to have a reference for what we do. You should be able to look in the mirror and tell what you'd be hitting on the invisible man. Actually you don't even need the mirror, just an imagination. In Escape from the Storm, turn all the way on the back scoop kicks and get the kick moving vertically. This is fitting, a form of contouring. The man's body creates a triangle with the crotch at the top point. Your foot needs to be vertical to fit. If you don't turn your hips enough, your foot comes up on an angle and usually strikes his inner thigh. Ask your training partner. They'll tell you if you have angle of incidence on the kick. I see this mistake all the time. Just slow down a little and it should cure itself because you'll have time to turn your hips.

Gun Techniques and Their "Extensions"

I have a problem with the gun techniques' so-called "extensions." I understand them but I don't like them. I think they are repetitive, having no real new information in them. What I see in the patterns are the same movements from other techniques, mostly just with a gun in your hand. That brings up ethical and legal issues that I have very rarely heard discussed by other instructors. In most states you are only allowed to use reasonable force to defend yourself. Kenpo may well be over-the-top from the start due to its overkill methods anyway. If an attacker points a gun at you and you decide that doing one of these techniques is the way to go, you may only go so far as to prevent him from doing anything else to you. I know, I know. You're probably thinking, "If it's him or me it's going to be him that goes down." I understand that. But if you poke his eyes, kick his groin, break his arm, knock his teeth out, disarm him AND THEN proceed to pistol-whip him four or five times as at least one extension teaches, you may be the one who winds up on the wrong side of the bar in court. The term the law uses is "molesting the corpse." We can go into a whole philosophical argument here about survival, quality of life, emotion, judgment, and more. My point is that once you have the gun, maybe you don't need to do all that to him. If you must, you learned all the lines to use with or without the weapon in the base techniques. Your instructor clued you in on that and how to do it.

The other question is moral. Should you do it? You know how and you've been given the when—which is the situation you're in. But should you? It's a judgment call. So many factors need to be considered. I've been trained to teach judgment in my role as a flight instructor. It's even fair game for testing a candidate on their judgment on a flight test. This is tough stuff.

Another thing I don't care for in the extensions is the gun handling at the end of the technique. Nobody who knows how to shoot holds a pistol as in the photo below. It looks nice and would be good for a demo. But it does nothing for a gunfighter.

Think about the fact that most people don't know how to handle a gun anyway. Get familiar with basic firearm safe-handling rules.

Did your teacher tell you to make sure you don't pass your hand in front of the barrel while doing any of this motion? To keep the barrel pointed away from you at all times and to make sure the opponent can't turn it back on you? Are you familiar with the operation of a revolver versus a semiautomatic weapon? Do you know how to de-cock, or clear a chamber? How to work a safety? Are you aware that you don't put your finger on the trigger until absolutely necessary and that you keep it outside the trigger guard until that time? All this takes training.

Let's assume you successfully did the technique. You didn't lose the gun; you have it in your hand and are pointing at your attacker who is in a crumpled heap.

Somebody saw this happening in the parking lot and called 911. They called in that they saw a man with a gun, and when the police roll up that's what they see, a man with a gun. The cops weren't there when it started. The officer does not know who had the gun in the first place. You could be the bad guy and have just beaten a non-compliant victim.

So Mr. Policeman is going to order you to drop the gun. This is a big-time stress event for most people. If you remember your physiological responses to stress you will recall that tunnel vision and hearing loss are some of the manifestations. It's like fighting in a tournament. You honestly may not hear the center judge tell you to break in the heat of battle. You may not see or hear the officer tell you to drop the weapon. He will usually tell you two or three times since it often takes that much to get it to register. Maybe you get the message and drop the gun, then sort things out. Maybe instead you get the vague impression that someone else is on scene. So you turn toward the source of the light, sound, or touch. What he sees is you turning toward him with a weapon. You're probably going to get shot. It's going to make a great war story, if you live. Maybe you should kick the gun away. Maybe you should empty the chamber. Maybe you should run like hell. Maybe you should not hold the gun by the grip. Maybe, maybe, maybe. . . . Get some sound advice and make your training decisions. I refer you to Counselor Triolo's contribution, "What Now?" on this very subject, found at the conclusion of this book.

8.

Forms Seven and Eight

Some Background on These Two Forms

Form Seven was originally a double knife form. The knife to be used was not an "Ed Parker" knife. That knife was designed by Gil Hibben as part of his black-belt thesis. The knife is now called the Kenpo Karate knife and has at least two versions. The Parker knife itself had several "mark" versions. The intended knife was smaller than the Parker knife, a double-edge dagger, to make manipulation easier.

The original Seven was not widely taught. The opening of the original Form Seven is what is done today to open Form Eight. However, that is where the resemblance stops. The tribal lore of our system says that the original Form Seven was only taught to seven people.

In Ed Parker's progression-type thinking, Form Seven was the next logical step in the forms. Form Six was defense against weapons that included knives. The majority of the techniques in Six are against a knife because he believed the versatility of a blade makes it the most dangerous of the weapons. If everything does have an opposite and a reverse, then we needed a form using the knife. In the 1980s, a stick form appeared and the original Seven was replaced by it. Form Eight was close behind. It was the new knife form, which supposedly is somewhat like the original Seven. Both forms use the weapons in both hands simultaneously. There are no single weapon forms.

If there is any confusion, it is because of the renumbering. The "new" Eight is a modified version of the original Seven. Today's Kenpo forms listing refers to Seven, the stick form, and Eight, the knife form. In my mind it is questionable whether Ed Parker created these forms or not. I tend to think that they were put together with his help by a senior student. I started learning Seven from him just before he died. I was a little disappointed. The forms just did not feel like an Ed Parker form. Sure, they have Parker techniques and some of his weapons concepts. But much of what is in Seven and Eight I just cannot see him doing in reality. There have been reports of people cutting themselves while doing Form Eight. They are violating the weapons rules used in edged-weapon systems. For example, you know the Kenpo rule of the new hand moving outside the old to keep the hand from being trapped. If you apply that principle to a bladed weapon, your blade remains inside, possibly resulting in injury, especially with a blade of stick length or longer.

Form Seven, Overview

As I wrote elsewhere, this form is known today as a double stick or club form, whereas Seven was originally a double knife form. Knowing how Mr. Parker thought in progressions, doing a knife form made sense in that Form Six has knife disarms in it, and if you get the knife you should know how to use it. Alternatively, in his thinking, the club being somewhat less deadly than a knife, an argument can be made that you should learn the club before the knife. Mr. Parker was very concerned about his information on using a knife getting out and into the wrong hands. Maybe this is what caused him to switch the form to a club form instead of a knife form. (I am using the terms "club" and "stick" interchangeably.)

From my familiarization with Filipino Martial Arts (FMA), I know that single stick is typically learned before double. In our system, we often don't do that, and this form is a double stick form. The form is composed of techniques very much like the empty-hand techniques to show that one can use a stick as an extension of the arm, a common martial arts concept. The problem I see with many who do this form is that they use the wrong size stick. Mr. Parker emphasized tailoring, and he had a formula for the stick as well. The stick should be as long as the distance from the tip of your longest finger to your elbow. When you palm the end of the stick it will protrude just past your elbow to protect it if you are using an inverted grip. This length also makes the stick very maneuverable and is much like that used in the Serrada FMA system. Serrada is a close-in system like Kenpo and so it makes sense to use a shorter stick. The longer stick tends to get one tangled up and makes it easier to be disarmed. If you buy escrima sticks to use, cut them down to size. Make sure the diameter fits you, too.

It is my belief that you should get trained in an FMA system if you want to know how to use sticks and knives since these practitioners are arguably the best at their use. However, if you do not have the time or opportunity to do so, learning to use a stick via our system is done by learning Form Seven and being overseen by a competent instructor. That instructor can guide you through the technicalities of proper grip, distance, striking methods, and other rules of motion appropriate for using this weapon. This is not intended to simply be Five Swords with sticks. There are other rules of motion that need to be learned and understood when using weapons. If you ignore that, at the very least your motion will be less than effective, and further, you can get hurt. For example, if you use the "new hand in front" rule here that you were taught as a beginner, you get trapped. Using it with a knife often results in getting cut. The rule about not stepping back when you strike in front due to body weight moving away from the strike can be "bent" or ignored when using a longer weapon due to reach and momentum.

Technique Sequence

Five Storms	Gathering Storm
Reversing Storm	Flashing Storms
Repeating Storm	Whirling Storms
Clashing Storm	Destructive Storms

Shielding Storms	Thundering Storms
Twisting Storms	Leaping Storms
Twirling Storms	Isolation
Criss-Crossing Storms	Close and salutation

Mr. Parker planned to write and publish *Speak with a Club,* a project unfinished at the time of his passing. Additionally, there are practitioners out there who say he taught them a club set as a foundation to this form. It's listed as a component of the system in one of his *Infinite Insights* volumes. Like the Nunchaku Set, which is also listed, they may be the Kenpo equivalent of Bigfoot—talked about, rarely seen, never captured.

Form Eight, Overview

Today, Form Eight is the double knife set—what Seven used to be. Like our other forms, it is intended to teach angles and methods of delivery as well as grips and transitions. Mr. Parker developed a vocabulary for the knives in which he described various additional methods of motion beyond hammering, thrusting, etc. They included filleting, tenderizing, and more. I was at his home as he went through his knife concepts with Mike Pick, and I was the body they worked on. If done on a body with a real blade, it is some pretty grisly work. I understood his concerns about the information getting out, and it showed his social conscience. He eventually planned to publish a book called *Speak with a Knife.* I had some of his completed work on it, and I do not know what changed his mind or how much he would have included.

The opening of the form shows how to use the knives with the blades forward and back, meaning blade forward like a fencer and back like a boxer. The FMA systems use the terms *sak-sak* and *pakal,* respectively. Within the form are switches from one to another to show the various configurations with which one can hold the knives such as both blades forward or both back, and one forward while the other is back. There are some manipulations I do not care for in the perspective that if one

has blood or sweat on the hands it
may increase the chance of losing
the weapon. A lot of work has been
done on using appropriate materials
on a grip to lessen or prevent this,
as well as customizing the shape of
the grip and guard. Which brings us
to knife selection.

Gil Hibben's Kenpo Karate a.k.a. Parker Knife.
Photo provided by Gil and Linda Hibben.

I made the mistake of doing the form with the Parker knives, those
designed by Gil Hibben back in the 1960s. These are big knives with thick
blades, meaty grips, and large guards. They do not lend themselves well
to manipulation, unless your hands are big. Ease of use will also depend
on whether you have a production knife vs. a custom knife. Mine were
custom-made by Gil and fit my hands. The production knife, therefore,
is probably not the best choice for most. This knife is superb for many
of the Parker applications using hammering, thrusting, slicing, and contouring methods. I don't think they should be used for the double (two
in one hand) techniques. The blade of choice for doing the set is Hibben's Silver Shadow or a similar knife. These are daggers with thinner
blades and grips. The blades are double-edged. The grips lend well to
rotation and manipulation. The guard keeps
the hand from slipping to the blade and may
be enough to prevent a counter-slice to your
hand. Hibben's big Parker knife is designed
for crushing skulls with the pommel, deflect-
ing and/or disarming a knife, and has a
heavy blade like a Bowie knife. Daggers are
a "sneak up and get him" knife.

Hibben Silver Shadow. Photo provided
by Gil and Linda Hibben.

There are some movements in the current version of Form Eight that
do not seem to consider what may happen after some of the cuts. Friends
in FMA have seen what most kenpoists do for application and have asked
why we would do something like position ourselves where we would

likely be sprayed with arterial blood. Or why we would switch hands in such a manner that the result is we still have a knife in each hand, which is where we started. I believe that the change from one form to another (the Seven I learned is not the same as the current version) added these moves, and maybe the transmission was not as accurate as it should have been. I was told that the original Seven was a "compliment" form, only being taught to a small few who Mr. Parker thought deserved it. The popular wisdom was that only seven were taught Seven. I have been told that by more than one person who knows the form. Huk Planas claims to have been one. When I asked why he didn't teach it to anyone, he replied that he "didn't know anyone worth teaching it to." Today there are plenty of instructors who can teach you a practical version.

Technique Sequence

The following was provided by Mr. John Sepulveda:

Twirling Lance

Finger Set

Destructive Lance

Shielding Lance

Flashing Lance

Snaking Lance

Hooking Lance

Slicing Lance

Deceptive Lance

Striking Lance

Protecting Lance

Thrusting Lance

Twisting Lance

Leaping Lance

Crossed Lance

Ending Moves

9.

The Sets

Mr. Parker told us that the forms and sets were designed to function like a dictionary, encyclopedia, or appendix. The sets, he said, are like an appendix; they contain additional, related information. I'd like to briefly cover what that information is.

Star Block

Typically one learns the Star Block, a.k.a. Blocking Set, as a beginner. This and the Finger Set are really isolations in that you stand in a horse as you work the hands and arms. The Star Block mainly shows how five major blocks and one hidden block are used in a flow and with zone changes. The back elbow is the hidden block, and the zones are the three horizontal ones (along with the basic Zone of Defense). The methods and angles of execution are reinforced and highlight Economy of Motion.

The inward block is interesting in that it's an anchoring inward, and we don't see that again until Form Four. Another way to look at it is that the first three moves are Lone Kimono components.

Regardless of how you do the set, you should run it with each hand, then both hands simultaneously. We then did it in reverse, single and both. Then you do one hand normally as the other runs in reverse. Then there's an offset timing version where you start the other hand two, three beats or more after the first. I have my students do it from a neutral bow as well as with foot maneuvers. I'll also throw a snap punch with a forward bow in between the blocks.

The objective is to gain familiarity with the blocks, develop speed and power, realize how the blocks match the zones, form the hands and arms, and exercise the brain with the body. This set will also be done with partners and can be done as an offensive striking drill, which requires a footwork angle change. These versions will provide the same benefits as doing the second set, those being majors and minors, dual movement (double factor), a more challenging coordination exercise, and timing changes.

Blocking Set Two adds stance changes, other blocks and combinations of blocks, reversals of sequence, and parries. Technically it's not a blocking set if there are parries.

Finger Set

Intermediate students learn this set. Many seem to think it's just to learn the hand formations, but there's a lot more. It is true that the fingers can do a tremendous amount of damage to an opponent but, conversely, they can be damaged easily. Bad formation of the natural weapon is usually the culprit, and that combines with the difficulty in hitting small moving targets such as the eyes.

The set really illustrates[15] angles and methods of delivery. All seven of the methods of delivery are used: hammer, thrust, whip, slice, roundhouse, hook, and claw. Single and dual usage are both shown, too.

It starts with thrusting methods delivered horizontally and vertically, palms up, in and down. The depth zones change as well, going from full extension to the obscure zone. Snapping follows along with the scissor, which is an interesting take on margin for error. This is followed by finger whips in the high and low zones.

Next we slice and rake. The use of finger surfaces being properly braced (slicing) and used in sequence (raking) with the proper travel and as an adjunct to a major strike is significant. I see many practitioners

---

15 I want to say "teaches" but the bulk of the hand formations should have been taught prior as part of the basics instruction.

do the slices improperly in that the hand is initially inverted to palm-down and that removes the brace. The rule is palm-up when going inward and palm-down, outward. The middle finger is then braced for impact since it is the primary weapon due to its being longer than the rest. Other formations slice with the palm down and moving inward, but there are subtleties in their formation in delivery that protect the hand. Raking is done following the roundhouse heel-palm to the jaw hinge. The sequential fingers to the eyes with the appropriate line, i.e., the rotation of the hand (inward line) or lack of (outward line), is what makes the rakes work.

Hammers follow with the claw formation. Since this is a finger set, the claw hand is used versus a heel-palm. The claw is unique and always uses the palm along with the fingers, which makes its own method of execution. Your hand should have an "iron ring" feel to it when the claw is right. Sloppily extending the fingers means your hand will meet the mass of the target while improperly formed. With your body momentum behind it and the likely use of borrowed force, that means everything will meet at your fingertips. If they are not right, they'll give, resulting in an ineffective strike or as much as broken fingers.

Hooking with two fingers to the eyes finishes the set. We do inward hooks in the set but outward inverted hooks were a favored Parker technique, and they're not shown. The major point on hooks compared to pokes is that hooks follow arcing paths while pokes are linear. We did the pokes at the start.

That completes what Mr. Parker outlined as the seven major methods of execution. See his *Infinite Insights into Kenpo, Volume 3*, for more on this. The three angles of execution, those being horizontal, vertical, and diagonal, are in the set along with using two and four fingers in a variety of ways, especially with double-factoring.

One of our system's seniors, Mr. Ron Chapel, speculates that when Mr. Parker took private lessons with Master Wong Ark-Yuey in Los Angeles, he may have gotten the set, or the idea of it, from him. There are Wing

Chun people who do a set very much like our Finger Set, too. They point out that the triangulation of the body and the natural weapons is the main idea. Mr. Chapel also mentioned that Ed Parker, when watching a film of himself doing the Finger Set, shuddered at his performance. I know the feeling, having had that experience watching myself doing forms in my early days. I saw the black-and-white 8mm film of Mr. Parker doing the set, and it was not executed in the manner he did it with me. Timing and zone placement of some of the moves were different. Mr. Parker picked up a lot of ideas by talking and "crossing hands" with many martial artists of many styles and systems. He was known to get an idea from someone, tweak it his way, and come up with a new technique. I dare say he could have done it with this set. I didn't think to ask him where it came from when I trained with him. It has been part of our system for many years and we need to understand it.

Finger Set Two

Often called the Moving Finger Set, that's just what this sequence does. It follows the basic hand pattern established in the Finger Set, with the addition of stances and foot maneuvers with the strikes. The warning I give on this is that you must watch to see that you don't break some basic rules as you move. I've seen people dropping rearward on some strikes without the proper timing, which detracts from power transfer. Their momentum is retreating as their strike is going forward, where the rearward movement should be to sink to set the base.

Striking Set(s)

The first Striking Set is useful in that the essence of what it teaches is possibilities of counters to counters. For example, in the first section you threw a straight punch and the opponent slaps it down, so you roll with it and turn it into a back-knuckle. The set covers the in/out/up/

down angle responses. "New" punches are practiced with an emphasis on being able to change lines quickly. The alternation and simultaneous punching segments are useful. Punching to the sides may be a new wrinkle for some, too.

When done to the sides, you use vertical punches instead of straight (as when you did the first sections). This is intelligent in that it considers how the shoulder moves when punching at that particular angle. If you do too many repetitions with a lot of power, and deliver the wrong punches, you can hurt the shoulder over time. The use of sequential and simultaneous timings is helpful as well, although I'm not convinced that doing it with your feet together has much value, as is called for at the close of the set.

The second set emphasizes elbows. There are some forearms and even an eye poke. The set puts together some combinations that you would find in the self-defense techniques and, like some of the other sets, doesn't really give you anything you wouldn't have elsewhere and may even be overly repetitious.

Two-Man Set (Black Belt Set)

I address this now because I broached the subject of adapted sets in our system when I wrote that Ed Parker may have gotten the Finger Set structure from someone else. Mr. Parker told me he thought that the Two-Man Set was taught to Professor Chow by his father. I've seen other systems do a two-man set that looks much like ours, and that makes me believe it was indeed a kung-fu set that has been "kenpoized."

This set is seen in Ed Parker's 1963 book, *Secrets of Chinese Karate*. In our system it is also called Black Belt Set because you learned it as a black-belt requirement. It's not complete in the book in that some moves that are done with two hands are shown with only one. I asked about that and Mr. Parker told me he did it that way so he could tell if someone learned the set from the book. If they had all the correct movements, those that were not shown in the book, he said he would know it was taught by "an authorized instructor" (his words).[16]

Most Chinese systems have at least one two-man set. They show how the solo routines could be done with a partner—in other words, there is application for the "dance steps." The main idea of ours is to show how important range (distance) is and to give an arena for Kenpo practitioners to practice adjusting to different-size partners. The focus of the set is on footwork. It also shows some of the exotic basics applications you don't see elsewhere, such as inverted web and thumb strikes, vertical upward parries, etc. There appears to be a lot of latitude in how the set is done (i.e., it seems to vary widely), with some preferring a harder version and adding the *kiai,* others using a softer flow. Some do it as prescribed and others like to put in more checks and inserts.

Two-Man Set has a lot of value gained in the effort to coordinate with a partner, and it makes a great demonstration or competition set.

Stance Set(s)

Which one? The first I learned was almost identical to the one shown in *Secrets of Chinese Karate.* I learned it from Mike Sanders, who called it "Chinese Leg Maneuvers." I have not been able to verify its origin. The versions today are very different. The focus on the set, obviously, is to practice forming the stances properly in a flow while advancing or retreating. The technical definition of a stance is that it is a frozen transition. That fact that you have to move to get to it means you are doing a maneuver. Therefore, I can see the value of calling it Chinese Leg Maneuvers. Put that aside as being a little too technical and accept that we're running the variety of stances without the "distraction" of arm movements. See my earlier comments on isolations starting in the chapter on Long Form One, and more in the chapters on Long Forms Two, Three, and above.

---

16 I met a senior Shotokan instructor in Germany who taught the set and said he got it from "the red book." Early editions of *Secrets* had a primarily red cover; others were yellow. I have one in French that has the yellow cover.

Originally it was done with hands placed on your hips. Today's versions have hand movements incorporated. Since they are stance sets, I think the original way places the focus where it should be. The forms are stances with handwork, so the student works for upper/lower body coordination. Without using the hands, the set is a great study in footwork transitions and provides a means of developing leg strength and flexibility while maintaining an anchored center. The set I first learned had different stances with today's names; a close kneel then was not the same as what we do now. In fact, I learned from Sanders that what we call a neutral today was not what they used to call a neutral. I think that may explain why some Kenpo schools teach a stance that looks like a neutral but may be called some version of a horse.

Kicking Set(s)

The Kicking Set as we know it today was developed by the late Mr. Tom Kelly, also known as *Sibok,* one of Mr. Parker's senior students. The set is constructed to show that one can step, shuffle, cross over, and spin with the kicks. The four kicks used are front, side, back, and roundhouse—our beginner-level kicks. You'll do them right and left in their variations for a total of twenty-four kicks.

Mr. Kelly used a four-sided box pattern for the set. This allowed incorporation of 90° angle changes, which means it takes a lot of space. For that reason, many instructors do the four sides in lines so the student travels along a 6:00–12:00 line, using the 180° cover to change direction.

While one of the main ideas is to show how, for example, a front kick can be done with a step-through, crossover, or shuffle, when he worked with us on it Kelly emphasized proper chambering, delivery, and recovery. His point on recovery was that you set your kicking leg down in a cat stance. This anticipated that an opponent was very likely to try to sweep the foot as it sits down. If you don't retract your leg properly, the weight and momentum tend to pull you forward and make it hard to plant without being in danger of the sweep, much less have margin for error to throw a different kick. In addition, he said that putting the foot down in the cat and sliding it forward to the neutral bow gave you that contact with the ground for stability and the aforementioned margin for error.

If you watch carefully, especially in many online videos, you'll see an extra step prior to the kick being delivered. The front foot turns out first and telegraphs the kick, increasing the probability that the opponent will see it coming. That foot should not turn until your body says it has to, which unifies the turn and increases power. Do the turn too late and over time it's bad for your knees.

In the early 1980s, when the system got rearranged, or resequenced, updated, modernized (pick your term), other kicking sets got integrated. Other kicks were used such as scoop and chicken kicks. It's the same idea as the original set, just more to remember and practice.

Coordination Set(s)

This set was originally required to move up to purple belt. It has two "sides" like some of the forms, those being a right and left side. There are five sections, the odd number being required to bring you back to the direction you started from. That's the same reason many systems have three repetitions of a move in a form.

This set reinforces the major/minor principle and shows how to attack all three horizontal zones. What is a stand-out within it is the last movement of each section in which you sit back as you punch forward. This would seem to break the rule of not moving back as you strike forward; however, it really is an example of the standard-oppose principle. That is the idea of opposite force, or yin/yang. The move is the same as one in which you would buckle as you strike, as in Dominating Circles. Once again, the lower-level sets and forms don't require an application. They are examples of how to move. Much of what this set does is in the One forms such as torqueing, moving forward and back, and majors/

minors. In addition, it shows how to change from defense to offense, like the Two forms, along with using opposite sides and/or hands and feet, simultaneously.

What is really good about this set and its variations such as Coordination Set Two is that it forces one to face the four walls. This throws off many students due to the change in orientation. As in the second side of Short One, Long One, and Short Three, the set is intended to force the brain to work versus going on automatic, in rote repetition. As I have written elsewhere, starting your forms facing the walls as well as corners is a great way to break the habit of having to always face one particular direction and to ensure that you really are better familiarized with the form.

The Coordination Set has a base in a stationary drill in which the same moves are done, only in a training horse. This drill doesn't seem to be done much anymore, but it's a good teaching tool if a student isn't getting the moving set due to the increased complexity of having to move the feet and change directions. This drill can be seen on my video site, www. wedlakekenpotv.com, in the drills section.

Coordination Set Two works the simultaneous aspect much more and requires better balance and counter-balancing movements. The addition of more movement in opposite directions and the timing changes make it a challenge.

Staff Set

The Staff Set is a weapon set using the long staff. In the Japanese and Okinawan arts it is called a *bo*. Some Kenpo schools insist on the set being called the "Bo Staff Set," which is like saying the "Staff Staff Set."

Chinese martial artists refer to the staff as "The King of the Weapons." This is due to its versatility and how many other weapons spring from it, such as a spear or halberd. The standard Japanese/Okinawan staff is almost six feet long (5.9 feet), while the Chinese staff is proportioned to the user, the exceptions being the nine-foot or longer staves. Mr. Parker told me the staff should measure from the ground up to the eyebrows, which is in line with both the tailoring concept of his Kenpo and the Chinese using the height of the practitioner, often called the "body ruler."

He made no mention to me about the material it should be made of. Stay away from the soft woods like pine since they break too easily and are dangerous when they do because they shear and have a nasty, ragged point. There is a vaulting movement in the set in which one supports all the body weight on the staff similar to what a pole-jumper does, and I've seen a staff break. It's easy to imagine being impaled. Stick with the standard materials used today to avoid this. I have a laminated staff of two woods made for me by woodworker Jeff Lewis in West Palm Beach, Florida, and it has stood the test of time. Today the suppliers sell weapons made of shiny and lightweight materials in order that they can be manipulated faster than a heavier weapon and catch the light to make your presentation flashy. They've catered to the younger and smaller students in that they are available in more variety of lengths and thicknesses, too.

The standard *bo* is tapered, that is, it is thicker in the middle than at the ends. The Chinese weapon may be tapered but is usually the same diameter along its length. The *bo* is tapered in order to focus more energy in a smaller contact area, much like a middle-knuckle strike transfers all the force of a straight punch but in one knuckle. You can certainly use a tapered staff for our set but the "traditional" one is not.

Speaking of traditional, where did this set come from? There was another, lengthier Chinese staff set taught in the first Ed Parker school in Pasadena. I've seen a video of it. Mr. Chuck Sullivan, one of the first black belts to come out of the Pasadena school, learned it there. The tribal knowledge of our system tells us that what we know as Staff Set was created by Mr. Sullivan; however, he told me personally that he based it on that longer form, taking out the bulk of the repetition to condense it. He said he took a chance and showed Mr. Parker what he had done and says he was told by him, "We'll use that." Therefore, it's correct that he created the Staff Set as it's known in Kenpo today.

Sets using the staff are generally considered to be either single-end or double-end. That's a confusing label since the staff obviously has two ends. What it refers to is the primary method of motion. The Chinese staff is seen to have more spinning and changing of the grip than its more linear Japanese/Okinawan cousin. The Kenpo staff falls into the double-end staff category.

As I was coming up through the ranks as a tournament competitor I heard hard-stylists refer to "baton twirlers," a reference to those who could manipulate a staff or nunchakus but seemed to be missing the requisite knowledge of application. I know from working with a staff combatively and by hitting a bag with one that certain movements look flashy but will often result in disarming yourself. Rebound, angle and method of delivery, grip, and timing are critically important. Even using a weapon of the wrong material makes a difference. The Filipino arts mention "dead" and "live" sticks when conveying how they feel when contact is made. There's a reason why rattan is used for practice with both a stick and a staff. Too hard of a material has a very hard feedback, one that rattles your teeth. When I trained with Danny Inosanto, we did staff *sinawalli* patterns, and the type of material makes a difference. It also gave me an appreciation for combative use of the staff. When I was young and crazy we would put on hockey gear and freestyle with the staff. That contributed to my understanding of application of the striking moves in the set.

When I first learned the set in an offshoot Kenpo school, there was no such thing as application for the moves, so we were the aforementioned "baton twirlers." None of the background information I have written here was given, either. I was fortunate to be able to work with many others at the Pasadena school where we could compare versions, and to get instruction on application from Huk Planas and *Sibok* Tom Kelly. It gave the set much more meaning and value. What I got from them were the counters to the attempts to grab the staff, use of contouring, and how to set up an opponent for the strikes.

I've seen countless versions of the set, from baton twirling to strong, positive executions. I won a lot of trophies running it in weapons divisions and attribute that to acquiring a good base on the principles in the set versus just knowing how to swing it around. Like any other form or set, if you have a good knowledge and execution of basics, this set will be better. There is a lot of nuance, starting with the salutation and running throughout. I don't think this set gets much attention. I believe that's because we have so much material to work on aside from this, and the set becomes kind of an adjunct. It takes space, is not easily done in groups, and more than one mirror has been broken from someone losing their grip. It's not concealable and you probably don't use one as a walking stick or to carry buckets of water. Its practicality is low, and with limited time we tend to spend it working other material. You have to stay on top of it or your proficiency slips, it being a perishable skill like your other material, only more so. On the plus side, it's good for the head-work, for competition and demonstration, has useful information, and one could use a broomstick or the like in self-defense.

In some schools a similar set called Spear Set was taught. I learned it and found it to be somewhat interesting although it's a pretty fundamental set and not Kenpo. A spear is just a staff with a point on the end, but you do need to know that you can't simply manipulate it as a staff; that point also has an edge and that's a need-to-know item.

10.

Capstone: The Thesis

Years ago there was an IKKA requirement for a candidate for first-degree black to write a thesis, ten pages, single-spaced. The subject was to be determined by the student in both consultation and agreement with the instructor. Educational background was taken into consideration. In addition, the candidate would create a physical thesis form.

There were several reasons for this. It is a mechanism for an instructor to see what comes out of what was put in. Did the student really integrate the concepts, principles, methods of motion, etc., and can he or she demonstrate that they really understand Kenpo? How well did they express that understanding? Did the student gain any appreciation for the efforts of those who had gone before, in many styles and systems, in the context of what is involved in creating such a work? What did the student really learn from their experience in the journey from white to black? It's said that two books were published that were originally a student's written thesis and thus contributed to our system—one on medical implications and the other on the nunchaku.

Ed Parker looked at this as being like a doctoral thesis, which must be created and defended. In our American educational system today we have the Capstone, a project or paper that demonstrates what one has learned in a program, similar to or the same as a thesis approved for those working to gain an advanced degree. Unfortunately for Kenpo, both the physical and written theses seem to have fallen by the wayside. I have seen many exams given without either of those requirements being met. Weighing both the physical performance and the thesis requirements, there are more of the physical being done than the written. I never wrote a thesis, but I was writing numerous magazine articles on the system and I like to think Mr. Parker was substituting that for the standard requirement. I also prefer to think that my books suffice as well for contributions to our knowledge base.

While many people have dropped the thesis requirement, others have made it optional, some have made it required for levels from blue belt and up, and some make it an either/or (choose the written, or physical, or both). I've done most of those variations and found that a thesis for black just has to be done, and most of my black belts elect to do a written thesis along with the form, since I give them a choice. It's a sticking point for brown belts, and many a green belt just gave up. Same for those going for blue and green belts. That's not so good for a commercial school. I'd make it optional for them since you'll get a good one once in a while who just loves to create stuff, so let them have at it.

I've had some cocky brown belts challenge the black thesis on the grounds that they already did one for brown. They missed the point. The black thesis demands that they not only make an original form, but develop original techniques to comprise that form—and both right-handed and left. The brown thesis as we do it now requires original techniques as well, but only ten instead of thirteen. The point is that good research is founded on sound results from past research. This is not just a matter of grafting techniques together, which is fine and has value. This requires a lot of thought—logical thought—and experimentation on a willing partner. Again, consultation with the instructor will yield much. Developing a thesis is an extremely fruitful endeavor when done as intended.

The Basic Thesis Form

There exist many people who are very creative and more who do not know they are. Creating a form can be a marvelous experience for them, discovering that ability. We have seen a wide range of ideas. I would like to discuss some used in the creation of these forms.

Mr. Parker felt it important that a student realize what it takes to put a form together in a logical manner. He mandated thesis forms for brown and black belt. Today some schools have every rank do this. That may be a bit much for a yellow belt, but it works for intermediate levels and above. The requirements were written down in an IKKA handout. The physical thesis required the candidate for black to create not only the form, but all the techniques within it. It's simpler for the lower ranks.

A basic thesis form covers the eight angles, walls and corners, to demonstrate an understanding of those angles. Other patterns are acceptable but are usually shown when creating a later thesis. This is comparable to doing the cross pattern in the One forms, and the overlaid X in the Two forms.

It's recommended that students graft standard techniques together to make their first thesis form. It's an easier way of introducing the concept of the thesis and helps to guarantee a greater measure of success. There are two approaches to this. One is to allow the student to take their eight or ten favorite techniques and string them together. People tend to practice things they like and avoid those they don't. Once again, it helps guarantee success. Alternately, having them do their least favorite techniques serves two purposes. First, it will strengthen those techniques. Second, it builds a discipline to do things that we really would rather avoid. That's part of character-building.

Students will typically then write down those techniques and try to run them in order, working to the eight angles. Most times that won't work. The big sticking point is the same as with the standard forms—the transitions. They will need help in getting from the end of one technique to the start of the next. The positions and angles throw them off. This is when they ask if they can add things to the technique. Great! They're making the technique fit the situation instead of making the situation fit the technique. Let them do whatever is needed to make it work as long as it's logical. They'll add chicken kicks, ground maneuvers, etc. As long as they have a reason with a good application, and the checks are there, what else do they need?

If the sequence still isn't working for them I suggest they run the list in reverse. That appears to change everything. Another way is to do technique numbers 1, 3, 5, 7, 9 and then 2, 4, 6, 8, 10. It shakes things up and students may see the opportunity they were looking for to make it work. Simple stuff but really helpful.

Personally, I like to build sequences with transitions that keep me from turning my back to the opponent and prevent stepping over him. Stomping on him is a different story. Other instructors don't agree, and both ways are fine. The objective is to get the students to develop the qualities I mentioned and to get the job done.

The Intermediate Thesis Form

I think it's cheating to take the basic form and build on it. I think the intermediate level is where we create the techniques as well as the form. I'd accept building the next level on this level, and I tell my students that this thesis form is a head start on the black-level thesis.

In the intermediate levels students will typically choose a group of techniques they like. Some techniques just feel good right away; they are "yours." People do what they like, so it is no surprise they do this. If the student asks an instructor for guidance and listens carefully, he or she may incorporate techniques that they do not do very well or don't like. The benefits of the exercise of creating the form will not diminish if using techniques that are not yours yet. The occasional student understanding this message will group their weak or even left-sided techniques into a form. This gives them the opportunity to improve those techniques and increase their understanding. The selection of a theme is generally limited, by the student, to these two ideas. Some will expand the ideas to those found at higher levels.

The brown-belt thesis consisted of ten original techniques, both sides. The term "both sides" here refers to the opposite side of a technique. If you do the standard technique Five Swords right-handed, the opposite side would be left-handed. The candidate chooses an attack scenario, takes components from their repertoire, and builds a self-defense technique. Frequent consultation with the instructor guides development. The instructor offers ideas and suggests alternatives based on the rules and principles of motion. Students often are not consistent in application and inadvertently leave gaps in their defense. Being students, they may also not have a firm grasp of what works in the real world. Although the techniques are simulations, they still must work in realistic situations.

The basic level got them introduced to the transition solutions. And as my Taiji teacher Tom Baeli likes to say, "The information is in the transitions." You're going to see more of the standard base techniques expanded on. It's not too hard to see the base moves within the techniques that the student creates. Yes, that's true of the things you'll see in the future, but not as much. This is the level at which the students often come to the teacher and say, "I can't do anything. Everything has already been done." We can help them by showing that the rearrangement principle is vital. I like to tell them that although there are only twenty-six letters in our alphabet, every day there are new writings published. It's just the rearrangement principle in action. Once they realize that they will naturally repeat learned basics—it's how they put them together that makes it theirs.

Gary Ellis, an excellent Kenpo practitioner in England, uses the analogy of a singer. The good ones have passion and they communicate it to the audience. Others can sing the words and hit the notes, but there is little or no life to it. Imagine your favorite singer doing your favorite song in a monotone. It's that infusion of passion that helps grab us and bring it to life, and it's the same with what we do in expressing ourselves through Kenpo. Everyone should have seen a performance of the arts that is just electrifying. It's inspiring, motivating, entertaining, and captivating. That's what we're looking for.

There is no doubt this project will take some time. Students are going to have to pick a theme or theme(s), lay out the roadmap of directions, and get to creating the techniques. Then they have to practice it enough to impress their peers and seniors and describe what they learned from the experience.

Creating the Techniques

This is second to developing a theme for the form. Once the theme is decided, the techniques will logically follow. Over the years I have seen many a creatively done thesis form. They have included fighting from the ground, barroom techniques, use of a briefcase, defending with only one arm, use of the stick, two-man defenses, and many laid out in the standard of defending against dead, semi-live, live, or combination attacks.

Once the attacks are chosen, the student will have to develop the defensive sequence and memorize it. At this point they should come to an instructor and get input on how well it works. Most times the instructor will seemingly tear the technique apart. This is a great time to learn something. While the mechanics may be right, it may be pointed out that alternate targets, weapons, or timing could be better used within the sequence. It often occurs that the student has developed a great technique (sometimes good enough to borrow for ourselves) but is using it for the wrong attack. I've seen many a technique they said they developed for a right punch that works even better for a left. It is these points in time that are helpful not only to the student but to the teacher. It gets us looking for alternatives, as it does for the student.

The techniques should be tested on partners to see if what you visualized and created actually works. Adjustments and changes are now made. You may even junk the technique and start over. Then the technique should be tested for holes, obvious openings in the defense. It should also be tested for ambidexterity. That is, it works for a straight right punch— does it work for a left without modification? This is not mandatory. It serves to open your eyes as to "sidedness" of techniques.

Once the techniques are created, you begin to lay them out in a pattern. The pattern can be whatever you want; it just needs to be justified.

You should not do anything like this randomly. It defeats the purpose of the exercise, which is to gain insight into what people before you did and why. I like to see intermediate students demonstrate an understanding of the eight angles presented to them in their early forms. I look for the lines and angles. If they are missing, I ask why to see what the student was thinking. Advanced and expert students use all sorts of patterns. We see lines, circles, the cross, X, and star pattern. But they all have a reason for using these patterns.

A note to the instructor: At this point the student is now an artist and that creation is their baby. No wonder they get a bit defensive when it is critiqued. That is to be expected, so keep this in mind during the process. There will be techniques that get scrapped, but most will make the cut with some guidance. If most of what you are getting is impractical, and you get it from most of the students, it might be a reflection of your teaching style. You may know what you're doing as a practitioner but may be having a problem getting it across. In fact, when a student fails at something, good instructors look at themselves to see where they could have done a better job. Yes, there are those students who just don't get it. They should be few and far between. When one of my candidates came to me and said he had a thesis technique ready to show me, I was disappointed to see that all he did was Delayed Sword with a back-knuckle instead of a chop. When I pointed that out he responded with "Oh. Yeah." He clearly didn't get it. But the next ninety-nine students came up with something good.

Once it seems the technique is working well, the advice of an instructor should be sought again. By now it's clear that this entire process should be a combined effort, the student working with the teacher along the way. Working it all out alone and then presenting it is usually a recipe for failure. Be assured that the people who developed reliable martial-art applications didn't do them alone; they had to try them on someone and get advice from more experienced people. You should do the same.

Application of Kenpo principles should go without saying. Mixing in elements of other arts the student knows will be appropriate if done logically. Sometimes people get so excited about being creative that they innovate themselves right out of the system. Ed Parker's ideas (but not all his ideas) are encapsulated in the system, and rolling around on the ground during a two-man attack wasn't one of them. However, if you are an excellent kicker with some tae kwon do experience and use it the way a Kenpo person would, fine.

When it comes time to demonstrate the form, you should be ready to explain and demonstrate each and every move as well as the theme and what you learned from the experience. Expect to perform your form just as well as standard forms, if not better—after all, it's YOURS! Remember, too, that nobody can help you if you get stuck. They don't know the form.

The Advanced Thesis Form

At the black-belt level more is expected from the candidate. The techniques should be well thought-out and practical. They will be consistent in principle. A formulation of previously introduced material should be presented that demonstrates an understanding of what Kenpo is about.

The requirement was written as being thirteen original techniques done on both sides. That means the candidate built thirteen techniques from scratch and did them right- and left-handed, even the two-hand attacks. That's a total of 26 sequences. This is expected to have black-belt knowledge and ability demonstrated. The process started before brown belt should make this relatively painless and highly educational. The most-heard comment from candidates at this level is about how the thesis work makes them appreciate just how much it took our predecessors to develop the forms of any system, and how impressive it is that they have lasted for many, many years. Ed Parker's Kenpo has only been around since the 1950s, which makes it a blip in the history of unarmed combat. For us to keep from simply disappearing off the screen we need to perpetuate ourselves through this art by keeping to its rules and principles, and adjusting as necessary to survive.

If techniques against non-standard attacks haven't been done in prior forms, they should be now. Suggestions include defenses for two-hand and/or rear hair grabs, inverted wrist grabs, defense from a seated position, working with your back against a wall, three- or four-man attacks, handgun in the "thug" grip, etc. I'm not saying the form should be composed exclusively of non-standard attacks but it should have some.

It is now more common to see the candidate present other ideas. Everyone has moves and sequences they prefer. It is important to break out of those on occasion and to develop ways to enter and exit those moves (prefix/suffix). There is a wide array of ideas to be used in the creation of a form. Some thesis forms have been dedicated to one attack, like right punches and the ways to handle that. Other common themes are defenses against kicks, clubs, combinations, pushes, and multiple attackers. Here are a few different ones.

Environmental consideration—the candidate specified he was in a close area, like a bar. Another carried a briefcase most of the time, so he developed techniques with it. He had a nomenclature and basics list as well. Position was included in one thesis done on the ground. Body momentum is used in everything, but one candidate included board-breaking during his form to show the power. Master knife maker Gil Hibben threw knives for his thesis to demonstrate the control, power, and possible methods of using the knife. My third-degree thesis included techniques when against a wall. Consult with your instructor and be creative!

Spontaneous Form

While not a thesis or a set pattern, a spontaneous form satisfies the definitions of a form. Skip Hancock of Spokane, Washington, used to compete in forms doing an extemporaneous sequence of Kenpo techniques. You use the principles, timing, visualization, and other qualities in a totally unplanned manner. It's explosive, somewhat unpredictable, and cannot be recreated.

I do this from time to time and it's a challenging exercise. Give it a try.

Author's note: This article is for discussion and educational purposes only. Nothing contained within it is presented as legal advice and should not be construed or relied upon as such. Anyone with questions regarding the law and its application to specific circumstances should consult a private attorney.

When Mr. Wedlake asked me to write a short essay on weapons defense legal issues, I was of course honored. Mr. Wedlake is the head of our system and has been my teacher, my friend, and a fellow aviator for many years. The book itself covers in great detail the technical and tactical aspects of Form Six. My dissertation concerns itself with the aftermath, i.e., you have been physically attacked by someone brandishing a weapon. You have defended (divert, seize, control, and disarm) successfully. You now have the weapon and the attacker under control. The question that I put to you is—How will you manage the situation as it develops?

Before you can answer intelligently, there are some things you need to know.

1. You must know the state of the law relating to self-defense in your jurisdiction.
2. You must understand that ignorance of that law is not an excuse or defense.

Jurisdictions differ in the law and its application, but generally you may use "reasonable" force in self-defense. You may only use deadly force if you are in "reasonable" (that word again) fear of death or great personal injury. Note: A full exposition of the law relating to self-defense is well beyond the scope of this general discussion, but you can see that knowing the law in your jurisdiction can be vital to your health, finances, and freedom. A very important concept in the law is the issue of "what is reasonable" concerning the use of force. Martial arts practitioners and

341

others (certain military specialties, security professionals, and police, to name a few) are held to a higher standard under the law when defining "reasonable" as it applies to a situational use of force and control. This is due to their perceived higher level of training.

Think About It

Who is the attacker, and what is the weapon? Would you use the same level of force and control on an old lady attacking you with a broom that you would on a thug with a gun?

So, back to the scenario. You are now in possession of the weapon—let's say it's a gun. The attacker has been immobilized or is otherwise compliant. By definition then, you are probably NOT in "reasonable" fear of death or great injury at this point. If you gave in to the feelings of anger, fear, and excitement resulting from the attack and shot him, could you be charged with one or more serious crimes? Arguably, you could. Moreover, even if you avoid criminal prosecution, you may still be liable for damages in a civil suit. What to do, what to do, what now?

I'm sure you realize there is no one right answer to the scenario issue. Even if there were, change the facts slightly and the answer would change. My own personal mantra for such situations is "less is better." By that I mean when able, use restraint in the application of the force required to maintain control of the attacker, the situation, and the weapon. Put another way: use all the force necessary, but only what's necessary.

Consider also: retreat if you can do so safely, call for help and medical attention if needed, and control the weapon as required.

None of this should be construed to mean that you shouldn't do what you think you have to do to defend against a weapons attack or any attack, for that matter. I believe Mr. Parker himself said, "It is better to be judged by twelve than carried by six." But in the aftermath, measured restraint consistent with the evolving facts of the situation will go a long way toward ensuring that those who judge you through the prism of 20/20 hindsight will find your actions "reasonable."

Appendix: General Rules (or Principles) of Motion

Instructors will give their students some general rules or principles of motion with which to work. As an example: for writing understandably in the English language, one rule is "I before E except after C." Kenpo is a language of motion. If you wish to be physically understood, you apply the Kenpo rules of motion. General rules are especially helpful in being self-correcting, what Mr. Parker often said he wanted us to be. Here is an example.

You go home to practice a new technique. You find that you cannot remember which stance to be in when you strike. You find yourself hitting with the front hand in a forward bow, which steals the power, and your body tells you something is not right. The general rule used here is "Front hand neutral, rear hand forward." You apply the rule, find your mistake (or vice versa), and correct it. Here is a list of some general rules. These will not make much sense to the uninitiated but will to anyone who has taken even a few lessons.

Rule Number One: Establish your base. This is primary in any system or activity. Without a strong base, everything else tends to not work as well. This applies to physical motion and to your knowledge base. As we teach beginners in a horse stance to widen, deepen, and strengthen their base, one should do the same for the mind and spirit.

"Always" means 99% of the time. Some rules are bent, not broken, but "bending" too much results in introducing another rule, I believe. Circumstances may dictate a departure from a rule. See the "New Hand" rule in Short Form One for an example.

Anchor your elbows. "When your elbows are in, you'll win. When they're out, there's some doubt." I first heard this quote from California's Howard Silva. Having your elbows out affects your breathing too.

Finish a pattern before starting a new pattern. Note the cross pattern established in Short One. See it overlaid in Short Two. You do the cross before the angles, thus finishing the pattern before starting the new one.

No two transitions are the same. You may find yourself in the opposite cat stance, but the way you got there is not the same as how you got in the first one. Sometimes the differences are very subtle.

The new hand goes in front. Exceptions are made under certain conditions, an example being when using a weapon. Look for others.

Blocks oppose force, parries ride force. Block with a closed hand, parry with an open hand.

Start on the strong side. This refers to the right side, since most people are right-handed. All the primary forms start with the right hand, a hammering inward block. Forms Three, Four, Five, and Six all commence with right-handed techniques. There are left-sided forms, if that makes you lefties feel any better. Short One, Long One, and Short Three were the left-handed forms we practiced. Some people have expanded on that to the other forms. Try the Finger Set starting with your left hand, or in reverse, for that matter.

The lower body sets the speed of the upper body. Many of us say "Speed Kills," meaning speed kills power since the upper and lower body can get out of sync when one moves too fast. Arms inherently move faster than legs, so you need to time them together.

Corollary: You only do the forms as fast as you can do them right. During group forms practice, the group ideally goes only as fast as the slowest person does. If the group gets away from you, do it at your own speed anyway—don't try to keep up. You'll normally be moving too fast to do it right if you try to keep up.

Front hand, neutral. Rear hand, forward. Both hands, either. Use a neutral bow when using your front hand. Use a forward bow when using your rear hand. Use either, depending on range, when using both together. Too often people use the rear hand without turning their body. Sometimes that's good, most times it's bad. It kills the reach and power when you don't. It's bad for your joints over the long term, as well.

When stepping forward, block with the same hand as the side you step with. When stepping back, block with the opposite hand.

When blocking inside, contact below the hinge (elbow); when blocking outside, make contact above the hinge.

Step directly when retreating. The first step back in Short One demonstrates this. Using this rule prevents extra movement that may actually take you closer to an opponent while in transition. Sometimes you want that, most times you don't—especially when working with the obscure zone.

Keep your center of gravity low as you move. Bobbing up and down is not what we do. There are exceptions—see the "99%" rule (above, second rule listed). There is a "float" technique in Short Three to show when/how to do that. Your center generally stays level or sinks.

Pain and realistic reaction are what make the techniques work. Remember this when working on the body in forms application practice.

Lower your stance when striking downward. Take advantage of gravitational marriage by adding it to the torque and/or back-up mass of your strike.

Finish a technique with your strong side.

Shuffles go where they are needed.

When using a knee strike, you should not be able to maintain balance; your momentum should carry you normally through the movement. You always bend the support leg for stability.

The "inside rule": When working on the inside, always break the opponent's height zone. It's a really good idea to break their posture regardless of what entry you use.

Use your elbows when too close to punch.

Every block position is a cocked position.

Strike high, check low. Strike low, check high.

Every move, concept, principle, or definition has an opposite and a reverse.

Stomp rule: Lift your foot three times the depth of the target. This helps ensure sufficient travel to cause damage, which is an example of economy of motion. If the target is three inches deep, lift to nine, then stomp. An average body is 10–12 inches thick, requiring a cocking distance of 30 to 36 inches. You may not be able to cock that high, but in the attempt you will get considerable travel and have the desired effect.

Standard oppose: Also known as opposing forces. It's what you learn on Day One with punching. One goes back as the other goes forward. Yin and Yang. It's an application of one of Newton's Laws of Motion—"Every action has an equal and opposite reaction."

Double cover outs are used to get a 360° view of the area. They're not just for show.

Don't lock your elbows. It can result in tennis elbow, an inflammation of the lubricating sacs (called bursa) in the elbow. The pain lasts for some time, usually months. Constant locking can be bad for your elbows over the long term, and you may regret it as you age. In addition, somebody like us might find it's easier to break your arm when it's straight. Don't give them the chance.

Keep your wrists straight. This is the converse of the previous rule. We do bend them in some situations, such as when using a thrusting chop as in Parting Wings or with a claw or heel-palm. However, you sure don't want them bent when you punch or block. The alignment won't support the impact. Remember, these are *general* rules.

Compact units are necessary to transmit force and prevent injury to self. This is an element of the above two rules on joint position.

Buckle at or just above the knee from the front, below from the back.

Borrowed force has borrowed reach. Borrowed reach doesn't have borrowed force.

Keep your eyes on the opponent. Maybe not a rule of motion but important.

Relax. Ed Parker said, "Tension is an intermission in relaxation." Breathe. Attempt to be conscious of this in all aspects of your life.

More General Rules, Pertaining to Weapons

The four rules in the weapons techniques are Divert, Seize, Control, and Disarm.

Keep the gun barrel pointed away from you at all times.

Keep the tip of the knife pointed away from you as much as possible.

Handle practice weapons as if they are real.

(EP) refers to a definition by Ed Parker; (HP) refers to a definition by Huk Planas

Accumulative Journal—Ed Parker's "Red Book," a notebook that a student would buy to hold manuals and other paperwork. As you progressed through the ranks you would *accumulate* the technique requirement booklets, which were written descriptions of techniques, etc. It was called "the manual" as well and was the forerunner of today's manuals, which are now into the 3.0 and higher versions. The system was written down about 1969–70 by Ed Parker, Tom Kelly, and Huk Planas. The technique booklets were marked with a copyright dated 1970. The manuals had coded alphanumeric markings and were also color-coded. The manual was rewritten and the curriculum reduced from thirty-two techniques per belt to twenty-four circa 1981, and later versions were largely based on that rewrite.

Angle of cancellation—an angle that closes one or more zones to prevent follow-up or retaliation. (EP)

Angle of deflection—the degree of deflection caused in a block, parry, or in the riding action of the body to dissipate energy. This may be your body or the opponent's. (EP)

Angle of incidence—the 90° (or perpendicular) angle of contact of a punch or strike. (EP)

Attack categories—generally they are "dead," "semi-live," and "live." "Dead" refers to grabs, "semi-live" to pushes, and "live" to punches, kicks, and weapons. (EP)

Back-up mass—the body momentum produced when the body weight moves in line with the strike, whether forward or back, changing depth. When used on the vertical or diagonal downward plane(s) is it called Marriage of Gravity or Gravitational Marriage, as it changes height and adds the power of gravity to the move. Back-up mass is introduced in the Two forms. (EP)

Body english—refers to moving with a strike but not so much that it requires a stance change. Rocking forward or to the side to engage your back-up mass without a shuffle is an example. (HP)

Borrowed force—the use of an opponent's force to defeat them. It may be used going against or with their force. Since momentum can be generated in three dimensions, we can use any or all of them in either way. Borrowed force always includes borrowed reach. (EP)

Borrowed reach—forcing a target into range but altering the timing to delay your follow-up. The delay eliminates the borrowed-force component, since momentum is allowed to stop. Borrowed reach does not include borrowed force.

Code words—an Ed Parker creation to label techniques to create an image in the mind, allowing the practitioner to more easily visualize the technique sequence. It is the reason for the "funny names" of our techniques. For our use here, wing is an elbow, twig is an arm, hoof is the foot, spear indicates a finger thrust, talon is a wrist grab. Probably based on the Oriental penchant for techniques having poetic names like "White crane cools its wings" or "Carry tiger, return to mountain."

Counter-rotation torque—when the body rotates in the opposite direction of the natural weapon. An example would be stepping back with your left foot and doing a right outward block, either a vertical or extended.

Directional harmony—when the total mass of the body moves in a single direction. (EP)

Direct-rotation torque—when the body (or its parts) rotate in the same direction as the natural weapon.

Double factor—entails dual movements of defense, which can incorporate any combination of blocks, parries, and checks. Also refers to sophisticated moves that are dually defensive and offensive. Involves the utilization of reversing motion as an answer in defending or attacking—thus opposite as well as reverse motion, since both supply answers in combat. (EP)

Dual movement—a sub-category of double factor. There is a difference in double-factoring by using two moves simultaneously, and using two moves in half-beat timing.

False travel—When the natural weapon looks like it is moving a lot but is, in reality, moving only inches. An example would be an inward elbow strike in which the hand does most of the movement (much like a hook punch), while the elbow travels very little. It's high intensity, but low yield. The elbow has false travel. The hand should be the center of rotation, with the elbow moving around the circumference.

Form—a short story of motion. These motions are offensive and defensive maneuvers incorporated into a dance for purposes of learning, home training, and exercise. They are usually done without a partner. (EP)

Head snap—a movement used by competitors to make a soft move look strong by suddenly snapping the head from one direction to another, sometimes seen in Protecting Fans or in the leg break in Escape from the Storm.

Isolation—a "signpost" of things left out, preview of things to come, additional related information. These are typically done in a horse stance. Having no motion of the lower body draws attention to what the hands, arms, and upper body are doing, "isolating" the upper body from the lower body. The Finger Set is an isolation, since it is practicing basics in a horse stance. (HP)

Minor moves—minor means hit "hard" and major means "harder."

Mass attack—refers to multiple-attacker situations. It is also the name of a form taught in many schools that is composed of techniques for two or more attackers.

Path of action—paired with line of action, it refers to using a wider swath in your movement for better Margin for Error. Mr. Parker sometimes called it the "squeegee principle." A squeegee is used to wipe water from a window in a wide "path of action." One would not turn it to use the end or tip, which would be a line of action. Using only the hammerfist portion of the hand to block with (line of action) is good if you are accurate. Allowing use of the forearm as well increases available surface area (path of action) and Margin for Error. It also is used to hit more than one target in a single move.

Penetration—in most cases you hit "through," not "to."

Principle of purposeful compliance—this may be considered as "going with the flow" when an opponent pulls. Instead of opposing the action, one moves with it. Purposeful *defiance,* which opposes the action, is often used to induce the opponent to pull and allow you to use that additional momentum to enhance your response. It is a facet of Borrowed Force, defined as using the opponent's force against him. The key difference is the tactical use of the opposition to induce the pull that allows one to use the compliance.

Re-orbit—when a force exerted on an attack or body causes the attack or body to continue on an arc or circle and return to the originally intended target.

Set—another term for "form" used by the Western Chinese. (EP) In our system it indicates a "form" containing additional related information such as Finger Set, Two-Man Set, etc. (HP)

Torque—rotation; this is the primary principle used in the One forms.

Web of Knowledge—a construction by Ed Parker to further break down the attacks in groupings such as hugs and holds, locks and chokes, grabs and tackles, punches, kicks, multiple attackers, and weapons. According to Huk Planas, a previous iteration was an actual physical object that he used to teach family groupings.

Recommended Reading

To get started, read the classics of Sun Tzu, including *The Art of War,* and Miyamoto Musashi's *Book of Five Rings.*

Cardoza, Monica McCabe. *A Woman's Guide to Martial Arts.* New York: Overlook Press, 1996.

Chuckrow, Robert. *The Taiji Book.* Boston: YMAA Publications, 1998.

Corcoran, John. *The Martial Arts Sourcebook.* New York: Harper, 1994.

De Becker, Gavin. *The Gift of Fear.* New York: Dell Books, 1997.

Ehrenreich, Barbara. *Blood Rites.* New York: Metropolitan Books, 1997.

Eyres, Linda and Richard. *Teaching Your Children Values.* New York: Fireside Books, 1993.

Grossman, David. *On Killing. The Psychological Cost of Learning to Kill in War and Society.* New York: Little, Brown and Co., 1995.

Grossman, David. *On Combat.* PPCT Publications, 2004.

Harrop, Grenville. *Parting the Clouds.* Dark Matter Books, 2011.

Heckler, Richard. *In Search of the Warrior Spirit.* Berkeley: North Atlantic Books, 1992.

Kane, Lawrence, and Wilder, Kris. *The Little Black Book of Violence.* Boston: YMAA Publications, 2009.

Miller, Rory. *Meditations on Violence.* Boston: YMAA Publications, 2008.

Morgan, Forrest. *Living the Martial Way: A manual for the way a modern warrior should think.* New York: Barricade Books, 1992.

Parker, Ed. *Kenpo Karate, the Law of the Fist and Empty Hand.* Alliance, Nebraska: Iron Man Industries, 1960.

Parker, Ed. *Secrets of Chinese Karate.* Englewood Cliffs, New Jersey: Prentice-Hall, 1963.

Parker, Ed. *The Woman's Guide to Self Defense.* Alliance, Nebraska; Iron Man Industries, 1968.

Parker, Ed. *Ed Parker's Guide to the Nunchaku.* Self-published, 1975.

Parker, Ed. *Infinite Insights into Kenpo, Vols. 1–5.* Los Angeles, Delsby Publications, 1982, 1983, 1985, 1986, 1987.

Parker, Leilani. *Memories of Ed Parker.* Los Angeles: Delsby Publications, 1997.

Waitzkin, Josh. *The Art of Learning.* New York: Free Press, 2007.

Wedlake, Lee. *Lessons with Ed Parker.* Ft. Myers, FL: Lee Wedlake's Karate Studio, Inc., 2009. (Available online at www.wedlakekenpotv.com/leewedlake/store)

Wiley, Carol A. *Women in the Martial Arts.* Berkeley: North Atlantic Books, 1992.

Wiley, Mark V. *Filipino Martial Arts, Cabales Serrada Escrima.* Vermont: Tuttle, 1994.

Wise, Jeff. *Extreme Fear.* New York: Palgrave Macmillan, 2009.

About the Author

LEE WEDLAKE, ninth-degree black belt in Kenpo Karate, has studied the martial arts since 1967. Originally from Chicago, Wedlake earned a bachelor's degree in Criminal Justice from the University of Illinois, opened a studio in 1976, relocated to Florida in 1991, and then to Texas in 2011.

Photo by Rich Hale

Wedlake is a first-generation black belt under Ed Parker, "The Father of American Karate." He is the author of *Further Insights into Kenpo* and *Lessons with Ed Parker*, as well as many martial art magazine and web articles. His work was included in Parker's *Infinite Insights into Kenpo* book series: he wrote the preface to Volume 3, was used as the model for the forms in Volume 5, and is named in the acknowledgments in Volumes 1 and 5. He wrote the article on American Kenpo for *Martial Arts of the World* by Thomas Green and Joseph Svinth. Wedlake is on the Board of Directors of the World Registry of Black Belts, Organizations and Federations (WRBBOF) and is recognized as *Hanshi,* Chief Grandmaster Instructor, by the prestigious Shidokan International group. In addition, he was included in both *The Journey* and *The International Journey* by Tom Bleecker, biographical books of the world's most proficient kenpoists.

In 1980 he was the first-ever Parker Kenpo stylist to earn a spot in the National Top Ten in men's black-belt forms. Wedlake served as the Midwest representative for Parker's International Kenpo Karate Association (IKKA) from 1979 until 1990. The IKKA named him to their Board of Examiners after Parker's passing. He continues today as senior advisor to Progressive Kenpo Systems, a group of Kenpo studios spanning the globe. His experience in other martial arts includes instructor certification and expertise in Russian Systema and Yang Taiji (Cheng Man-Ching style), among others.

Today Wedlake lives in Round Rock, Texas. He is on the international seminar circuit, has filmed a DVD series and produced an online learning website on the Kenpo system, and continues to write about the Parker system.

To learn more:

www.wedlakekenpotv.com/leewedlake

www.wedlakekenpotv.com